S0-DTD-120

Exploratorium Learning Studio
3601 Lyon Street
San Francisco, CA 94123
phone: 415-561-0343
email: studio@exploratorium.edu
http://www.exploratorium.edu/ls/

# THE ROLE OF SCIENTISTS IN THE PROFESSIONAL DEVELOPMENT OF SCIENCE TEACHERS

Committee on Biology Teacher Inservice Programs
Board on Biology
Commission on Life Sciences
National Research Council

NATIONAL ACADEMY PRESS
Washington, D.C. 1996

LC+
QH
315.25
R64
1996
(GN)

**NATIONAL ACADEMY PRESS   2101 Constitution Avenue, N.W.   Washington, DC 20418**

NOTICE: The project that is the subject of this report was approved by the Governing Board of the National Research Council, whose members are drawn from the councils of the National Academy of Sciences, the National Academy of Engineering, and the Institute of Medicine. The members of the committee responsible for the report were chosen for their special competences and with regard for appropriate balance.

This report has been reviewed by a group other than the authors according to procedures approved by a Report Review Committee consisting of members of the National Academy of Sciences, the National Academy of Engineering, and the Institute of Medicine.

This study by the Board on Biology was supported by the National Science Foundation under grant TPE-9150186. Dissemination of the report was supported by the National Research Council's Frank Press Fund for Dissemination and Outreach.

### Library of Congress Cataloging-in-Publication Data

The role of scientists in the professional development of science
    teachers / Committee on Biology Teacher Inservice Programs, Board on Biology,
    Commission on Life Sciences, National Research Council.
        p.   cm.
    Includes bibliographical references and index
    ISBN 0-309-04999-7
    1. Biology teachers—In-service training—United States.
    2. Science teachers—In-service training—United States.
    3. Biology—Study and teaching (Continuing education)—United
    States.  4. Science—Study and teaching (Continuing education)—
    United States.  I. National Research Council (U.S.) Committee on Biology Teacher
    Inservice Programs.
    QH315.25.R64   1996                                                        96-4530
    574'.071'55—dc20                                                              CIP

Copyright 1996 by the National Academy of Sciences

Printed in the United States of America

# COMMITTEE ON BIOLOGY TEACHER INSERVICE PROGRAMS

SAMUEL WARD (*Chairman*), University of Arizona, Tucson, AZ
JEAN BEARD, San Jose State University, San Jose, CA
ROBERT D. BONNER, Hampton University, Hampton, VA
JAMES M. BOWER, California Institute of Technology, Pasadena, CA
COLEMAN GENN, Center for Educational Innovation, New York, NY
GEORGE B. JOHNSON, Washington University, St. Louis, MO
JOSEPH D. MCINERNEY, BSCS, Colorado Springs, CO
DAVID MICKLOS, DNA Learning Center, Cold Spring Harbor, NY
WENDELL G. MOHLING, National Science Teachers Association, Arlington,
    VA
GARY NAKAGIRI, San Mateo County Office of Education, Redwood City,
    CA
NANCY RIDENOUR, Ithaca High School, Ithaca, NY
BARBARA SCHULZ, Shoreline High School, Seattle, WA
MARE TAAGEPERA, University of California, Irvine, CA
JON THOMPSON, Silverthorne, CO

*National Research Council Staff*

DONNA M. GERARDI, Study Director
NORMAN GROSSBLATT, Editor
KAREN GOLDBERG, Research Assistant
ALVIN G. LAZEN, Study Director for completion of the report
KIT LEE, Administrative Assistant
JEFF PECK, Project Assistant
KIRSTEN SAMPSON, Special Assistant

**BOARD ON BIOLOGY**

MICHAEL T. CLEGG (*Chairman*), University of California, Riverside, CA
JOHN C. AVISE, University of Georgia, Athens, GA
ANANDA M. CHAKRABARTY, University of Illinois Medical Center, Chicago, IL
GERALD D. FISCHBACH, Harvard Medical School, Boston, MA
DAVID J. GALAS, Darwin Molecular Corp., Bothell, WA
RICHARD E. LENSKI, Michigan State University, East Lansing, MI
BARBARA J. MAZUR, E.I. du Pont de Nemours and Co., Wilmington, DE
DANIEL MORSE, University of California, Santa Barbara, CA
DANIEL SIMBERLOFF, Florida State University, Tallahassee, FL
ROBERT R. SOKAL, State University of New York, Stony Brook, NY
SHIRLEY M. TILGHMAN, Princeton University, Princeton, NJ

*National Research Council Staff*

ERIC A. FISCHER, Director
PAULETTE ADAMS, Administrative Assistant

# COMMISSION ON LIFE SCIENCES

THOMAS D. POLLARD (*Chairman*), Johns Hopkins Medical School, Baltimore, MD

FREDERICK R. ANDERSON, Cadwalader, Wickersham & Taft, Washington DC

JOHN C. BAILAR III, McGill University, Montreal, Canada

JOHN E. BURRIS, Marine Biological Laboratories, Woods Hole, MA

MICHAEL T. CLEGG, University of California, Riverside, CA

GLENN A. CROSBY, Washington State University, Pullman, WA

URSULA W. GOODENOUGH, Washington University, St. Louis, MO

SUSAN E. LEEMAN, Boston University, Boston, MA

RICHARD E. LENSKI, Michigan State University, East Lansing, MI

THOMAS E. LOVEJOY, Smithsonian Institution, Washington DC

DONALD R. MATTISON, University of Pittsburgh, Pittsburgh, PA

JOSEPH E. MURRAY, Wellesley Hills, MA

EDWARD E. PENHOET, Chiron Corporation, Emeryville, CA

EMIL A. PFITZER, Research Institute for Fragrance Materials, Inc., Hackensack, NJ

MALCOLM C. PIKE, USC School of Medicine, Los Angeles, CA

HENRY PITOT, University of Wisconsin, Madison, WI

JONATHAN M. SAMET, Johns Hopkins University, Baltimore, MD

HAROLD M. SCHMECK, North Chatham, MA

CARLA H. SHATZ, University of California, Berkeley, CA

JOHN L. VANDEBERG, Southwestern Foundation for Biomedical Research, San Antonio, TX

*National Research Council Staff*

PAUL GILMAN, Executive Director

ALVIN G. LAZEN, Director for Program Operations

SOLVEIG M. PADILLA, Administrative Assistant

The National Academy of Sciences is a private, nonprofit, self-perpetuating society of distinguished scholars engaged in scientific and engineering research, dedicated to the furtherance of science and technology and to their use for the general welfare. Upon the authority of the charter granted to it by the Congress in 1863, the Academy has a mandate that requires it to advise the federal government on scientific and technical matters. Dr. Bruce Alberts is president of the National Academy of Sciences.

The National Academy of Engineering was established in 1964, under the charter of the National Academy of Sciences, as a parallel organization of outstanding engineers. It is autonomous in its administration and in the selection of its members, sharing with the National Academy of Sciences the responsibility for advising the federal government. The National Academy of Engineering also sponsors engineering programs aimed at meeting national needs, encourages education and research, and recognizes the superior achievements of engineers. Dr. Harold Liebowitz is president of the National Academy of Engineering.

The Institute of Medicine was established in 1970 by the National Academy of Sciences to secure the services of eminent members of appropriate professions in the examination of policy matters pertaining to the health of the public. The Institute acts under the responsibility given to the National Academy of Sciences by its congressional charter to be an adviser to the federal government and, upon its own initiative, to identify issues of medical care, research, and education. Dr. Kenneth Shine is president of the Institute of Medicine.

The National Research Council was organized by the National Academy of Sciences in 1916 to associate the broad community of science and technology with the Academy's purposes of furthering knowledge and of advising the federal government. Functioning in accordance with general policies determined by the Academy, the Council has become the principal operating agency of both the National Academy of Sciences and the National Academy of Engineering in providing service to the government, the public, and the scientific and engineering communities. The Council is administered jointly by both academies and the Institute of Medicine. Dr. Bruce Alberts and Dr. Harold Liebowitz are chairman and vice chairman, respectively, of the National Research Council.

# Preface

The Committee on Biology Teacher Inservice Programs was a combination of teachers, research scientists, teacher educators, and educational administrators. As we worked together with our combined experiences and observations to learn how to improve biology teaching, we recognized that our efforts in learning to understand each other's perspectives were a microcosm of how science-education reform must proceed: with mutual understanding and respect.

When research scientists involve themselves intensely in science-education reform, their perceptions change. Improving science education is not as simple as doing experiments in the laboratory. Data are harder to collect and interpret. Educational improvement is difficult to quantify, and the important variables are hard to sort. Scientists are accustomed to science as the "art of the soluble," where formulating a problem correctly often leads more or less automatically to its solution. In science education, both problems and solutions are embedded in the context of the individual teacher, his or her classroom, and the school and school district. Formulating problems correctly does not necessarily lead to their solution. In fact, the simple logic of problems and solutions can often impede reform. As Sheila Tobias has put it, "since [scientists'] thinking is in terms of solutions rather than strategies, their recommendations are not expressed as options; nor are they rooted in the pragmatic, the real, the here and now. They do not offer people in the field (as one person I interviewed put it) any suggestions as to 'what we can do tomorrow.'" (Tobias, *Revitalizing Science Education*, p. 16)

We have prepared this report as a guide to help scientists and other science educators know "what they can do tomorrow" to support the professional development of their teacher colleagues. Our analysis and recommendations are based on review of almost 200 programs for teacher enhancement and the collective experience of the committee members. Although we focused our study on biology-education programs, and the name and makeup of our committee reflect this focus, we found that many of the issues we address apply to education in all sciences. Thus, we chose a broader title addressing all scientists to encourage their interest in professional development.

Our findings reveal several contradictions. On the one hand, much effort and much money are going into professional-development activities for teachers; hundreds of scientists, thousands of teachers, and scores of federal and local funding agencies are involved. Many dedicated people have worked diligently to improve how teachers teach and how students learn science. On the other hand, few programs last more than a few years, and even fewer are linked with lasting reform. Substantive program evaluation has been scanty because appropriate methods are lacking and funding is inadequate. Thus, the conclusions we have reached cannot be established with the certainty we are accustomed to in science laboratories. Yet the committee has come to a clear consensus about what works and what does not and how scientists can contribute most effectively to the professional development of teachers. We need not wait for the definitive proof of what program works best. Many programs work. Use this guide now to develop practical strategies for scientists and teachers to work together to promote their own professional development and thus enhance the education of their students.

The committee met and wrote its report between November 1991 and October 1993. Unanticipated circumstances delayed its release. As this report was nearing completion, the National Science Education Standards underwent their national review and redrafting. By that time, however, our committee had finished its deliberations. As a result, this report refers to the Science Education Standards but does not fully integrate them into the description and discussion of professional-development programs we describe. I and several other committee members were involved in the national review of the standards draft between December 1994 and February 1995. I am confident that this report is consistent with the content and teacher-preparation sections of the national standards. It will provide valuable guidance for scientists and teachers as they work together in professional-development programs to improve science education for all students.

I thank the members of the committee for the collegial spirit in which they addressed our tasks. The comments of the anonymous reviewers were thoughtful and thorough, and we thank them for their contribution to this report. Special thanks are due the Commission on Life Sciences staff: Donna Gerardi, whose familiarity with all the communities involved in education greatly assisted the committee in its work; Norman Grossblatt, who edited the report; Karen Goldberg, who served as research assistant; and Jeff Peck, who was the project assistant. We also thank Kirsten Sampson, who updated Appendix A.

> Samuel Ward, *Chairman*
> Committee on Biology Teacher Inservice Programs

# Contents

# Summary

Stimulated by concern for the state of biology education nationally, a National Research Council committee in 1990 prepared the report *Fulfilling the Promise: Biology Education in the Nation's Schools*. The centerpiece of the report was the call for leadership from the scientific community, "as both guide and goad, both resource and participant," to promote sustained reform in science education at all levels. Among its recommendations was that improvements be made in "inservice" education—the activities engaged in by teachers as they continue to learn. The present Committee on Biology Teacher Inservice Programs was formed in the Board on Biology of the National Research Council's Commission on Life Sciences to pursue that recommendation by examining a sample of programs for the inservice training of biology teachers, determining which of the programs worked best and why they worked well, and preparing a report that would guide scientists as they work with science teachers for the improvement of biology education.

This report is not about the need for educational reform. Educational reform is vital, but many other reports address it—the *National Science Education Standards* and the Project 2061 *Benchmarks for Science Literacy* of the American Association for the Advancement of Science, to name only two. This report is instead a practical "how-to" guide, primarily for scientists but also for teachers and administrators, on how to design, implement, and evaluate professional-development programs. This committee's use of the term *professional development* instead of *inservice* emphasizes its belief that the science teacher and the practicing scientist are full partners in a professional community dedicated to improving science education and that each brings different strengths and resources to the process.

*1*

In addition to the goal of guiding scientists and teachers about professional-development programs, we hope to communicate to the National Science Foundation and other funding agencies our findings concerning the breadth and scope of professional-development activities for science teachers and to offer our assessment of where more information, attention, and funds are needed to promote sustainable programs that work.

Our subject is important. Any society that is serious about the education of its children must be equally serious about supporting the continuing education of those charged with that task. If we are to meet the needs of diverse students and the nation's needs for scientifically literate citizens and skilled workers, it is essential that teachers have the opportunity to continue to expand their knowledge and develop their pedagogical skills and laboratory expertise from their undergraduate education throughout their professional career.

The committee reviewed almost 200 professional-development programs nationwide and examined a number of these programs in detail, including site visits and interviews. The reviews, combined with our professional experience and knowledge, helped us to define the desirable characteristics of programs and to judge the effectiveness of programs by how well they achieved the desirable characteristics. This summary provides only a taste of the detailed guidance provided in the text and appendixes of the report.

## CHARACTERISTICS OF EFFECTIVE PROFESSIONAL-DEVELOPMENT PROGRAMS

Our review of programs revealed that each of the most effective professional-development programs shared the following characteristics:

- Scientists, teachers, and administrators collaborated in the program's development and implementation.
- Participating teachers were treated as professionals.
- The program was designed to meet important school-based needs.
- Opportunities were provided for continuing involvement among participants.
- Evaluation was a continuous process and was used to improve the program.
- New partnerships, projects, and networks were stimulated among participating teachers and between teachers and scientists.
- Program directors used effective publicity and recruitment strategies.
- The program was encouraged and supported by school districts and school administrators.
- Effective dissemination strategies were used.
- Program directors had practical knowledge of the process of change.
- A charismatic person or group provided strong leadership.

# THE SCIENTIST'S ROLE

Scientists have an obligation to assist in science teachers' professional development. Many scientists recognize the obligation and are ready to get involved. Scientists can provide opportunities for teachers to learn how the scientific process works—what scientists do and how and why they do it. They can provide research opportunities for practicing teachers; act as scientific partners; provide connections to the rest of the scientific community; assist in writing grant proposals for science-education projects; provide hands-on, inquiry-based workshops for area teachers; and provide teachers access to equipment, scientific journals, and catalogs not usually available in schools. They can help teachers to review educational material for its accuracy and utility.

When scientists teach their undergraduate classes and laboratories, potential science teachers are present. Scientists should recognize that as an opportunity to promote and act as a model of both good process and accurate content teaching and so strive to improve their own teaching.

Most professional scientific societies have recognized the importance of the involvement of their members in programs to improve education. Nearly every one has an office dedicated to "education." Some also organize special workshops at annual meetings directed to scientists interested in K-12 education or workshops and scientific sessions directed at teachers. The professional societies can help teachers to secure funding, coordinate summer research opportunities for teachers in members' research laboratories in a way that relates to the classroom environment, publicize and disseminate effective supplementary curricular materials, and encourage and welcome teacher membership in societies by reducing fees, publicizing meetings in science-education journals, and including teachers on education committees. Professional societies can devote sections of scientific-research journals and newsletters to education articles and refereed educational-research papers. Such a change in editorial policy will help to reduce the barriers between teaching and research.

# GETTING STARTED

Given the numerous ways for scientists to involve themselves in professional-development programs, how do they get started? Before planning a professional-development program, a scientist should initiate interactions with teachers and school administrators to become familiar with the needs of elementary- and secondary-school science teachers and learn about the realities of the school system. Many a scientist's first inclination is to volunteer to give a 1- to 2-hour class presentation and discussion of his or her own research or discipline. That can provide contact with teachers and is a good starting point if the scientist recognizes and respects the needs of the teachers. A valuable next step would be to visit the elementary- or secondary-school science classroom of one of the teachers for at least an entire day. That gives the scientist a realistic view of schools and allows him or her to see teachers at work in the environment of the classroom.

As a followup activity, the scientist can invite local teachers to campus and structure special seminars and demonstrations at times convenient for teachers. The scientist can foster open discussions about teachers' needs, explore opportunities for future activities, and discuss the implications of collaboration for K-12 science teaching and learning. The scientist can also invite teachers to the research laboratory to participate in experiments. The one-on-one interaction between teacher and scientist can develop into work with postdoctoral fellows, graduate students, and technicians. Teachers become members of a community of people "doing science."

## INVOLVING TEACHERS AND ADMINISTRATORS

Teachers who are already actively involved in professional organizations or have actively sought professional-development opportunities generally receive a wealth of information on workshops, conferences, and summer institutes. Many of them consistently attend such professional-development programs and are among the most enthusiastic participants. The challenge is to identify and attract the much larger potential audience of teachers who are less active professionally. They can be reached through use of school-district and teacher's-union mailing lists, but programs must be well designed and rewarding to attract and retain the teachers.

Once teacher participants have been recruited, program organizers should treat them as colleagues and partners. In many programs, teachers conduct some of the program activities. Teachers are encouraged to participate in programs if the programs offer continuing-education or college credit and financial support.

Support from administrators—such as district superintendents, principals, assistant principals, and counselors—is essential for the continued success of new programs. The administrators must agree that the programs will make their schools more successful. If they do agree, they can attach high priority to science education and budget appropriate funds, recognize that *all* students benefit from quality science education and provide a variety of opportunities for students to become successful in science, take leadership for developing orientation programs for parents and encouraging parents to advocate science education, support professional development of science teachers, and commit appropriate administrative personnel to support professional development of teachers and to support such followup activities as networking, peer coaching, and seminars to continue professional development. Administrators can also strive to improve dissemination of information to teachers about opportunities for professional development.

Professional science-education organizations can help to build bridges between teachers and scientists by inviting scientists to teachers' conventions, involving scientists in such organizational activities as workshops, and inviting scientists to write articles for the organizations' journals. The science-education organizations can encourage and welcome academic and industrial scientists by publicizing their meetings in journals read by the scientists. They can appoint appropriate scientists to committees to help plan science-based educational activities for teachers, and they can recognize and reward scientists for outstanding accomplishments in science education.

## ENCOURAGEMENT THROUGH REWARDS

The institutional culture of nearly every university requires that faculty contribute by research, teaching, and service, but few institutions reward research and teaching equally, and fewer reward service at all. Although research has a wide range of external rewards (such as grants, national and international prestige, and meeting invitations), good teaching is rarely rewarded externally and is often underappreciated internally. The lack of recognition and rewards, particularly for junior faculty at research universities, is a major impediment to scientists' participation in professional development of teachers.

To encourage the involvement of scientists in professional-development programs, their efforts must be treated as a part of their professional responsibility, recognized, and rewarded. University and college administrators and faculty can help by rewarding participating faculty through the promotion and merit-increase processes. The administrators can support partnerships with schools and school districts by providing on-campus facilities and support for K-12 teachers, by promoting cooperation between schools of education and science departments, and by participating in national reform efforts. Professional scientific societies can recognize and reward scientists for outstanding accomplishment in science education.

Teachers need to be recognized and recompensed for their participation in professional-development programs. Tangible ways are to provide continuing-education or college credit for the programs, room and board for participants in programs when appropriate, and funds to purchase equipment and supplies for use in the teachers' classroom. No less important is that administrators show through the promotion and merit-increase processes that they encourage and reward teachers' participation in professional-development programs.

## INDIVIDUAL-BASED AND SYSTEMIC PROGRAMS

Most professional-development programs are designed for individual teachers and reach only a few teachers. A major challenge for professional-development programs is to get *all* teachers involved. Various systemic reforms designed to link teachers in whole schools, school districts, and states are attempting to do that. Both individual-based and systemic forms of professional-development programs have merits, and both are needed to drive education reform.

However, we believe that systemic programs can contribute more effectively to science-education reform; most important, they have the prospect of reaching all teachers and not just those motivated and able to participate in individual-based programs, and they have better potential for becoming institutionalized to provide continuity and ensure long-term support.

Our survey of effective individual-based programs showed that they are not imposed from the top down but are instead built on the efforts of small partnerships of dedicated teachers, scientists, and administrators. The overwhelming majority of those programs' activities involve specific topics, such as molecular biology, biotechnology, genetics, or ecology. Most common are lectures or lecture series, courses with lectures and laboratory activities offered for course credit or continuing-education credits, topical workshops during the summer, summer research experiences in academic or industrial laboratories, sabbatical years spent in research or working in a university department, workshops at scientific-society or teachers-association meetings, state workshops, and local school-district workshops. Although some programs are open to teachers in specific regions, schools, districts, or states, others draw participants from a national pool through a selective application process. Generally, those who planned and funded the individual-based programs that we surveyed did not belong to local school administrative structures. Teachers and scientists involved in the programs often benefited greatly, but the programs rarely became self-sustaining. Many lasted only until the first round of funding disappeared—usually no more than a few years—and few of these offered followup activities to teachers after their participation in the programs.

The focus of systemic efforts for science-education reform, and for education reform more generally, goes beyond the individual teacher; systemic efforts are aimed at improving the organization of an educational system so that it can function more effectively. Professional-development programs that embrace this approach are linked to larger systemic efforts that aim to improve all components of an educational system—such as teaching, student achievement, curriculum, administrative leadership, and school policies and practice—and to institutionalize changes that prove effective. An underlying assumption in this approach is that members of different parts of the system—such as principals, teachers, parents, and university faculty—are included in the planning of the change process from the outset. This inclusion allows the effort to obtain the massive support it needs by providing stakeholders with a sense of ownership.

Scientists who involve themselves with either individual-based programs or systemic programs should first learn about the current science-related programs and projects that involve their local schools or school districts. Relationships must be nurtured so that all parties become better acquainted and have time to develop a working relationship. In addition to involving key teachers early in the planning process, early inclusion of school and school-district administrators is important. An adept administrator can help to develop an effective school or district partnership by facilitating communication and obtaining support.

The more realistic and better-focused are the goals of a program, the easier it will be to recruit supporters and advocates. District commitments—especially financial commitments—are sometimes difficult to obtain. Scientists must have realistic expectations of how long it takes to facilitate change and must be sensitive to political realities. Reform is often easier in elementary schools than in secondary schools, and elementary schools might be better places to start.

Whatever form a professional-development program takes and whatever organization sponsors it, it will be more effective if it is institutionalized to provide continuity and ensure long-term support. This message is vital.

## EVALUATION

Large amounts of federal and private money are being spent on innovative programs for the professional development of K-12 science teachers, and many people are devoting much time and energy to this critical component of excellent science education. But we need to be able to identify programs that work and programs that do not, and evaluation is a daunting and expensive task. The primary question to be answered is, "Has the professional-development program being evaluated helped teachers to create a high-quality learning environment so that their students are doing better in science?" The answer is difficult to obtain because long-term followup is required and it is hard to know whether improvements are the result of participation by teachers in professional-development programs or something else.

It is important to establish an evaluation plan from the outset of program design. This process forces clarity in thinking about program objectives and activities in much the same way that careful planning of scientific research forces clarity of thinking about experimental design. Comprehensive evaluation is not necessary or cost-effective for every program. Instead, selected programs, such as biotechnology programs or systemwide programs or all programs in a geographic region, could be reviewed as a group. The goal is to learn about the net effect of a program on teachers and students and to identify strengths, weaknesses, and gaps in content, pedagogy, or geographic distribution. Although long-term followup evaluation is desirable, continuing, short-term evaluation is also critical and was used in every effective professional-development program that we reviewed.

Program directors and principal investigators should not have primary responsibility for followup evaluation of their own programs, but they should have a major role in continuing evaluation. Evaluation is a specialized skill best applied by persons with a background in the methods of social-science and education research. Furthermore, program directors might be too close to their own programs to evaluate them objectively.

## FUNDING

Science-related professional-development activities are funded by a variety of federal, state, local, and private sources. The primary direct sources of federal funding for professional-development activities are the National Science Foundation and the Department of Education, but other federal agencies have education activities at the K-12 level. The Department of Education's Dwight D. Eisenhower Professional Development Program is an important source of funds that states use locally for the training and professional development of elementary- and secondary-school science and mathematics teachers.

Private foundations are an important source of local funds for professional-development activities, as are local and regional philanthropic organizations and, increasingly, local businesses and industry.

At a time when both national government and local governments face severe financial stringency, priorities for expenditures must be established. Our recommendations are aimed at making available funds go as far as possible. Expenditure for professional-development programs is an investment in the future. The investment will earn the greatest possible return if we

- Increase the duration of education grants so that professional-development programs have time to build partnerships and become self-sustaining.
- Provide supplements to research grants to encourage scientists to participate in professional-development programs.
- Fund professional, third-party evaluation to determine the effectiveness of major programs.
- Encourage programs that focus on systemic change.
- Fund programs that eliminate barriers to and stimulate cooperation between science and teacher-education departments at colleges and universities.
- Earmark substantial grant funds for supplies and equipment to support implementation of programs by teachers in their classrooms.
- Link funding of curriculum development with professional development.
- Involve both scientists and educators in the peer-review process for education grants.
- Fund activities that are aimed at creating methods of evaluating how professional-development programs affect students' learning of science.
- Fund the establishment of an information and dissemination center for professional-development programs.

We urge scientists to step out of their laboratory, classroom, or field site and to adopt our vision of scientists and teachers working as colleagues in the continuum of science education. This report is intended as a road map to help that happen.

# 1

# Introduction

I believe that scientists have a crucial role to play in precollege science education reforms. But it is not easy to know how or where to begin. . . . The scientists . . . can come from either industry or academia, but in either case they must be well-informed and prepared in order to play an effective part. . . . The problem we face is a huge one, and there will be no quick solutions. But I believe that a properly organized group of scientists can be effective in catalyzing meaningful and lasting changes in this badly neglected area. [Bruce Alberts, 1991]

Stimulated by concern for the state of biology education nationally, the National Research Council in 1987 appointed a committee of scientists, K-12 teachers, teacher educators, science publishers, and school administrators to examine the scope of biology education. That committee's 1990 report, *Fulfilling the Promise: Biology Education in the Nation's Schools,* highlighted the need for sustained educational reform, rather than idiosyncratic efforts. The centerpiece of the report was the call for leadership from the scientific community "as both guide and goad, both resource and participant" (p. 103) to promote sustained reform in science education at all levels. The report offered strong recommendations for improving biology curricula, laboratory activities, tests and testing, school administration, teacher preparation, licensing and certification of teachers, and leadership in science-education reform. It also recommended that improvements be made in "inservice" education–the activities of teachers as they continue to learn.

## CHARGE

The present Committee on Biology Teacher Inservice Programs was formed, in the Board on Biology of the National Research Council's Commission on Life Sciences, to pursue the above recommendation by examining a broad sample of programs for the inservice training of biology teachers. The specific charge to the committee was as follows:

- To identify existing inservice programs (templates) that can readily be used elsewhere with minimal changes and to provide guidance on establishing new programs.
- To identify essential aspects of inservice programs.
- To identify elements of inservice programs that address the needs of different cultural and ethnic groups.
- To recommend a desired level of teacher participation, including advice about the level of necessary funding and means of increasing teacher participation.
- To examine ways to increase the involvement of the scientific-research community and research universities in providing and supporting inservice programs, including ways of institutionalizing this involvement.
- To provide recommendations about the design of inservice programs that include both content and pedagogy and are conducted with the collaboration of experienced science teachers, teacher educators, and scientists.
- To develop criteria for evaluation of inservice programs.
- To examine innovative ways to incorporate research on how students learn biology into inservice programs.
- To review the emerging fields of biology with a view to what teachers should know in coming years.[1]

## THE COMMITTEE'S METHODS

In response to its charge, our committee examined a sample of almost 200 professional-development programs to determine how they work, to identify characteristics of effective programs, and to recommend how the effective elements can be replicated elsewhere. The programs were identified in several ways. We requested information by advertising in a variety of journals and newsletters of

---

[1]Since this committee began its work in 1991, the American Association for the Advancement of Science has further developed its Project 2061, and the National Research Council has developed and published the *National Science Education Standards,* which provide the criteria and framework for high-quality science programs and the policies necessary to support them. Our report does not discuss biology content but defers to the other reports, which have been prepared by committees dedicating all their effort to defining science content.

professional teacher and scientific organizations. The same request was sent directly to the members of many organizations and to principal investigators of programs sponsored by federal agencies and private foundations. It was also posted on electronic bulletin boards. Some of our committee members had first-hand experience with the programs examined.

Almost 200 programs responded to our requests for information. They included a wide range of activities: short topical workshops, 1- to 3-week institutes during the summer, lecture series during the academic year, and programs designed to influence systemwide reform. And they were in a variety of locations: university science departments, schools or colleges of education, community colleges, museums and science and technology centers, nature preserves, professional societies, and industry. The programs that responded are listed and described in Appendix A; not all programs responded, but the ones that did constitute a sample of the types of programs active across the country.

A questionnaire (Appendix B) was sent to all programs that responded to our initial request for information. It was designed to collect specific information about each program and to help identify exemplary programs for further study. It was not feasible to conduct a thorough review of all programs that responded to the questionnaire. Instead, committee members reviewed the responses and selected 15 programs for followup telephone calls and seven to visit. Programs were selected for further review on the basis of the following characteristics: each had been in existence for a number of years, each had a continuing evaluation process, and each used the results of the evaluations to revise and improve itself. Few programs met the criteria; most did not because they had not been in operation long enough or did not have adequate evaluation programs. During a visit to a selected program, committee members met with both program directors and teachers who had participated in the program and collected copies of written evaluations. In several instances, committee members talked directly with teachers separately from program directors. Positive responses of the participating teachers and their description of how the professional-development program had improved their teaching and student learning were important in defining "effective" programs in the eyes of the committee.

The generalizations about professional-development programs found in this report are derived from the information gathered from the program review and from the committee members' professional experience. The committee could not quantify the results of the program review for statistical analysis, because the programs were diverse, because few programs had quantifiable evaluations, because few programs had been in operation for more than a few years, and because a program often changed as participants gained experience with it. Nonetheless, there was sufficient consistency in the reports from the teachers, program directors, and scientists about factors that made their programs effective for the committee to be confident about its findings and the recommendations that emerged from them.

As we examined programs for secondary-school biology teachers, we also learned about successful programs for elementary-school teachers, some of which programs were structured differently from those for secondary-school teachers. We also saw excellent programs for teachers in the other sciences whose structural components would work well in biology. And like the preceding Research Council committee, we discovered that the "ecology of science education" consists of complex relationships among all levels and components of the school system—

> how failure of learning in high-school science has its origins in elementary school, how texts, tests, teacher education, colleges and universities, and political and economic assumptions all contribute to the status quo, and how difficult it is to alter any one element alone and expect any meaningful change in the entire system. There is of course a history, too—how the nation's educational system got into its present state, and why previous efforts at reform of science education have been so ephemeral. [National Research Council, 1990, p. vii]

We interpreted the charge to the committee to be that we produce not another study of science-education reform, but a report that would serve as a handbook—a resource and practical guide for professional-development programs. This report's first goal is to guide scientists who want to become involved in professional-development programs and to serve as a resource for scientists who are already involved; it gives scientists practical information on how to participate effectively in such programs and initiate constructive communication between scientists and teachers. Its second goal is to help teachers and administrators, both in schools and in universities, to develop, promote, and use effective professional-development programs. Its third goal is to describe the breadth and scope of professional-development activities for science teachers; to show where more information, attention, and funds are needed; and to recommend how to target funding to innovative and sustainable programs that work.

In the "Issues in Professional Development" section of this chapter, we present our understanding of the status, needs, opportunities, and problems in science education and in the professional development of science teachers. Chapter 2 offers detailed descriptions of characteristics that make programs effective. Chapter 3 is a guide for scientists to get started and participate effectively in professional-development programs. Brief vignettes of the daily activities of an elementary-school, a middle-school, and a high-school teacher are included to illustrate some of the realities of classroom teaching and to set the stage for scientists who want to become involved in professional-development activities. Chapter 4 is addressed to university administrators and scientists who try to encourage more scientists to participate in professional development. Chapter 5 describes ways to initiate and promote effective interactions for professional development between scientists and elementary- and secondary-school educators; it also highlights the need for administrative support for science-based professional-development programs for teachers. Chapter 6 discusses the differences between programs that focus on improving the professional lives of individual teachers and systemic programs that are parts of a broader effort toward reform of science education. Chapter 7 focuses on program evaluation. Chapter 8 is a vision of how professional-development activities could support science education in the future.

In addition to the already-cited Appendixes A and B, this report contains appendixes to assist those interested in learning about education-reform efforts and about specific professional-development programs around the country. The appendixes include a glossary of terms used in this report (Appendix C); an annotated list of suggested readings for scientists to help them to learn more about schools, teachers, students, and their needs (D); copies of guidelines related to science education from two institutions of higher learning (E); a list of professional organizations actively involved in science education (F); a National Science Teachers Association (NSTA) statement on teacher professionalism (G); examples of laboratory exercises (H); and information about the funding of professional-development programs (I).

## INSERVICE AND PROFESSIONAL DEVELOPMENT

> Teaching involves life-long learning. The professional education of teachers should be a seamless experience, beginning with college preparation, extending through the first few years of teaching, and providing opportunities to extend knowledge and skills throughout a career. Teachers with this professional experience will be equipped to meet the needs of all students. [National Research Council, 1993, p. 3]

At the beginning of our deliberations and in accord with our charge, we used the term *inservice* to describe the broad range of teacher involvement in out-of-school professional-development activities. Other terms commonly used for those activities are *staff development* and *teacher enhancement*. In the process of examining programs in a variety of institutions across the country, we found that we needed to think about not only isolated inservice activities, but the continuing process of professional development of teachers. We use the term *professional development* in this report to mean a long-term commitment on the part of scientists and teachers. Improving professional development, not just inservice activities, is the goal of this report. For scientists, participating in professional-development activities that are useful for teachers involves taking the time to learn about teachers' educational backgrounds and teaching environment, recognizing teachers' needs, helping to articulate clear programmatic goals and ways to achieve them, and learning more about teaching and education. For teachers, effective professional development means recognizing the importance of participating actively in professional-development activities, including the design of programs. We also see teacher professional development as an integral component of science-education reform.[2]

We use the term *teacher preparation* (instead of *preservice*) to describe prospective teachers' formal coursework at the undergraduate level. We use the term *teacher* to refer to a K-12 classroom teacher, *scientist* to refer to someone professionally trained in science who might also be engaged in scientific research, *research scientist* to refer specifically to persons whose main occupation is the practice of scientific research, and *science educator* to include anyone involved in science education, including teachers, scientists, and school science coordinators. The terms are not exclusive. We recognize that many people play several of those roles concurrently—scientists teach and teachers do research. Those and other terms are included in the glossary in Appendix C.

NSTA has published a statement on teacher professionalism that points up the importance of professional-development programs. It is excerpted in the following box and presented in detail in Appendix G.

## ISSUES IN PROFESSIONAL DEVELOPMENT

Throughout its deliberations and review of programs, the committee repeatedly discussed its perceptions of the current state of science education. It identified key problems, needs, and opportunities for improving professional-development programs. Our framework for thinking about these issues is presented below.

### Goals for Students

*Preparation for Life*

Students will face continual changes in society, technology, families, health, and the workplace. Professional-development programs might vary in their immediate goals but should have the common goal of *enhancing teachers' abilities to improve student learning* so that students will be prepared to deal with those challenges. If teachers are prepared to teach well-designed science courses, *all* students might acquire the tools to think creatively; to gain an appreciation of the

---

[2]This report focuses on science and leaves considerations of such general topics as school structure and student readiness for schooling to others. Because of its charge and expertise, the committee concentrated on professional development of teachers with little attention to the specifics of teacher preparation or science curriculum. The focus on professional development is complementary to the work of other groups, including the National Research Council's National Committee on Science Education Standards and Assessment, the American Association for the Advancement of Science's Project 2061, the National Research Council's Committee on Undergraduate Science Education, and Project Kaleidoscope.

## Preamble and Conclusion of the National Science Teachers Association Statement on Teacher Professionalism

Preamble

The teacher is the key to making science teaching a profession and to providing quality science education. For American society to accept science teachers as professionals, science teaching needs to conform to society's professional practice model.

Society's professional practice model is knowledge based and content oriented. It is a pact between society and members of an occupation whose work "requires discretion and judgment in meeting the unique needs of clients . . . (A profession organizes itself) to guarantee the competence of its members in exchange for the privilege of controlling its own work structure and standards of practice. The profession assumes collective responsibility for defining, communicating, and enforcing professional standards of practice and ethics. It develops and maintains a process which ensures both the research and craft knowledge accumulated in the field are communicated and used effectively by all its members. That knowledge is also used to prepare, induct, certify, select, and evaluate new members. Further, the profession ensures continuous generation of new knowledge. Differences in knowledge levels, expertise, responsibility, and productivity result in differentiated roles, status, and compensation.

Science teaching requires an individual to exercise discretion and judgment in meeting the needs of students. Thus it is fitting for science teachers to assume the rights and responsibilities of professionals in our society. To do so, the educational enterprise in the United States must eliminate the existing hierarchy. The roles of all participants in the enterprise must change. Such initiatives are emerging throughout the country and are supported by research publications and position papers from professional societies. This position statement *describes changes in structure and expectations which must occur* to enable a science teacher to assume the role of a professional within society's professional practice model.

Conclusion

NSTA supports the restructuring of schooling necessary to enhance science teacher professionalism so that:

• Science teachers collaborate with each other and with stakeholders to make decisions about policies and regulations for science teaching.

• Science teachers allocate their time among students, parents, peers, administrators, scientists, and other community members.

• Science teachers have both technical and staff support in order to be available for interaction with students and other stakeholders.

• Science teachers' professional growth continues throughout their careers. They select learning opportunities that meet their needs. They are reflective and share research findings from both their own and their students' experiences.

• Science teachers use society's symbols such as business cards, displaying diplomas, certificates, and awards to reflect professional images.

• Science teachers assume responsibility for enabling learners to reach their potential. Science teachers collectively establish and continually revise standards of practice, model ethical behavior, and account for their actions.

–Adopted by the NSTA Board of Directors in January 1992.

natural world; to appreciate the role of humans in the biosphere; to understand fundamental scientific concepts; to become familiar with the processes of science and scientific thinking; to collect, organize, synthesize, and interpret data; to solve problems; to make decisions on the basis of analysis and interpretation of information; and to know about science-related career choices. These goals are in accord with those of the National Science Education Standards.

*Opportunity for All Students*

The committee believes that all professional-development programs should support teachers in maintaining high expectations for all students while considering the individuality of each student and the diversity among groups of students. For the purposes of this report, student *diversity* refers to sex, language, ethnic, racial, cultural, and economic differences.

The committee recognizes that some professional-development programs address "diversity and equity in individual classrooms" (Little, 1993, p. 3), but it believes that greater attention must be given to those issues by teachers, administrators, and scientists. Because the committee lacked adequate expertise to address appropriately the important question of how diversity among teachers and students affects classroom teaching and learning, we refer the reader to special readings on the subject. The references are included in Appendix D, in a section on "Diversity and Equity in Science Classrooms." In the words of Dennis Tierney, professor of teacher education, San Jose State University,

> both pre-service and in-service teacher education can benefit from increased attention to the challenge of providing effective content instruction to a multicultural student population. This will likely require that instruction in multicultural issues be more closely tied to instruction in lesson planning so that teacher education students understand that cultural pluralism is simply one of the variables that must be addressed in every part of every lesson. . . . Clearly, more research is needed to determine the full scope of this issue. [Tierney, 1988, p. 15]

## Goals of Professional Development

The primary goal of professional-development programs is to improve teachers' interest in and ability to teach science. Programs vary in their emphasis. Some of the aims are

- To improve teaching skills (pedagogy).
- To increase teachers' knowledge about subject matter in science or to update teachers' knowledge about current issues and practices in science, including effective ways to teach particular subjects.

- To offer laboratory or field opportunities to participate in scientific research so that teachers will understand more about the process of science.
- To build discipline-based scientific collaboration that provides K-12 science teachers and scientists with opportunities to meet regularly for collegial discussion about scientific ideas and materials.
- To assist teachers in learning about and implementing school- or curriculum-reform efforts.
- To prepare mentors to train other teachers in subject matter, teaching strategies, or ways to adapt teaching strategies to the curriculum.

Many programs have more than one of those objectives. Specific descriptions of various kinds of programs are found in Chapter 3.

### Relationship Between Teacher Preparation and Professional Development

The kind of professional development needed by teachers today depends not only on their teaching assignment but also on the kind of science and science teaching that they had as undergraduates. Teacher preparation in American colleges and universities has generally consisted of three elements: study of disciplines that teachers will teach (subject-matter preparation), study of teaching and learning (pedagogy), and a brief classroom apprenticeship (student teaching).

#### Science Subject-Matter Preparation

Only 26 states require any science courses for persons preparing to be elementary-school teachers, and only 29 require these persons to complete coursework in both science and mathematics teaching methods (Blank and Dalkilic, 1992). As noted by Raizen and Michelsohn (1994), "both quantity and quality are lacking in the science-content and science-education components of teacher-preparation programs for prospective elementary-school teachers." In contrast, nearly 80% of secondary-school science teachers majored in a scientific discipline; it varies from 58% in Alaska to 91% in Maryland (Blank and Gruebel, 1993). As science majors, they took standard science classes with no particular attention to whether they intended to teach. Many of their science courses presented science as a body of factual knowledge that was usually taught in didactic lectures rather than in a spirit of inquiry. The need for improving those science courses and suggestions for changes in college and university rewards for teaching that will be necessary to induce improvement are discussed in Chapter 4.

#### Pedagogy

Preparation in educational theory and teaching strategies (pedagogy) varies from state to state. In most states it is still possible to major in elementary education. Only six states now require elementary-school teachers to major in a field other than education (Raizen and Michelsohn, 1994, citing Mastain, 1991). In most institutions a science-methods course is required for elementary-education majors although it is not coordinated with science-content courses (Mechling, Stedman, and Donnelan, 1982). Some elementary-school teacher candidates are taught science with teaching methods in a college of education. Elementary-education teachers are prepared to teach other subjects as well, including methods, which are also useful for activity-based science teaching.

Secondary-school teachers usually have had a course in curriculum and instruction or science methods. They studied inquiry-based teaching but often had little teaching experience to correlate with the theory. A single course in teaching pedagogy that stresses hands-on inquiry and problem-solving is not enough for most people to supplant their own experience in college lectures and demonstration laboratories. The high-school science curriculum resembles the biology, chemistry, and physics taught in college. But elementary-school, middle-school, and integrated high-school science combines concepts and activities quite differently from college offerings. Because few science courses are designed with teacher candidates in mind, they usually do not provide effective models of teaching strategies or concept development that can be used in teaching in K-12 teaching. All too often, undergraduate science majors have no research experience and so are unprepared to teach an open-ended inquiry activity or course.

Greater communication between teaching faculties in the sciences and teacher preparation could result in more effective teaching and learning in both K-12 and college science. Many scientists "discover" teaching methods and curriculum materials in professional-development activities even though the knowledge of the teaching methods and curriculum materials had been readily available elsewhere on their own campuses.

## Student Teaching

Student teaching or internship in a classroom setting usually occurs in the final undergraduate year or during a fifth year of specialized teacher preparation. It might be limited to one or two periods of teaching for one term or semester or culminate in full-day teaching for several weeks. Few efforts assess the teaching practices of mentor teachers with whom student teachers work. And few colleges or universities have mechanisms for involving master teachers officially in student teaching or assessing student teachers. There is little coordination of the education and science curricula with the real-life situations that will be faced by future elementary- or secondary-school science teachers. It is difficult to include enough appropriate experience in a 4- or 5-year teacher-preparation program. For that reason, several teacher-preparation programs continue to assist teachers for a few years if they take positions near the university.

## Content and Process in Science Teaching

It has long been debated whether elementary- and secondary-school science teaching should be mostly content-oriented or process-oriented. At present, much of secondary-school science teaching consists of lecturing on science content, a situation that is a direct reflection of how science is taught in most undergraduate courses in colleges and universities. Lectures might be an efficient way to communicate with a large group of students, but lectures alone do not reveal the excitement of the process of *doing* science.

It is here that scientists can perform a unique service by helping teachers to experience the solution of scientific problems through research. By using intuition and methods of approaching a problem, a scientist can both illustrate the processes of science and introduce content. Such professional-development activities could model, to the extent possible, the most appropriate instructional methods for best teaching both science process and content. For content, the National Science Education Standards are an excellent source. Teachers tend to teach the way they were taught, and scientists who use inquiry-based teaching will communicate the value of this method to their students.

The focus on inquiry-based learning is not new. Paul Hurd, professor of science education, emeritus, at Stanford, has reviewed science-education reform efforts over the last century and noted how similar are their recommendations for inquiry-based science (see box). Thirty years ago, in reaction to overambitious content-based curricula, inquiry-based approaches were developed. *Inquiry-based* means teaching science in ways that emphasize the process of *doing* science. In some inquiry-based curricula, content became almost irrelevant. That goes too far: the content of science is indeed essential. But content is most easily

---

**Suggestions for the Improvement of
Biology Courses from the Central Association of
Science and Mathematics Teachers, 1910**

   1. More emphasis on "reasoning out" rather than memorization.

   2. More attention to developing a "problem-solving attitude" and a "problem-raising attitude" on the part of the students.

   3. More applications of the subject to the everyday life of the pupil and the community, and "this does not mean a commercialization or industrialization of science . . . although these are practical phases of this life value."

   4. More emphasis on the incompleteness of the subject and glimpses into the great questions yet to be solved by investigators.

   5. Less coverage of territory; the course should progress no faster than pupils can go with understanding.

[Hurd, 1961, pp. 25-26]

understood if connected to process and to the student's own inquiry. The two laboratory exercises shown in Appendix H illustrate the differences between a traditional, teacher-directed laboratory exercise and a student-generated, inquiry-based laboratory exercise. The former allows a student to follow directions, collect data, and learn laboratory techniques, but it does little with analysis and application of information. The latter allows the teacher to help students to generate hypotheses and encourages the students to cooperate in designing experiments to test their hypotheses and then, in interpreting the results, to decide which hypotheses are most promising.

Other approaches to balance process and content in science teaching include the science-technology-society (STS) approach, which was developed in the 1980s. Current problems and societal issues directed the content with emphasis on science and technological processes that students could use in everyday life (including decision-making skills and cost-benefit analysis) (Yager and Zehr, 1985). Another approach, the "conceptual-change perspective," suggested that the goal of science education is to help students to develop a meaningful, conceptual understanding of science and its ways of describing, predicting, explaining, and controlling natural phenomena (Roth, 1989). Proponents of the conceptual-change perspective argued that science teaching should integrate conceptual knowledge and science processes in ways that better reflect the richness and complexity of science itself. These approaches have laid some of the groundwork for the current renewed efforts in science-education reform.

## Needs of Individual Teachers

Teachers' needs for professional development vary with their backgrounds, school environment, motivation, experience, and resources. Teachers have the complex task of integrating teaching methods and science content mandated by state and local curricular frameworks for science. Often, the mandated content and curricula are presented differently from the way they were taught in college; and sometimes, they cross customary disciplinary lines. Here we address the needs of individual teachers.

### Teacher Isolation

Irrespective of educational or scientific background or level of experience, science teachers in both elementary and secondary schools suffer from isolation. They have no regular contact with the rest of the scientific community. They often work in buildings with no peers who teach similar courses. Many teachers, at all grade levels, work long hours with inadequate resources, insufficient funds for laboratory materials, and large classes. One report estimates that, on the basis of an average of five classes per day, high-school biology teachers (grades

9-10) are responsible for an average of 217 students and middle-school science teachers (grades 7-8) 177 students (Blank and Gruebel, 1993).

Proximity fosters the sharing of ideas and materials, but innovative and successful teachers find ways to establish communication with kindred spirits, either at their own school, with teachers in other schools, or even with teachers in other parts of the country. Professional-development activities can provide immediate and cost-effective opportunities for teachers to communicate with each other both informally and formally about subject matter and teaching and learning techniques and can help to develop professional relationships and information-sharing among teachers and scientists.

*Increasing Teachers' Knowledge About Science*

Many teachers try to stay current in science by reading scientific publications, but elementary- and secondary-school teachers are responsible for such broad fields of science that they cannot hope to be at the cutting edge of any discipline. Nor do they have to be. But they must be familiar enough with current science to incorporate topics and applications that are of current interest to the general public into the curriculum, especially laboratory investigations. The fields of molecular biology and biotechnology, for example, are moving so quickly that the information available to the general public exceeds what a biology teacher learned in college just a few years ago.

Elementary-school teachers become certified with little or no undergraduate preparation in science, and many do not teach science, often because of a lack of confidence. Many middle- and high-school teachers are asked to teach courses for which they are inadequately prepared. A teacher who majored in biology, for example, whose undergraduate chemistry courses also certify him or her to teach chemistry might need to take a refresher course when assigned to a chemistry class. A general-biology teacher who is assigned to teach a second-year physiology course might also want to upgrade his or her background in the more specialized field. Many middle-school teachers of life or physical science are now being asked to teach integrated or general science and need additional work in the other sciences.

Some teachers (and some scientists) hold misconceptions about science, and some hold unscientific beliefs. For example, some believe pseudoscientific explanations and misconceptions about evolution, and others equate scientific theories with guesses. It is often difficult to motivate those teachers to participate in professional-development programs, because the programs introduce information that challenges their unscientific beliefs. Unlearning and replacing misconception is more difficult and time-consuming than learning about something new and can be a challenge for professional-development programs.

*Elementary-School and Secondary-School Science Teachers*

Many argue that the needs of elementary-school and secondary-school science teachers are fundamentally different because of their preparation and classroom responsibilities. However, both kinds of teachers can improve their teaching skills and their students' learning by engaging in professional-development programs. In most elementary schools, the teacher is responsible for teaching all subjects, including science. Because most elementary-school teachers have had little or no preparation in the sciences, they do not consider themselves science teachers. In some elementary schools, a "science specialist" is responsible for teaching science to all classes. That reinforces the idea that science is a "special" subject rather than a core subject, or that science is not accessible to the average teacher. Most secondary-school teachers' undergraduate preparation included a grounding in science content. However, many teachers at this level have not experienced inquiry-based laboratories or individual research projects. Some might have knowledge of this approach but have chosen not to use it, because of lack of class time, preparatory time, and resources.

*Beginning Teachers*

Effective professional-development activities in the first few years of teaching can help teachers to adapt their generic undergraduate preparation to concrete teaching situations. Activities can help new teachers to develop effective teaching strategies, supplement their knowledge of both content and pedagogy, and link them with experienced teachers. Each activity can help to reduce the frustration and dropout rate of beginning teachers. As noted earlier, some teacher-preparation programs include followup activities that extend through the first few years of teaching. Often, however, teachers take positions far from the institutions that prepared them and are left without this support.

Secondary-school science teachers might teach general science, biology, chemistry, or physics. They might also teach other subjects and coach a sport during each season. Beginning secondary-school teachers are most likely to draw diverse subject-matter assignments and to have little control over their schedules. They might teach several subjects each day, each requiring a different class preparation, and have extracurricular duties, such as monitoring the halls, cafeteria, or student activities. They might or might not have their own classrooms; many must cart materials from classroom to classroom every day.

Whether the elementary- or secondary-school teacher's undergraduate program was stellar or mediocre, it was not adequate to prepare the beginning teacher for all his or her duties during the first few years. For example, one of the most difficult tasks for new teachers is to set up and sequence classroom activities in an efficient manner. Preparation for class takes time—time that teachers do not have. In addition, teachers need to know a variety of techniques to teach students with different abilities. Teachers often learn these and other skills through on-the-job training. Many become overwhelmed by all the teaching and nonteaching tasks that they must juggle and with which they are unprepared to deal and drop out after a few years of teaching.

## Experienced Teachers

In addition to learning the needs of individual new students each year, teachers often master a repertoire of classroom-management strategies and school politics. Like other professionals, experienced teachers need to stay up to date in their subjects. They also need to learn new teaching techniques and practice incorporating them into their classroom activities.

With the explosion of new scientific information, the veteran biology teacher, for example, has had to incorporate new information about DNA and recombinant-DNA techniques, accelerated extinction rates and endangered species, reproductive technology for humans and other organisms, and the discovery of much older fossils that has led to taxonomic reordering. The new information has been added, often with little integration, to curricula and to science textbooks. New information has also affected the development of teaching materials and local or state initiatives directed at improving science education.

Some teachers watch educational television and read scientific periodicals and professional journals. Others attend professional meetings and courses where they learn new subject matter. Still others work with scientists and other educators to develop ways to incorporate new information into K-12 curricula. In addition to learning new scientific information, teachers need to learn how to use the information in inquiry-based activities that stress critical thinking by students.

## Science Enthusiasts and Other Teachers

Teachers who are science enthusiasts participate actively in professional development to increase their knowledge of science and to improve their teaching. A large percentage of both enthusiasts and less-involved teachers, however, do not engage in professional-development opportunities, because of other school duties, family obligations, prohibitive cost, lack of time, lack of interest, or burnout. Of the nearly 47,000 high-school biology teachers and 46,500 middle-school science teachers in the United States (Blank and Gruebel, 1993), only about 10% belong to professional science teachers organizations. Most professional-development programs do not address the less-involved teachers, but these teachers must be taken into account if efforts to improve science education are to reach the majority of students.

## PROFESSIONAL DEVELOPMENT AND
## SCIENCE-EDUCATION REFORM

Science-education reform is not being pursued on the basis of an integrated set of changes designed to enhance the learning of science by all students. Professional development designed to promote reform would need to be more extensive than traditional programs. Effective professional-development programs can prepare teachers to participate in reform or empower them to become leaders of reform. It takes time to adjust to the major changes in curricula and instructional materials called for by standards-based reform and to learn to use them effectively. The changes called for by the major science-education reform efforts—most notably the National Research Council's National Science Education Standards, AAAS's Project 2061 and its Benchmarks, and NSTA's Scope Sequence and Coordination Project—require individual teachers to adopt new curricula and teaching strategies. In particular, standards-based reform requires teachers to be involved in the changes that result in new curricula and instructional materials and to implement those changes. Teacher leaders can become advocates of change and assist in the professional development of their colleagues. Although we do not consider curriculum development specifically in this document, we acknowledge that participation in curriculum development, implementation, and evaluation is in itself a rich professional-development experience for teachers.

## INDIVIDUAL AND SYSTEMIC PROGRAMS

Most programs that we examined in our review of programs fit a particular profile—they were designed for and attended by teachers who were self-selecting. They are *individual-based*. A fundamentally different kind of program is designed to affect a connected group of teachers in a school or school district. The eventual goal of *systemic reform* is to extend exemplary teaching and learning to the entire educational system. Although there is no consensus on its definition among educators, a common theme is that systemic reform efforts must address all students, encompass all components of the educational system, be understood and supported by people from all segments of the community, and cascade through all levels of education and school governance (Kober, 1993). We use *systemic* in a sense that applies to smaller elements of the system—such as departments, individual schools, and school districts—because professional-development programs designed for related groups of teachers have common elements irrespective of the size of the group. Examples are presented in Chapter 6.

Science education can be a starting point for systemic reform, and several efforts around the nation are working toward that end. Professional-development activities can be designed to help science teachers to participate in systemic reform. If scientists choose to become involved in this kind of professional development, they must have clear goals and understand how their efforts fit into the larger context of school reform. Scientists must know about the needs of teachers and students, be aware of the level of commitment required, and solicit the support of both school and university administrators for systemic activities within universities, schools, and school districts.

## USING EDUCATIONAL RESEARCH

Scientists who want to become involved in K-12 education have much to learn from the educational-research community. Research on teaching and learning has identified numerous techniques and strategies that influence how teachers teach and how students learn, for example, the benefits of cooperative and collaborative learning, the importance of active learning, and the value of recognizing different learning styles. Scientists and most other university faculty are not aware of this literature as it applies to their own college or university teaching and not aware of its value to elementary- and secondary-school teachers and their students. There are several reasons for that. Most scientists do not have the inclination or training to be directly involved in educational research themselves, nor are they motivated to read the available literature. They have difficulty in assessing the quality and applicability of the research. There is also a widespread misperception that "there is no good educational research out there anyway." That misperception is particularly strong in experimental scientists who design and interpret controlled experiments; they find it difficult to evaluate outcomes of research that deal with the complexity of the real classroom.

Although we do not explore educational research in detail in this report, we have compiled an annotated reading list in Appendix D that provides a starting point and resource for scientists who want to become more informed about research in science education.

# 2

# Characteristics of Effective Professional-Development Programs

In our survey of almost 200 programs, we found that professional-development activities for science teachers occur in a variety of institutions, including research universities, research institutes, comprehensive universities, liberal-arts colleges, community colleges, industrial settings, science centers, museums, and zoos. They have a wide range of formats, such as evening and weekend lectures, short and long summer workshops, and various one- to several-day followup activities. Some were directed to individual teachers, others were systemic. Irrespective of that variety, however, the programs involving scientists that were most effective, as judged by longevity and evaluations by program participants, had many of the following characteristics:

- Scientists, teachers, and administrators collaborated in the program's development and implementation.
- Participating teachers were treated as professionals.
- The program was designed to meet important school-based needs.
- Opportunities for continued involvement with program staff and other participants were provided.
- Evaluation was a continuous process and was used to improve the program.
- New partnerships, projects, and networks were stimulated among participating teachers and between teachers and scientists.
- Program directors used effective publicity and recruitment strategies.
- The program was encouraged and supported by school districts and school administrators.

- Effective dissemination strategies were used.
- Program directors had practical knowledge of the process of change.
- A charismatic person or group provided strong leadership.

*Scientists, teachers, and administrators collaborated in the program's development and implementation.* All were involved in planning the program from the outset. Teachers and scientists worked in partnerships to determine the focus of the program and to develop laboratory activities appropriate to students' level of understanding. Teachers provided insight about the appropriateness of activities for teachers' needs, creative ways of disseminating information about the program to improve participation, and advice regarding practical laboratory activities. Scientists helped the teachers to learn more science content and the processes of science—which together can improve teaching and student learning. The scientists benefited from participation by gaining a better understanding of the school setting and respect for teachers. Many scientists from colleges and universities reported that their own teaching skills had improved because they had worked with outstanding K-12 teachers. Programs improved over time when former participants became part of the program's leadership.

*Participating teachers were treated as professionals.* The tone of a program as transmitted by its directors and instructors was critical to its success. Teachers welcomed and responded positively to the opportunity to meet and become colleagues of scientists. Participants usually received stipends or honorariums (especially during the summer), college or continuing-education credits, and access to needed supplies or equipment during the school year. Programs in which participants and scientists were treated as equals often developed collegial relationships that extended beyond the program itself.

*Opportunities for continued involvement with program staff and other participants were provided.* Regardless of a program's format, followup activities were necessary to extend and reinforce its content and teaching strategies. Followup opportunities allowed participants to continue and solidify their connections with their scientific and teaching colleagues and furthered the establishment of collaborations and partnerships.

Followup activities included classroom visits by program staff, weekend events for alumni to share new laboratory projects and content, return visits by the participants to the laboratories of their mentors, weekly or monthly sessions for all participants to review progress on new teaching strategies or curriculum materials, establishment of newsletters and computer networks, and reunions for teachers at state and national professional conferences. A 1-week intensive course in biotechnology, for example, might use followup activities to help to solve practical problems and ensure that teachers are comfortable in implementing "wet" laboratory exercises. Visits to classrooms by scientists or technicians and reconvening of participants at a university, industrial site, professional-organization meeting, or convention allowed teachers to share their experiences with each other, to renew acquaintances, and to modify curricular materials.

Followup activities must provide a support system for teachers who were using materials for the first time. Support might include an equipment-sharing consortium that provided equipment to teachers or a program coordinator who could assist teachers when they were doing the new laboratory exercises and, when necessary, suggest alternative activities. Computer networks were an effective way to provide such support and keep teachers connected to each other and to scientists.

*Evaluation was a continuous process and was used to improve the program.* Both informal and formal evaluation made it possible to obtain participants' responses and make adjustments in the activities. Through informal evaluation, specific difficulties were identified during the life of a program, and program organizers changed the program accordingly. Followup activities also provided program organizers with an opportunity to obtain information about the program's strengths and weaknesses. Regular self-evaluation enabled organizers to recognize situations where there was a need to alter the program to meet teachers' needs.

*New partnerships, projects, and networks were stimulated among participating teachers and between teachers and scientists.* Some programs provided leadership-training sessions for selected teachers. Those teachers then worked with colleagues in their home institutions or school districts to implement new teaching methods and curricula. The process often stimulated the creation of spinoff projects that gave teachers access to the equipment required to do laboratory investigations in their classrooms or to implement particular teaching strategies more effectively. In some cases, local companies or universities donated equipment. Partnerships between scientists and teachers were fostered by collaboration in planning both the initial program and followup activities.

*Program directors used effective publicity and recruitment strategies.* The program had effective strategies for teachers to learn about it. Direct mailing to teachers and word of mouth were effective in creating interest. Successful programs made advocates of their participants, who eagerly spread the word. Professional organizations, such as the National Association of Biology Teachers and the National Science Teachers Association, and state and local organizations, such as a state science-teachers association and a local alliance, provided valuable information about professional development. Some school districts used local newsletters to spread information about professional-development activities.

*The program was encouraged and supported by school districts and school administrators.* The program encouraged or even required a particular amount of administrative support or participation in its activities. Support ranged from providing a number of release days (paying for a substitute teacher's coverage of a classroom) to commitment to purchase instructional materials, equipment, or supplies or holding a special session for administrators. Commitment and support were contagious; some of the most effective advocates for effective continuing programs were district or school administrators, who encouraged teachers who usually did not participate in professional-development programs.

*Effective dissemination strategies were used.* Such strategies assisted participants in spreading the program to other teachers. Followup sessions provided opportunities to practice dissemination strategies, such as workshop presentations, facilitation skills, and practical implementation plans that helped teacher-leaders to become more effective in working with their colleagues. Providing financial, material, and networking access was important for effective program dissemination.

*Program directors had practical knowledge of the process of change.* Understanding some of the basic tenets of change helped to support both participants and their colleagues as they tried to implement in their classrooms what they learned. Program directors understood that the more important the curriculum and methodological change expected, the more difficult and time-consuming the process would be.

*A charismatic person or group provided strong leadership.* In a single program, a school, or even a whole school district, education was improved throughout by virtue of the energy and dedication of a few teachers and scientists who listened to each other and were willing to share ideas. A successful program began with visionary, informed people who were able to take their message to the local community. Rather than being authoritarian or autocratic, those persons or small groups of them were able to convince skeptics of the value of the program and to sustain the program during the difficult beginning periods.

Those desirable characteristics will guide the discussions about programs found in the rest of this report.

# 3

# A Guide for Scientists

Any society that is serious about the education of its children must be equally serious about supporting the continuing education of those charged with that task. If we are to meet the needs of diverse students and the nation's needs for scientifically literate citizens and skilled workers, it is essential that teachers have the opportunity to continue to expand their knowledge, pedagogical skills, and laboratory expertise from their undergraduate education through their professional careers.

Rapid and extensive improvement of science education is unlikely to occur until it becomes clear to scientists that they have an obligation to become involved in elementary- and secondary-level science. In this chapter, we describe ways to interest more scientists in becoming involved in professional-development programs for science teachers, suggest ways that scientists can contribute most effectively, describe various types of programs, and suggest ways to gain administrative support for these programs. This chapter builds on the summary of characteristics of effective programs in Chapter 2.

## GETTING STARTED

Many scientists are ready to get involved, but few know where to begin. Scientists from both academe and industry describe several common motivations for their involvement in professional development. Many say that they "simply love to teach" and believe that science education is so important that they will take an active role, whether or not they are rewarded externally. Others discover from their own children or grandchildren in school how poor science education

---

**How Scientists Are Stimulated to Participate**

In response to an invitation to teach an adaptation unit to elementary-school teachers at a summer science institute, the biologist replied, "But I can't do it." "Why not?" "Because I have never taught elementary-school teachers before."

After considerable negotiations and assurances that the biologist would be team-teaching with an experienced teacher, the course-planning meeting started. The biologist came in with an outline of the subject matter to be covered in 30 contact hours. The teacher suggested, on the basis of his experience, that there was "no way" the prescribed outline could be covered. Painstaking negotiation started about what could be left out and which student activities ("hands-on" activities or "experiments") needed to be included to develop conceptual understanding. There were other considerations: What materials were typically available in schools? How did the life-science unit fit into the state science framework? How could the life-science unit be integrated with physical and earth science? Were there activities in which the teachers needed to participate as adult learners? This give and take between the content expert and the pedagogy expert is necessary to produce a curriculum that teachers find not only "fun" (i.e., nonthreatening), but also appropriate for developing conceptual understanding in science.

---

can be and how their children are turned away from learning science. Many scientists want to do something because they have found that many students in introductory undergraduate courses are poorly prepared and not motivated to learn science. Industrial scientists, in particular, share the widespread concern that the schools are not producing the workforce that industry needs—both trained scientists and technicians.[1]

## Self-Education

As a first step, scientists thinking about getting involved in the professional development of science teachers should assess their own teaching to determine whether they are using effective methods of science education. They should educate themselves about the professional lives of elementary- and secondary-school teachers and about classroom science teaching. To assist in the process, this chapter includes three vignettes describing a day in the life of an elementary-school teacher, of a middle-school teacher, and of a high-school biology teacher; they show some of the varied teaching experiences in American public schools

---

[1]For more information about industry's role in science education, we suggest *Business and the Schools,* a guide to programs run by businesses for schools, published by the Council for Aid to Education (1992). Because of the availability of this excellent publication, this section focuses primarily on ways to involve academic scientists.

today. Scientists should also familiarize themselves with school organization and the roles of teachers, administrators, and parents.

Although there are many effective partnerships between teachers and scientists, to expand effective professional-development programs teachers' and scientists' understanding and appreciation of each other's responsibilities must be improved. Their misconceptions about each other exist partly because there are few opportunities for them to interact. Our discussions with teachers around the country revealed that scientists were often perceived to be "threatening" and "not interested" in working collaboratively. That stereotype is perpetuated by misconceptions held by some scientists that cause misunderstandings between them and teachers, including the following:

- Because scientists understand a topic, they know how to teach it.
- Because a topic is a scientist's lifelong interest, it will be interesting to precollege teachers and students or be an appropriate part of the science curriculum.
- Because a topic is new, it must be better and should be included in the curriculum.
- If teachers understood the scientific content better, they would automatically be able to teach more effectively and to create new and better curricula.
- If students and teachers are merely told correct information, they will acquire the skills necessary to recognize correct information when they encounter it.

Working collaboratively with teachers will help to dispel some of those misconceptions. Several professional societies have workshops for teachers and scientists to foster partnerships. These are described below. In addition, the annotated reading list found in Appendix D should help scientists to minimize misunderstandings and educate themselves about the world of teachers and students, issues of teaching and learning, educational research, and current efforts in science-education reform.

### Initial Involvement

Before beginning work with teachers to plan a professional-development program, scientists should initiate interactions with teachers and school administrators to become familiar with the needs of elementary- and secondary-school science teachers and learn about the realities of the school system. If possible, they should visit other programs or participate in workshops, for example, at professional meetings. Most scientists' first inclination is to volunteer to give a 1- to 2-hour class presentation and discussion of their own research or a review of their subject. That might be a good starting point if planned in conjunction with the teacher. A valuable next step is to visit the elementary- or secondary-school science classroom of one of the teachers for at least an entire day. That gives the scientist a bird's-eye view of schools and allows him or her to witness teachers' motivation in the face of the physical and financial constraints of the classroom.

As a followup activity, scientists can invite local teachers to campus and structure special seminars at times convenient for teachers and on topics decided on in consultation with the teachers. Scientists can foster open discussions about teachers' needs, explore opportunities for future activities, and discuss the implications of collaboration for K-12 science teaching and learning. Scientists can also invite teachers to a research laboratory for a demonstration that emphasizes the processes of science. The one-on-one interaction between teachers and scientists can lead to the involvement of teachers with postdoctoral fellows, graduate students, and technicians. Teachers can gradually then become members of a community of people "doing science."

The following vignettes describe a day in the life of school teachers at various levels. They provide a snapshot of the nation's public schools through the eyes of teachers and give scientists a glimpse of day-to-day life of the teachers.

## A Day in the Life of One Elementary-School Teacher

I teach fourth-graders in an urban elementary school serving about 500 students. My class of 32 students represents over 10 ethnic groups. Among my students are several limited-English speakers, two former special-education students who have been "mainstreamed" for the first time this year, and 14 from families who live below the poverty level.

I have taught for 10 years. For 5 years, I taught at the second-grade level only; since then, I have been assigned a different grade level each year. This summer, I spent a good deal of my vacation preparing to teach fifth-graders; unfortunately, 2 weeks before school began, the principal placed me with a fourth-grade class instead.

As always, I report to school a week early to put up attractive bulletin-board displays (to hide the ugly walls), organize my ancient desks and tables, and prepare instructional materials.

The first day arrives, and I learn that the district computer has miscalculated: the number of students in my class is 32, not 30. The janitor quickly brings in two additional chairs (no tables or desks are available). Of these students, 12 are newly assigned. This year the school has many unexpected new students, forcing the creation of a new class, which will be taught in the school library. Since the library has fallen into disrepair over the last few years, there are no objections from the staff.

I sign in at the office well before 8:00 a.m., the required time for teacher arrival. I hurry to my room to complete some last-minute preparations.

About 40% of the students take district-provided buses. If the buses are late, so are the students. Today, as the first bell rings at 8:25, most students enter the old, two-story building. Teachers stand just outside their doors, as expected, to welcome their classes and to monitor the halls. When the tardy bell rings at 8:30, the halls are filled with the sound of doors slamming shut.

I begin the day by assigning several math problems to students divided into small groups. The problems contain material that will be covered later that morning on a math test. Ten minutes pass, and I ask each group to present its work. The presentations are interrupted when the cafeteria "count" person comes by and yells out to one of his friends.

After presentations, I go over the math problems with the students and give them individual math tests. I provide bilingual versions of the test to several limited-English-speaking students and another version for two special-education students. The latter version includes a section for discussing the math problems with me directly. The test takes approximately 30 minutes. The children then take their morning recess.

Next, I facilitate literature-reading groups. Students are grouped by what they choose to read—that leads to a wide range of abilities in each group. Reading activities last until 11:00, when students march to the multipurpose room serving as our cafeteria. I take a hurried 20 minutes for lunch, then return to my classroom to prepare for the afternoon. Thirty minutes later I monitor the halls with other teachers as the children come in from the playground.

Using several types of materials, I set up learning stations focusing on science and art. Today, students have time to rotate through several stations. Next, we spend 30 minutes discussing the history and culture of California, and I send them out again for the designated afternoon recess.

The children return tired and hot from their combined "recess and physical education" period. During the last period, I alternate daily between teaching "art and music" and "science and health." Today I teach science. By the time the students have completed their science activities, the 3:00 p.m. bell rings. I quickly review homework assignments, pass out notices for parents, and dismiss the students for the day.

All students have gone now, except for one who has been asked to stay late. As he does his homework, I start my preparations for the next day. Next on my "to do" list is to notify several parents by phone about some of my concerns about their children's behavior in school. To get to the phone designated for teachers (limited to local calls), I would have to go to the central office. I decide to remain in the classroom with the detained student and make the calls later that evening.

After sending my student home at 4:00 p.m., I hurry down the hall for the monthly meeting of fourth-grade teachers. I am already familiar with the topic ("preparing students for next month's standardized tests"), and so I try to grade a few math tests during the meeting. Afterwards, I duplicate handouts for tomor-row's activities, finish classroom preparations, and gather today's math tests to grade. I hope I have time to finish them before the "Open House" that evening at the school of my own children.

## A Day in the Life of One Middle-School Science Teacher

My day begins at 6:30 a.m. On the drive to school, I mentally review my plans for the day. I think of my two seventh-grade environmental-studies classes for which I have planned an activity on carbon dioxide. I remind myself to make sure that I have enough solutions for the 34 students in the first class and the 31 students in the second class and enough on reserve for the occasional accident. Next, my thoughts turn to my three eighth-grade classes on plant science. The Fast Plants unit has been a great success so far. Students have been coming into class early to check the progress of their plants, comparing the growth of various sets and asking me to have a look at them. I enjoy watching the students interact; their enthusiasm makes the class fun for me. As I drive, I am aware that this commute is the only quiet time I will have to reflect all day.

I arrive at school and check the mail, finding the usual plethora of catalogs and brochures filled with goodies that our small budget—$100 per year—cannot afford. At 7:00 a.m., I go to the weekly faculty meeting, which offers a brief chance to speak with colleagues. This week several teachers give small committee reports on the designated meeting topic: integrated curriculum.

The meeting adjourns at 8:10 a.m., and I rush down the hall to unlock my classroom door. Students pour into the room—giggling, pushing, and shoving each other playfully (for the most part). The first bell rings; 5 minutes later, we hear the second bell and the school day begins. There are now 34 active bodies in my small room. In 50 minutes, this group of students changes places with a group of 31 students, entering with the clamor of simultaneous chatter. At least five students are calling my name or asking questions with urgency ("What are we going to do today?" "Is this right?"). During this period, we have two interruptions over the loudspeaker: a break to read the morning bulletin and a timeout to recite the Pledge of Allegiance to the Flag. Another 50-minute period ends with the bell.

Five minutes later 33 eighth-graders enter the room. I turn my attention to a new topic, using different equipment and teaching strategies to communicate the appropriate concepts. This class, stocked with changing hormones, seems more social and more boisterous than other classes. The unique challenge of this age group is to keep up with the emotional roller coaster that dominates the dynamics of the classroom; it calls for more of what I refer to as "nurturing and social work." Another bell announces the 25-minute lunch period. There is no phone in my classroom, so I rush to the school office to make some important parent phone calls during this time. I have 10 minutes left for a cup of coffee with colleagues before the next class begins.

After lunch, a group of 24 students comes into the room for "silent reading." During this 20-minute interlude, the entire student population spends time reading or doing homework. I am not in charge of assessing the students' work, but I am often called on for assistance and attention. At the next bell, my conference period begins. During the next 50 minutes, I talk with counselors about problems related to my students, call more parents, mix solutions for laboratory exercises, read mail, plan lessons, and grade papers. Unfortunately, I am unable to work in my classroom because it is being used by another teacher.

Two classes later it is 3:00 p.m. By this time, I have met with 194 students who have worked with me, leaned on me, laughed with me, and learned with me. At 3:30 p.m., I leave school for a meeting at the central office. Like all my colleagues, I serve on several districtwide committees. Today, I attend a meeting on technology in the classroom.

Later, as I head home, I reflect on this day's events for the first time. I have spent at least a third of my time on "social work" (negotiating conflicts between students, learning about difficulties that have kept students from completing their homework, listening to problems at home, listening to jokes, trying to get kids to focus, and disciplining those who get out of line), about 90 minutes in meetings, and 10 minutes conversing with colleagues. I have had no "think time"—no time to reflect on my teaching, my students, or other areas of my life. I have a stack of 97 papers to grade, and I still have to stop by K-Mart to get materials for the next day's lab with my own money.

## A Day in the Life of One High-School Biology Teacher

When I began teaching at Normal High School, I did not have my own classroom. I used a cart for my laboratory supplies. I would set up a laboratory exercise in one classroom before first period, teach the lab, dismantle it, and rush to the next class. This took place for three consecutive periods. After several years of teaching, I now have my own classroom and I no longer use a cart to store my supplies. I am teaching an advanced-placement biology course and two honors courses.

At 8:20 a.m., my day begins with a free period. I prepare laboratory exercises during this time and then teach classes during the next three periods. After three morning classes, at 11:35 a.m. I become a lunchroom monitor. I have no time during this period to review teaching material, work with students, or prepare for afternoon activities.

At 12:15 p.m., I use my own lunch period to prepare for the upcoming double period of AP biology. The laboratory exercises for this class require significant preparation. I try—with little time, microscopes that were purchased in the 1960s, and no teaching assistant—to simulate a college-level laboratory experience. There is no time for the five biology teachers at Normal to assist each other with these kinds of preparation or to share our teaching experiences. Last summer I made an attempt to collaborate with some colleagues on the revision of a laboratory manual with funding from an Eisenhower grant. The project was not entirely successful, because of administrative criticism and lack of support.

The labs take me straight through to the end of the school day. I clean up, prepare materials for the next day, schedule guest speakers for future AP classes, correct labs, grade exams, work with student leaders in the National Honor Society (for which I am the adviser), collect new laboratory materials in local stores or ponds, and purchase pet food and shavings. I use my own money to purchase these supplies because the money is not available from the school district. I am owed over $100 that I spent on materials; I do not expect to be reimbursed.

Since I began at the school, the expendable part of the AP budget has been reduced to one-fourth, and the laboratory exercises have become more sophisticated. Colleagues at the local university have donated some of the reagents and supplies for the exercises; others have been given by ABC Research. The local university has recently started to give area teachers its excess equipment and glassware from its laboratories. Unfortunately, these supplies are scarce. There is a circulating rumor that there is going to be another cut in the district's science budget.

I spend the evening preparing classroom materials for the following day.

## CONTRIBUTING MOST EFFECTIVELY

Roland Barth, a former principal, wrote in *Improving Schools from Within* (1990):

Perhaps the most influential contribution a university can make in assisting teachers, parents, and principals in improving their schools is to convey prestige and respectability to them. . . . Recognition these days is the commodity in greatest supply in universities and in shortest supply to teachers and principals.

Scientists can contribute to the professional development of teachers in many ways. They can contribute directly by sharing their scientific knowledge, their understanding of the processes of scientific research, and their individual professional experience. They can also contribute in less-tangible ways. For example, scientists' involvement builds teachers' optimism about the eventual success of a program and builds the program's credibility among parents, administrators, students, and even funding agencies. Scientists' specific contributions can be summarized as follows:

• Scientists can *support good science-process teaching* by modeling scientific processes—what scientists do and how they do it. Scientists can work with teachers to design inquiry-based laboratory exercises for use in K-12 classrooms but should be careful not to underestimate the time that will be required for field testing and development. This kind of collaboration helps to build a broader base of investigative approaches in K-12 science laboratories. Scientists can also help teachers to evaluate existing laboratory experiments, interpret data, and find relevant connections to current research. In this way, student laboratory exercises can be put into a research-oriented context.

• Scientists can *provide accurate scientific content that also adds to the teachers' understanding of scientific process.* Content learning is an essential part of science education, but content is best learned and retained when presented in the context of the processes of science—how science works. Directors of programs that focus on inquiry-based and hands-on learning have observed that once teachers have developed an understanding of scientific processes, they often begin to seek out the content knowledge that can be used as a basis for inquiry into real and immediate scientific questions (J. Bower, personal communication). When teachers seek information themselves, it is likely to be successfully connected to what they do in the classroom. The search for content to elucidate inquiry-based teaching reverses the common approach of teaching content first. The scientist can become an invaluable resource for teachers and their students when the impetus to acquire content knowledge comes from inquiry-based experiences. More important, this approach ensures that the content is relevant to the teacher in the classroom, not just to what the scientist thinks the teacher should know.

• Scientists can *ensure the accuracy of scientific content of existing curricula* by working with teachers to evaluate the accuracy of existing curricula and textbooks. Scientists can help teachers to identify existing curricula and tailor them to local needs. Developing new curricular materials, however, must be done cautiously and with appropriate expertise because good curriculum design takes money, many iterations, field testing, and dissemination. New discoveries do have an intrinsic interest to students, but they need to be incorporated into a coherent curriculum and be developed in an age-appropriate manner.

• Scientists can *provide research opportunities for practicing teachers.*

Participating in laboratory or field research can provide teachers with experiences that foster understanding of and excitement about the processes of science—the kinds of experiences that often are missing from their undergraduate education. Research experiences, however, do not translate automatically into improved inquiry-based teaching in the classroom, even if the teacher is invigorated. For teachers to incorporate a new teaching strategy into classroom activities, they must practice, be coached by a team member, and analyze outcomes (Joyce and Showers, 1980; Showers, 1985). Once they have experienced and accepted inquiry-based laboratory exercises, they are more likely to pursue new content to elucidate the exercises, design their own laboratory exercises, and teach in innovative ways. This scenario is enhanced through long-term support and networking between teachers and scientists.

• Scientists can *act as scientific mentors.* Mentoring relationships can develop early in the interactions between scientists and teachers, and these relationships can grow into continuing, mutually beneficial partnerships. Many scientists have reported that their interactions with teachers have resulted in improved teaching in their own classes. Many teachers have reported that they have developed collegial interactions with scientists in university or industrial settings. These professional relationships can lead to research experiences for teachers during summers and other times convenient to teachers, collaborative review of curricula, and grants for new scientific or educational projects.

• Scientists can *provide connections to the rest of the scientific community.* Teachers are often isolated from the professional scientific community, so collegial relationships with scientists can be an important link between the science and science-education communities. Scientists can foster this linkage by including teachers in seminars or lectures at the university or research facility, by inviting teachers to spend time in research laboratories, by providing teachers with electronic-mail addresses at the university so that they can be connected to the scientific community throughout the country through electronic networking, and by encouraging and sponsoring teachers to become members of scientific and science-education professional organizations.

• Scientists can *assist in planning, conceptualizing, and writing grant proposals for science-education projects.* Successful professional scientists today must have effective grant-writing skills. Teachers often do not have the time, nor have they had the need, to develop those skills. The current financial conditions of most public schools, however, make the need for outside funding of new projects, or even of basic science instruction, critical. Scientists can provide a valuable service by working with teachers to prepare grant proposals. Teachers who develop these skills are in the best position to take advantage of federal and private resources directed to science education.

• Scientists can *provide teachers access to equipment, science journals, and catalogs not usually available in schools.* A particularly effective way to do this is to prepare "kits" of equipment with everything needed for a group of students and to arrange for teachers to receive the kits when they are needed for an exercise. This economizes on equipment cost by ensuring that equipment is available when needed but does not need to be stocked and stored. It also makes it possible for the teacher to concentrate on teaching, rather than on the logistics of setting up a laboratory.

## TYPES OF PROFESSIONAL-DEVELOPMENT PROGRAMS

Once scientists become interested in professional development they can become involved in many kinds of programs that will promote their effective contributions. The overwhelming majority of programs that we reviewed were designed for individual teachers who chose to participate. The various types of programs for individual teachers are described below. In Chapter 6, we discuss alternative types of programs designed for systemic reform of education through programs that focus on groups of teachers or larger parts of the education system. We believe that such systemic programs hold the greatest promise for an eventual reform of science education that reaches all teachers and all students, but such programs are complicated to initiate and sustain.

Scientists and teachers can choose from various professional-development activities. We list here categories of individual programs in order of increasing need for commitment on the part of the teachers and scientists involved. The most common professional-development programs focus on activities in specific topics, such as molecular biology, biotechnology, genetics, and ecology. Some programs are open to all teachers in a specific region, school, district, or state; others draw participants from a national pool through a selective application process. Many kinds of institutions participate in professional-development programs for science teachers. They include 2- and 4-year colleges and universities, museums, zoos, and science and technology centers.

### Lectures and Seminars

Local universities, museums, and professional societies often sponsor individual public lectures, lecture series, and seminars for science teachers. Individual lectures usually occur during the school year on Saturdays, in the late afternoons, or in evenings. The lecturer, usually a research scientist, often uses the situation to introduce teachers to up-to-date science content. The effectiveness of this approach depends on the lecturer's ability to communicate complex research results in a way that meets the needs of the audience.

The same organizations often offer continuing seminar series that include lectures followed by participant discussion. Sometimes, teachers find this format on university campuses, where they can interact with faculty and graduate students. Teachers are most likely to participate in these events if they take place after school hours, if universities advertise them widely, if the teachers consider the subject matter to be important, and if they can be used to obtain continuing education or graduate credit.

Lectures can be convenient and easy ways for scientists to begin their involvement, but they might not be as effective in yielding classroom impact as types of programs that promote more active participation. Lecture or seminar content and presentation can often be irrelevant to the needs and interests of the teachers, especially if they have not been adequately planned. If opportunities to meet and plan with key teachers are provided, guest lecturers are more likely to match their expertise to their audience and be able to engage its active participation. Some experienced scientist-speakers have incorporated classroom visits and meetings with teachers as part of their presentation preparation.

## Short Workshops

A common professional-development activity is a workshop, usually a 1- to 6-hour exploration of a specific topic. Workshops usually occur during staff-development days allocated by school districts. They can be held at a school site, a nearby college or university, a statewide professional-development gathering, or a state or national teachers' convention. A common source of funding for such workshops has been the Department of Education's Dwight D. Eisenhower Mathematics and Science Education State Grants program (see Appendix I for a discussion of funding). Teachers typically receive continuing-education credit recognized by local and state education agencies for attending these workshops.

The location of a workshop can have an impact on teachers and scientists. For example, workshops held at a college or university can give the teachers a chance to visit research laboratories. Workshops held in the schools give scientists a chance to learn about teachers' working conditions and laboratory resources. Exposure to elementary- and secondary-school teaching situations also helps scientists to accommodate their strategies to teachers' circumstances.

Some colleges, universities, and other organizations have promoted both lecture series and short workshops by establishing speakers' bureaus. Teachers are encouraged to select from a list of scientists, often identified through professional societies. Scientists then help teachers to supplement their classroom material by visiting classrooms or inviting teachers to visit their laboratories. Communication between scientists and teachers helps scientists to present material that fits into existing curricula.

It is often through short workshops, and thus interactions with teachers, that scientists gain appreciation for the needs of teachers and become more interested in and committed to science education. Poorly planned workshops can have the opposite effect, disengaging both scientists and teachers.

## Summer Workshops or Institutes

National Science Foundation (NSF) summer institutes of the 1960s and early 1970s were popular and effective in increasing teachers' knowledge and enthusiasm for science, even if effects on students could not be measured (GAO, 1984). Similar content- and inquiry-based workshops have been developed in recent years, and many are supported by NSF and other federal agencies.

Some institutes address misconceptions or lack of knowledge in specific fields. In the life sciences, programs have focused on evolution, ecology, genetics, or molecular biology and the techniques for gene isolation and manipulation. Others have provided updates of basic concepts in light of modern information or have focused on learning to use new tools in the classroom. Still other programs have focused on the bioethical implications of new knowledge, particularly in genetics, and exposed participants to techniques of ethical analysis and strategies for conducting effective classroom discussions about ethical public policy.

Of the institutes we examined, the ones that best met our criteria for effectiveness reinforced the processes of science by using activities that caused teachers to rethink their own knowledge. Such programs incorporate both new information and new interpretations. The continuing challenge for scientists and teachers is to adjust their courses so that they examine the processes of science through experiments and demonstrations for their students. Demonstrations without experiments are discouraged in favor of real experiments. A number of summer institutes and workshops (and some school-year workshops) offer intensive hands-on laboratory training in new techniques and are designed to promote transfer of laboratory skills and techniques to schools. In some instances, hands-on laboratory exercises have been developed that are readily transferable to high-school or even middle-school classrooms. Many of those exercises, however, are expensive to implement, especially in school districts where science budgets are low or nonexistent. Some of the best institutes included laboratory investigations that tested hypotheses; these were developed through teacher-scientist partnerships. The institutes promoted teacher comfort with the procedures and interpretations, thereby increasing the likelihood of their use in the classroom. Specific kinds of workshops are considered below.

## Learning to Use New Tools in the Classroom

In some school districts, computers have become an integral part of elementary- and secondary-school education. Nelson et al. (1992, p. 85) reported that 61% of eighth-graders and 79% of twelfth-graders attended schools that had a computer laboratory (although there are few data on the use of computers specifically for science classes). Computers as a teaching tool are far more useful in the science classroom—although still uncommon—than in a separate laboratory. Professional-development programs have been designed to familiarize teachers

## Using Computers for Teacher Networking

A program at Cornell University arranges with Apple Computer, Inc. for teachers to purchase with their grant money computers and modems that they can use at home. Cornell University pays the bulletin-board, network, and telephone fees, so there is no cost to the teachers. Teachers exchange information about their experiences with new laboratory exercises learned in summer workshops, share their ideas about innovative exercises, and solicit suggestions from university faculty. The university posts notices about availability of surplus scientific equipment, seminars, and other activities of interest to teachers; this mechanism is intended to promote long-term interactions among teachers and scientists and to reduce teacher isolation.

with computers and their appropriate applications in classroom activities. Some applications beyond word-processing are to collect real-time data, generate charts and graphs for laboratory reports, analyze statistical data, and measure precisely in the science laboratory.

Instruction in computing technology and networking through the modem can be part of programs (see box). Every day, more information becomes available on the Internet and World Wide Web. Laser disks and interactive videos are also becoming more available in schools. Programs are available to assist teachers in using these tools thoughtfully in the classroom and not merely as entertainment devices. Their effective use depends greatly on the instructional strategies embedded in the software or video or in the print materials that accompany them and on adequate preparation of teachers. But poorly conceived educational software abounds.

The experience of several programs has shown the difficulty of providing basic computer services in schools. It is particularly difficult to secure funds and permission for additional telephone lines for modem use. And teachers do not have time to use computers at school even if they are available. Thus, providing teachers with computers and modems for home use to promote their networking with other teachers and with scientists is another effective use of computers for teachers.

### Development of Supplemental Curricula

Another type of professional-development program focuses on involving science teachers in curriculum development. The underlying principle is that teachers know best about teaching strategies and scientists about science. By working together, they can develop or improve classroom and laboratory activities. Teachers who are involved in the programs then pilot test the materials in their own classes and in some cases ask other teachers to field test the materials to identify problems. The result is new materials to supplement established curricula. Teachers become both advocates of new curricula and trainers of other teachers. Although workshops might be a good way to develop supplementary curricula, we caution against the use of professional-development activities to develop curricular activities de novo. Curriculum-development programs are expensive and take time. If quality control is not emphasized, new materials can be used incorrectly and the programs might have little lasting impact.

### Hands-on Programs Promoting Science Inquiry

A growing number of programs are designed to provide science teachers with experiences that translate science into tasks that actively engage students in the learning process. Science is taught by challenging students to explore scientific concepts by engaging their senses of touch, sight, smell, and sound. These activities have come to be known as "hands-on" science. Effective programs have used the hands-on experience as a basis for student inquiry and developing critical thinking skills. Professional-development programs built around hands-on participation by teachers are designed to help teachers learn pedagogical techniques that bring children into contact with the physical world. Hands-on activities have been shown to be an effective way to achieve inquiry-based learning, especially in younger students. Increasingly, hands-on professional-development programs involve teams of teachers from the same school or school district and focus primarily on elementary-school teachers. These hands-on programs are likely to lead to minds-on learning experiences for students.

### Research Experiences for Teachers

Local universities, research institutions, and industrial and national laboratories have increasingly become providers of summer research experiences for science teachers. Teachers who work in scientists' laboratories are usually funded by a stipend that comes from supplements to federal research grants, by grants from professional societies, by special grants to national laboratories, or by industry. Successful programs take into account that a stipend must correspond to a teacher's earning potential in other summer jobs. Research experiences typically last for 3-8 weeks in the summer. In the most effective programs, a teacher becomes a part of the research-laboratory team. Such programs increase teachers' understanding of the processes of science, expose them to the teamwork required in modern research, and involve them in both the frustrations and failures and the rewards and successes of experimental science. Many scientists who invite teachers into their laboratories find that such experiences educate the scientists about teachers' needs and scientific backgrounds.

Some have found that the value of the research experience can be enhanced

---

### Resources and Partnerships

The Association for Science and Technology Centers has established a Teachers Education Network (TEN) that is developing professional-development programs for teachers in science and technology centers.

The Exploratorium in San Francisco, although focusing primarily on the physical sciences, has developed programs that use hands-on experiments nearly exclusively. Staff have developed an effective mechanism for networking with the teachers and encouraging them to return for additional experience and to share the practical problems encountered when they implement their experiences in the classroom. The Exploratorium's Snackbook is a plan for replicating museum exhibits in the classroom.

The Lawrence Hall of Science's Scientists and Teachers in Educational Partnerships (STEP) program in Berkeley, California, is developing individual partnerships between teachers and scientists and others with expertise on the societal issues raised by specific technological and scientific advances.

The National Science Resources Center (NSRC), operated jointly by the Smithsonian Institution and the National Academy of Sciences, develops and disseminates exemplary teaching resources, including many imaginative and classroom-tested "kits" of experiments for hands-on inquiry experiments. It also has week-long "institutes" to inform teachers and scientists about getting involved with local schools and a national outreach to create networks of individuals and organizations to promote exemplary science teaching.

---

if several teachers are supported in a laboratory setting and then meet regularly during the summer to exchange their experiences and to discuss ways to translate the experiences into lesson plans. That process is an effective way to promote direct transfer of new information into the classroom. Scientists' involvement in the process gives them the opportunity to recognize the difficulties that teachers face when transferring their research experiences into elementary- and secondary-school classrooms.

Examples of programs that bring teachers into research laboratories are the Industry Initiatives for Science and Mathematics Education program in the San Francisco Bay area, the Department of Energy's national laboratories, and the Summer Scholars programs of the American Society for Biochemistry and Molecular Biology, the American Society for Cell Biology, and the American Physiological Society. Not all of them have been as effective as they might have been, because real partnerships have not been formed.

### Comprehensive Programs

In some institutions, a comprehensive set of complementary professional-development programs in which many things happen simultaneously have been developed. Such programs typically are housed in research institutions or sci-

---

### Examples of Comprehensive Programs

California's Statewide Systemic Initiative includes an elementary-science implementation component called the California Science Implementation Network (CSIN). The primary mission of CSIN has been to assist districts and schools in implementing effective, high-quality, hands-on science programs. That has been accomplished through a systemic process of training a statewide network of teacher consultants, staff developers, and school-site teacher leaders in science content, inquiry teaching strategies, and facilitation skills. This process was developed and "field tested" in local areas before expanding statewide. Scientists have been key partners in the process by serving as content specialists in collaborative "presentation teams" for the various institutes scheduled throughout California each summer. For example, a geologist from the U.S. Geological Survey collaboratively plans a 2-week series of lessons on plate tectonics appropriate for use by elementary teachers with a CSIN teaching consultant and an elementary-science mentor teacher. Where CSIN has been implemented effectively, schools and districts have developed science curriculum guides, short- and long-term staff-development plans, and, most important, an excitement and commitment to teaching elementary science effectively.

The University of California, Irvine has a program that has been institutionalized through coordination by science faculty whose specific responsibility is teaching. Science-faculty members, as content experts, can be called on to team-teach with experienced teachers in workshops or summer institutes. The interface between the K-12 levels and postsecondary institutions benefits both K-12 level and college teaching and, most important, student learning. This comprehensive program provides a mechanism for continuous promotion of the public understanding of science at the local and regional levels.

---

ence centers, where many resources are drawn on to create a science-rich environment for teachers. Comprehensive programs can accomplish the difficult task of developing and maintaining communication networks among teachers, who then are able to support one another continually. Those programs are characterized by a high degree of collaboration with other professional-development programs. Partnerships can be established between teachers and universities, museums, zoos, industrial settings, and extension services of federal agencies. Comprehensive programs can help to promote systemic change (see Chapter 6) if they work together with all elements of a school, district, or region to promote systemwide reform.

### Duration of Programs

The goals of a program will dictate its length, but the duration of the program affects its accessibility to all teachers. Short workshops need to be scheduled at a time and place convenient for the teachers. A summer program designed to last

4 weeks or longer will not reach the many teachers for whom 1-3 weeks is a more attractive option, given family considerations and the need for summer employment. Many teachers feel the need for a break in the summer and are reluctant to participate in longer professional-development programs, and longer programs must pay enough to compensate for loss of employment income. If professional-development programs are to be truly effective, they must reach *all* teachers, so a range of durations, daily hours, and locations should be available.

### Support and Participation of School Administrators

Many of the program developers in our survey initially planned and secured funding for the programs independently and were not part of the local school administrative structures. Teachers who later became interested in the programs learned about them directly from the organizers, local universities, other teachers, professional-education publications, or pre-existing networks. In many cases, programs functioned without the attention of school administrators, union leaders, parents in the surrounding community, or even awareness on the part of the school district's central office. Although teachers and scientists involved in the programs often benefited tremendously from them, they rarely became self-sustaining. Many lasted until the first round of funding disappeared—usually no more than a few years—and among those programs, few offered followup activities to teachers who completed the programs. Individual-based programs should aim to include administrators and policy-makers in their planning and development so that the programs have a greater likelihood of being incorporated into the practices and budgets of schools or school districts.

### Examples of Effective Professional-Development Programs

Although many programs that were examined benefited from some of the scientist contributions that are necessary for effective programs, few exhibited them all. We highlight here examples of different ways that scientists have contributed to effective professional-development programs.

• *The North Carolina Biotechnology Center (NCBC), Research Triangle Park.* The initial planning of the program was done by teachers; current administrators of the program are former research biologists. These scientist-administrators help to nurture support for the program in the state legislature. Their knowledge about the educational system in North Carolina has facilitated the involvement of scientists at state universities, and most of the administration and consensus-building is done by NCBC staff. Scientists are provided with all the materials needed to conduct the biotechnology-oriented activities for teachers within their own universities, and the NCBC administrative center provides continuing support. Scientists are allowed to do what they do best: illustrate the process of science to teachers and share their enthusiasm for science with them.

• *Iowa Chautauqua, University of Iowa.* This program involves research scientists on its advisory board. The scientists' role is to help to conceptualize the program, aid in grant procurement, and make departmental resources available. Community-college faculty serve as consultants in the development of curriculum units.

• *The Exploratorium, San Francisco.* Research scientists with expertise in the physical sciences are the teachers of teachers in a summer program with followup activities throughout the school year. Research scientists with different teaching styles model the inquiry-based strategies used in the conduct of research to demonstrate to teachers how to phrase leading questions to engage student thinking. Lectures are avoided.

• *Fred Hutchinson Cancer Research Center (FHCRC) Science Education Partnership, Seattle.* FHCRC's programs involve research scientists at many levels. This one was initiated by a research scientist who organized a small planning committee of teachers, FHCRC public-relations staff, and research scientists. The scientists' interest, creativity, and tenacity resulted in institutionalization of the program. One indicator of institutionalization was the creation of a new position: Science Education Partnership program director. Within the program, research scientists are both mentors and resource persons for the teachers. Through collaborative activities, a mutual exchange of professional expertise has developed. As resource persons, scientists also provide content-update lectures for teachers.

• *Cornell University.* Research scientists initiated and direct summer institutes for teachers from the surrounding area of upstate New York. These institutes have created partnerships between scientists and teachers to develop new laboratory materials for teachers attending the summer programs. The network, both personal and electronic, promotes communication among teachers about their classroom experience with new laboratory and content updates. An electronic bulletin board, maintained by Cornell faculty and support staff, promotes communication among the whole group and allows posting, for example, of used equipment available from university laboratories. Scientists also respond rapidly to teachers' technical questions via the bulletin board.

• *Lansing Community College Hands-on Science Workshops.* The Science Department of Lansing Community College, through its Teacher Education Project, offers inquiry-based workshops for K-6 teachers. The workshops are designed with science-shy teachers in mind. The goals are to help teachers to become more confident about their knowledge of fundamental concepts in biology, chemistry, geoscience, and physics and to encourage them to integrate process-oriented activities and student investigations into their own classroom instruction. Workshop leaders demonstrate research-based teaching strategies and provide ready-made materials for classroom use, which reflect the new science objectives of the Michigan Department of Education.

• *University of Illinois.* The University of Illinois in Urbana has an excellent "footlocker program" to support molecular biology and other experiments in local schools. Complete footlockers of equipment with everything needed for experiments are loaned to the schools. An alternative is a traveling equipment van that can go from school to school. The program requires administrative support from a college, university, or industrial company.

## RECOMMENDATIONS

• More scientists should become involved in professional-development programs for science to help ensure substantive improvements in science education.

• Scientists should educate themselves about K-12 education and not assume that they know or understand the problems and issues involved. That requires learning about teachers' needs and working cooperatively to form partnerships with teachers and science educators. It also requires learning about the educational research on how students learn science and how to teach most effectively.

• Scientists should examine their own teaching in undergraduate classes and laboratory exercises. Their classes include potential science teachers, so scientists should be aware that their teaching will be modeled by these teachers and ask themselves whether they are promoting active learning and good process and content teaching.

• To promote better science education, scientists should

—Become champions of science education in their own institutions and professional communities.

—Respect and support colleagues and students who become involved in science education.

—Join professional organizations concerned with science education, such as the National Association of Biology Teachers and the National Science Teachers Association.

—Work with their own professional organizations to support K-12 science education.

—Support reciprocal interchanges of scientists and other science educators at their own conferences.

# 4

# Administrators' and Others' Responsibilities for Encouraging Scientists' Participation in Professional-Development Programs

University leaders must make it clear to their science departments that the quality and quantity of the service that each department provides to precollege science teachers (both preservice and inservice training) and in the general education of nonscience majors will be important considerations in the distribution of university resources and faculty positions. [National Research Council, 1990, p. 75]

Participation by scientists can become the rule rather than the exception if universities provide more recognition and reward both internally (on campus) and externally (in the scientific community)[1] to faculty members who participate in professional-development programs. The lack of recognition and rewards, particularly for junior faculty at research universities, is a major impediment to scientists' participation in professional development.

## INTERNAL REWARDS

The nation's colleges and universities have intensified discussion and debate about the relationship between teaching and research (Boyer, 1990; Kennedy, 1990; AAHE, 1993). The institutional culture of nearly every university requires that faculty contribute by research, teaching, and service, but few institutions

---

[1]The need for increased recognition and reward applies to other kinds of teaching at research universities as well, for example, undergraduate teaching. This matter is being addressed by the National Research Council Committee on Undergraduate Science Education.

reward research and teaching equally, and fewer reward service at all. A central issue is that research has a wide range of external rewards (such as grants, international prestige, and meeting invitations), whereas teaching is rewarded externally or internally only rarely and sometimes by no one but appreciative students. Faculty members, therefore, routinely undervalue undergraduate teaching, including the teaching of future science teachers. Even more discouraging is that at many research universities, working with teachers in professional-development programs is not even valued as teaching, but as "service" to the community.

To increase professional rewards for scientists who are involved in professional development of teachers, universities must show that they value and reward their faculty members' participation. The following are examples of how universities have recognized the importance of closer connections between K-12 education and universities.

• The Department of Molecular Biotechnology at the University of Washington School of Medicine established a program that began by asking questions of educators about their needs and then designing a partnership that addressed those needs. Department members, with the encouragement and endorsement of the department chair, can become involved in professional-development activities for K-12 teachers. Because it looks at teachers' needs and then finds appropriate funding sources, the program has the potential to have a positive impact on education in the Seattle area. The department is also planning a course with teachers and faculty of the College of Education for elementary-school teacher preparation, a summer program with middle-school teachers, and a secondary-school teacher program involving specific topics.

• As a part of the academic senate's committee structure at the University of California, Irvine (UCI), a committee on community education was established in 1985. The committee is responsible for promoting educational activities for teachers and for informing the faculty of the importance of these activities and recommending how to improve them. The committee serves as a forum for discussing the continuity of courses and teaching in K-16 subjects. The impetus for the program is the recognition that as the K-12 system undergoes educational reform, it becomes more important than ever for college and university faculty to be aware of the changes. It might also be critically important for faculty to become involved in the decision-making processes so that the postsecondary institutions have some impact on the future directions of K-12 reform. The committee on community education has requested that faculty receive teaching credit, not service credit, for teaching professional-development courses for teachers. The University of California has discussed awarding points to faculty for the teaching of professional-development courses. The point system might be based on numbers of students taught and their level. (See Appendix E for more information about the UCI committee program.)

• At the University of Arizona, promotion and tenure guidelines for the faculty were revised in 1992 to define inservice education of teachers as teaching, rather than service, so that faculty participation could be better rewarded. The faculty of science also has approved special promotion and tenure guidelines for faculty who take a major role in K-12 teacher education. (These guidelines are included in Appendix E.)

University administrators can support programs in other ways. They can provide space and joint appointments, thereby allowing university staff to spend time in teaching or research and time in outreach programs. That would give staff an academic home; built-in contacts with faculty, graduate students, and postdoctoral researchers in their departments; academic credibility; and accessibility to scientific research.

Administrators can also allow program participants to work with as many groups as possible across a campus. For example, a land-grant institution's cooperative extension service could help to establish ties with teachers in rural areas, and human-relations offices could help to recruit teachers from urban schools with large minority-group populations. Administrators can help to promote activities both on and off campus.

## EXTERNAL REWARDS

The national concern about science education has generated many sources of grant support for educational programs, particularly through the National Science Foundation. Private organizations, specifically the Howard Hughes Medical Institute in the life sciences, have also committed more of their resources to this issue. The impact on science faculty in recent years, when federal appropriations for basic research have been flat, has been immediate. Science faculty members are now obtaining large grants to support educational programs. The hope is that university administrators, who presumably share the desire to improve science education, will support and reward these scientists in tenure and promotion decisions. In addition to receiving science-education grants, however, a simple and effective way to promote scientists' involvement in science education would be for federal agencies to promote more educational supplements to research grants that can support teachers working in research laboratories. Scientists can use the suggestions in Chapter 3 to make such interactions as productive as possible and use the information in Appendix A to learn about their colleagues' efforts around the country.

## PROFESSIONAL-SOCIETY RECOGNITION

Scientific professional societies have become more involved in science education. Nearly all professional societies have education as one of their stated goals. In the physical sciences, the American Chemical Society and the American Physical Society have special precollege-education committees and programs that have made substantial efforts to reach out to the precollege teaching community. The American Chemical Society has a separate section for precollege education. The American Physical Society has created a program with the American Association of Physics Teachers to link the professional development of physics teachers more closely with the physics research community.

The life-science community, however, has a wider diversity of professional organizations. Rather than having a single broadly encompassing organization, the life sciences have hundreds of smaller organizations. Most of the programmatic focus of life-science education programs has been on graduate and post-graduate education. In recent years, interest in K-12 education has increased dramatically, as evidenced by an increase in the number of precollege-education committees. Special symposia and workshops for *teachers and students* at national meetings are becoming more common. These can be an effective way to interest scientists in professional development and an efficient way for them to educate themselves about the issues. Some of the activities of professional societies, however, assume that scientists already know the best ways to become involved. Professional societies should offer workshops and symposia on science-education reform *for scientists* so that they can understand the needs, the opportunities, and the most productive ways to become involved.

Some societies (such as the American Society for Microbiology, the American Society of Human Genetics, and the American Society for Cell Biology) have begun to feature educational activities in their newsletters or monthly news journals; others (such as the Genetics Society and the American Association for the Advancement of Science) have spun off separate education newsletters. Some (such as the American Physiological Society, the American Society for Biochemistry and Molecular Biology, and the American Society for Cell Biology) provide grants for teachers to work in research laboratories. The Society for Neuroscience has begun a collaboration with the National Association of Biology Teachers to develop teaching materials in neuroscience. Some societies (such as the American Society for Microbiology, the American Physiological Society, the American Chemical Society, and the American Institute of Physics) have hired staff to focus specifically on education issues.

The Genetics Society of America has several education programs. It occasionally includes education papers in its professional journal, *Genetics*, and disseminates information about outreach programs in a booklet titled *GENeration* and another titled *Genetics in the Classroom*. Similarly, the American Society for Cell Biology includes education articles in the essays section of its journal, *Molecular Biology of the Cell*. Scientists rarely read education journals and are more likely to read and learn about science education if articles about it are included in the specialized scientific journals. *Science* includes some articles on science education, and the AAAS Directorate for Education and Human Resources Programs publishes *Science Education News* eight times a year. If more-specialized journals published articles on science education and science-education research, artificial barriers between teaching and research might be lowered. At the same time, such publication would legitimize and give broader recognition to creative teaching. (Specific information about how to get in touch with scientific and science-education organizations is found in Appendix F.)

The American Society of Human Genetics (ASHG) conducted a full-day program for 25 high-school biology teachers and 50 of their students on the day before the official beginning of its 1993 annual meeting, in New Orleans. ASHG collaborated with the state affiliate of the National Association of Biology Teachers (NABT) to identify teachers and students; the state affiliate arranged for transportation to the meeting for teachers and students from areas outside New Orleans and worked with the education committee of ASHG to develop the program. During the morning program, ASHG provided three brief descriptions of subjects of current active investigation in human genetics. The focus was on open questions and the different ways in which scientists are approaching them. Some exhibitors donated examples of technologies used to investigate the questions highlighted during the morning presentations, and students and teachers used those technologies during the afternoon sessions. One of the afternoon sessions provided a simulated genetic-counseling clinic to demonstrate the use of data derived from the technologies in counseling sessions. All the teachers and students received free registrations to the annual meeting, and each one attending was assigned an ASHG member as a mentor to serve as a guide and interpreter for the scientific sessions. ASHG also provides—at its own expense—two speakers for each annual meeting of NABT and one speaker for the annual meeting of the National Science Teachers Association (NSTA).

## RECOMMENDATIONS

### University Administrators

University administrators in research universities, comprehensive colleges, liberal-arts colleges, and community colleges should support K-12 teachers' professional development by

• Becoming involved in professional-development activities in local communities.
• Forming partnerships with schools and school districts and working with school administrators.
• Providing incentives for faculty to be involved in K-12 science education by recognizing faculty involvement in teacher professional development, rewards through promotion and tenure decisions, and recognition of professional development as a legitimate teaching activity of university science faculty.
• Providing on-campus facilities and support for K-12 teachers.

- Examining undergraduate science teaching to see whether their institution is preparing future science teachers effectively.
- Promoting cooperation between science departments and schools of education to improve science education at all levels.
- Participating in national science-education reform at all educational levels and facilitating the participation of their faculty.

## Scientific Professional Societies

Scientific professional societies can do a number of things to promote scientists' involvement in improving science-rich opportunities for K-12 teachers. They can

- Organize special workshops at annual meetings for scientists interested in K-12 education.
- Organize workshops and scientific sessions directed at teachers at annual meetings.
- Secure funding and coordinate summer research opportunities for teachers in members' research laboratories.
- Publicize and disseminate effective supplementary curricular materials.
- Encourage and welcome teacher membership in societies by reducing fees, publicizing meetings in science-education journals, and including teachers on education committees.
- Recognize and reward scientists for outstanding accomplishment in science education.
- Arrange for and subsidize speakers at teacher professional meetings, such as those of NABT, NSTA, and state science-teacher associations.

Professional societies should devote a section of scientific-research journals and newsletters to education articles and refereed education-research papers. Such a change in editorial policy will help to reduce the barriers between teaching and research.

Professional organizations that have memberships drawn from many disciplines or subdisciplines of biology (such as the American Association for the Advancement of Science and the American Institute of Biological Sciences) should increase their efforts to create networks among scientists committed to education reform. The networks could improve communication among biologists and between biologists and scientists in other disciplines.

# 5
# Strategies for Attracting Teachers to and Involving Them in Professional-Development Programs

Previous chapters focused on how scientists can most effectively work with teachers and how universities and professional societies can encourage scientists' participation in professional-development programs. This chapter focuses on strategies that have successfully attracted and involved teachers. The examples are drawn from some of the current programs noted in Appendix A. Without substantial teacher involvement, even the most carefully designed program will have little success, simply because teacher involvement to help ensure that the program will have an impact on the educational system at which it was directed.

## HOW TO ATTRACT TEACHERS

Teachers who are already actively involved in professional organizations or have actively sought professional-development opportunities generally receive a wealth of information on workshops, conferences, and summer institutes. Many of them consistently attend those programs and are among the most enthusiastic participants. It is more difficult to attract the much larger potential audience of teachers who are less active professionally and who are on few, if any, professional organizations' mailing lists. The following are some suggestions for ways to identify and recruit the potential audience:

• *Use a number of channels to reach potential participants.* For instance, mail materials directly to teachers, science supervisors, and principals; distribute materials at teachers' meetings and conventions; work with teachers' unions; make presentations at professional meetings and inservice events; and advertise in teacher professional publications, newsletters, and electronic bulletin boards. Direct mail to targeted teachers is probably the most effective of all enlistment strategies. However, only a 5% response rate can be expected, even from a well-targeted mailing. Lack of communication between administrators and teachers is common, and one cannot depend on science supervisors or principals to relay information to teachers.

• *Use information available in county offices or other intermediate state-government units.* In California, for example, 58 county offices can provide various types of educational support services to school districts. Most have extensive countywide address-label mailing lists that can be used for mailing flyers, brochures, and even conference programs to teachers. A few have comprehensive lists of all secondary-school science or mathematics teachers in the county divided according to subject matter taught. Nonprofit organizations can usually gain access to those mailing lists free or inexpensively. Many county offices also publish a catalog or booklet of future professional-development activities, including regional conferences and workshops sponsored by other organizations.

• *Identify mentor or lead teachers for assistance.* Each school district usually has teachers who have served in leadership positions for specific subjects, such as school science-department heads, mentor teachers, science-resource teachers, and teachers who have been active on district science-curriculum committees. Any of those teachers might have the expertise to recommend strategies to publicize professional-development programs and attract teachers to them. Some would be ideal candidates for participating on planning or advisory committees that are developing programs. Names can usually be obtained from school principals or district administrators responsible for curriculum, instruction, or staff development. Examples of programs in which teachers are used as lead teachers are the Evolution and the Nature of Science Institute at Indiana University and San Jose State University; Teachers Teaching Teachers: National Leadership Program for Teachers at the Woodrow Wilson National Fellowship Foundation; City Science at the University of California, San Francisco and San Francisco Unified School District; the UCI Summer Science Institute at the University of California, Irvine (UCI); and the Cornell Institute for Biology Teachers.

• *Organize special orientations at meetings of continuing programs.* The Science Research Expeditions program offered by the University of California Extension Program uses its orientation meetings each fall to publicize and promote interest in its summer research activities. Past participants present brief slide talks about their summer work. Brochures and applications for the following year's programs are distributed at the meetings.

## HOW TO INVOLVE TEACHERS IN PLANNING AND DEVELOPING PROGRAMS

If several teachers have agreed to serve on a planning or advisory program committee, there are several effective ways to use their skills and expertise:

- *Treat the teachers as colleagues, not as subordinates.* Make them feel comfortable and valued as members of the committee. Listen carefully to their comments and suggestions. They should be fully involved in all planning activities—not just the "teaching" component.
- *Solicit teachers' opinions about their needs, interests, and problems.* Partnership with teachers in developing programs will ensure that the programs provide the help they need and want.
- *Use the teachers' experience and knowledge to learn how they and their colleagues will react to the program being planned.* These teachers might have made presentations to their colleagues and acquired a feel for what will be seen by teachers as workable. The teachers can provide realistic feedback on proposed activities. Input from teachers can, for example, help to develop programs that are intellectually challenging and rigorous, yet appropriate to the backgrounds of the participants.
- *Have teachers conduct some of the program activities.* Effective teachers can serve as models to demonstrate how particular teaching strategies should look in the classroom, as facilitators for discussions about classroom implementation strategies, as communicators of science content when they are competent to do so, and as teachers of laboratory investigations.

## PRACTICAL CONSIDERATIONS

To attract the largest number of teachers, program planners should consider offering

- *Continuing-education or college credit.* Teachers who are earning credits for salary placement are more willing to participate in programs that offer credit. Program organizers should work with local and state administrators or university administrators to ensure that their programs meet credential and course requirements.
- *Financial support.* Extended summer institutes (2 weeks or more) usually offer some type of stipend or honorarium. Ideally, the level of financial support matches teachers' per diem and is another attractive factor to entice potential participants.
- *Room and board for participants.* Some programs draw participants within commuting distance of the program site, traditionally a local college or university. When teachers live beyond commuting distance, however, room, board, and

travel should be provided.    During the summer, economical rates often are available.

• *A budget to purchase equipment and supplies for use in the classroom with students.*  Money for or access to materials and supplies is essential for implementing new activities.  School budgets that typically allow only $1-5 per student per year for science, however, are frequently not sufficient to purchase the quantities of materials necessary to implement even the least-expensive hands-on laboratory investigations that teachers might be exposed to during professional-development programs.  A small expenditure will enable teachers who become informed and excited about new techniques to implement them in their classrooms.  For sophisticated laboratory activities that require special purchases, like those involved in recombinant-DNA technology, teachers should be provided information about grant-writing opportunities or fund-raising strategies at the local level.

• *Access to equipment needed for laboratory activities.*  Providing equipment or teaching kits can help teachers to implement hands-on activities learned during other professional-development programs.  Some programs that we examined allowed teachers to share truckloads of scientific equipment, such as electrophoresis equipment, video equipment, and microscopes.  Equipment-sharing consortia, in which complete sets of laboratory equipment are rotated among several schools, have proved especially effective in supporting laboratory activities in molecular genetics.  Equipment-sharing is part of the programs at the University of Illinois, the North Carolina Biotechnology Center, the Fred Hutchinson Cancer Research Center, Cornell University, and San Francisco State University.

## ENLISTING THE SUPPORT OF ADMINISTRATORS

Support from administrators—such as district superintendents, principals, assistant principals, and even counselors—is essential for the success of new programs.  Many teachers reported that support from school principals is the most important factor in improving science in the schools.

The support of administrators must be cultivated from the outset. It must be made clear to administrators how the programs will make their schools more successful.  Once a program is started, organizers should ask administrators to visit the program in action and to talk with the teachers and scientists involved.  It is even better to ask administrators to participate.  In general, administrators are concerned about their school's progress and image in the eyes of parents and other community members.    Therefore, any strategy that includes generating favorable publicity will have a better chance of success.  Including special events for parents as part of program activities and inviting the news media to cover them and other aspects of the program will help in achieving success.

The statement (see box on p. 60) adopted by the Board of Directors of the

---

**Involving Administrators**

One teacher successfully implemented a collaborative professional-development program this way:

> She identified the most important obstacles to implementation as the teachers' unwillingness to change their teaching styles and the administrators' lack of understanding of the nature of science; administrators did not support a program that would lead the teachers to change their styles. To help to overcome the administrative barrier, she regularly supplied the school administration with articles supporting the desired program. She then took administrators to see a similar program that was being successfully used in a nearby school district. After a year of intense advocacy, she submitted a proposal with goals, budget, management plan, and all possible benefits. The administrator granted approval.

---

National Association of Biology Teachers provides relevant guidelines for administrators' support of life-science teachers.

## RECOMMENDATIONS

Professional development should be viewed as a continuous process that includes appropriate staff, administrative, and community support. With that support, teachers will accept more responsibility for their own professional growth and actively participate in appropriate professional activities.

### K-12 Teachers

Teachers should view professional development as a continuous process and become active members of their professional organizations; establish contacts with local scientists; attend appropriate meetings, workshops, and conferences; read and analyze professional journals and newsletters; recruit and act as mentors for new teachers; collaborate with their colleagues; and recognize the important relationship of professionalism to high-quality teaching and learning for their students. Scientists should play an important role in this process by providing opportunities for collegial relationships and by inviting teachers to attend special events and opportunities to learn more about the work of professional scientists.

### School and School-District Administrators

School and school-district administrators should attach high priority to science education and budget appropriate funds, recognize that *all* students benefit from quality science education and provide a variety of opportunities for students

## Administrative Support for Life Science Teachers

NABT firmly believes that science teachers, at all levels of instruction, must be supported in their teaching positions by all administrators (principals, science supervisors, etc.) to successfully fulfill their professional responsibilities.

**Professional Development.** Teachers should be supported financially and encouraged to continue their professional development. They should receive incentives, both monetary and psychological, for taking courses; attending workshops, conventions and local in-service training; and for being an active member of professional societies. This support could be in the form of providing paid substitutes for time off to attend workshops and conventions. Administrators should also consider providing subscriptions to science education journals for the school's science faculty to share.

**Equipment, Supplies and Space.** Classrooms and laboratories should be provided with equipment and supplies for hands-on science teaching. There should be a source of funds for the incidental supplies which so many science teachers must purchase with their own money. For middle and secondary teachers, laboratory space should be made available on a regular basis, at least one-third of the instructional time.

**Preparation Time.** Laboratory science teachers should be given sufficient preparation time to implement a laboratory-oriented, hands-on science program. The additional time required for this should be taken into account when schedules are prepared and duties assigned so that the teacher has adequate time for both planning and laboratory preparation. Laboratory setup and cleanup take place during the school day and time should be allowed for this.

**Development of Science Curriculum.** Science teachers should be involved in determining the science curriculum for the school/district and be encouraged to provide significant input to this process. Teachers should be supported when they try innovative ideas and new methods and be encouraged to share this new information with their colleagues in both formal and informal settings.

—Adopted by NABT Board of Directors in November 1991.

to become successful in science, take leadership for developing orientation programs for parents and encouraging them to advocate science education, support professional development of teachers of science, and commit appropriate administrative personnel to support professional development of teachers and to support such followup activities as networking, peer coaching, and seminars to continue professional development. Administrators can also strive to improve dissemination of information to teachers about opportunities for professional development and indicate where the science programs fit with professional development.

## Professional Science-Education Organizations

Professional science-education organizations should involve more scientists in organizational activities, such as holding workshops at annual meetings, writing articles for journals, and hosting scientists at their conventions. Those organizations should encourage and welcome academic- and industrial-scientist membership in societies by publicizing meetings in science journals and including practicing scientists on appropriate committees. They should appoint K-12 education committees that include scientists to plan effective science-based educational activities for teachers and recognize and reward scientists for outstanding accomplishments in science education.

# 6

# Systemic Professional Development and Science-Education Reform

There is, in my judgment, no agenda more important to the future of this country than improving the educational system. . . . To bring that change about—both to deliver the collective shove necessary to get the educational system rolling and to provide the support to keep it rolling—will require enormous efforts from us all. . . . That, in the end, is what partnerships are all about. Through very flexible vehicles we can unleash the creativity and harness the energy that normal institutional relationships can crush. [Haycock, 1990, pp. 9-10]

Professional development of science teachers is one component of the entire educational enterprise. In this chapter, we describe professional-development programs that are designed to link groups of teachers in whole departments, schools, and school districts. These are commonly called systemic or systemwide programs. Systemic professional-development programs involve changing (or attempting to change) multiple components of a total system, whether the system is a school, a school district, a group of districts, a region, a state, or a nation. They require collaboration among several groups or organizations and can include elements of curriculum development and implementation, in addition to continuing, long-term professional development. We compare the goals and effectiveness of such systemic programs with those of the programs that we have previously described, most of which have been individual-based programs, designed to enhance the skills of individual teachers. The distinctions are obviously not absolute, and both types of programs and combinations of them can enhance teachers' professional development. We believe that systemic programs can contribute more effectively to science-education reform because they deal with

"It seems to me that one test of teachers' professional development is its capacity to equip teachers individually and collectively to act as shapers, promoters, and well-informed critics of reforms." (Little, 1993)

more of the issues that affect the success of professional development. Most important, they have the prospect of reaching all teachers, not just those motivated and able to participate in individual-based programs.

Whatever form a professional-development program takes and whatever organization sponsors it, it will have a lasting effect only if it is institutionalized to provide continuity and ensure long-term support. That message is vital. Teachers become hesitant to participate in professional-development programs if they have been part of new programs that disappeared quickly, especially if they disappeared just when support was most needed. Teachers are more willing to make substantial commitments of time and energy if an institution also shows a commitment in the form of continuing support and collaborative efforts among colleges and universities, school districts, and industry. Although time-consuming and difficult to develop, collaboration provides a broad base of program support, in case a primary source of funding disappears.

## THE PAST AS PROLOGUE

Paul Hurd, professor emeritus of science education at Stanford University, and others have observed what appears to be a 30-year cycle of science-education reform (Hurd, 1984; Atkin, 1989). Many experienced teachers, science educators, and scientists participated in the last era of major curriculum reform in the late 1950s and early 1960s and became familiar with the major science-curriculum projects, such as the Biological Sciences Curriculum Study (BSCS), the Chemical Education Materials Study (CHEMS), the Chemical Bond Approach Project (CBA), the Elementary School Science Project (ESSP), the Earth Science Curriculum Project (ESCP), the Intermediate Science Curriculum Study (ISCS), the Physical Science Study Committee (PSSC), Science–A Process Approach (SAPA), and the Science Curriculum Improvement Study (SCIS). Those projects provided updated and accurate information for textbooks that were outdated at the time. Many efforts were devoted to designing inquiry-based laboratory activities (and materials for them) that were meant to be the focus of K-12 courses. Most were designed as sets of courses emphasizing processes of science, as opposed to the content texts that they were designed to replace.

The National Science Foundation (NSF) was the major source of funding for those curriculum-reform efforts. Summer teacher institutes during the 1960s and 1970s were the primary mechanism by which teachers were prepared to use the new curricular materials. The goals were to prepare teachers to teach science through inquiry-based methods and to deepen their content knowledge of science. At the same time, the Office of Education (now the Department of Education) was authorized, through the National Defense Education Act, to buy science equipment and improve K-12 science-teaching facilities. Thus, several mechanisms were put into place to reform science education on a national level.

Unfortunately, funding for NSF's teacher institutes was reduced in the 1970s, and the reform movement faded into the background and stalled when NSF's Science and Engineering Education Directorate was essentially disbanded in 1982. A major stated reason was that NSF was using the institutes as a way to promote curricula–some of which contained controversial material—whose development it had funded. The use of NSF funds to prepare teachers to use programs developed with NSF funds was seen by some as promoting a national science curriculum.

After the elimination of the institutes, many of the curricular programs were not sustained. Most teachers never had the opportunity to experience the new curricula at all. Teachers who adopted the new curricula had little opportunity to learn how to incorporate them into their classrooms. Teachers who had fully adopted new science curricula continued to use them well, but those who were not comfortable with the changes that required inquiry-based classroom activities tended to slide back to the old styles of teaching. The reform effort led to revision of many of the old standard textbooks to incorporate much of the new content information from the curriculum-reform efforts but few of the inquiry-based activities for teaching the process of science. An important lesson learned from that period of major science-education reform is that if teachers themselves are not prepared to make and are not directly supported in making changes in their classrooms, change will not occur. Thus, effective professional-development programs are essential to prepare and support the teachers who will be responsible for reforming science education.

## SYSTEMIC CHANGE

The five "streams" used to describe combinations of school-reform efforts have been identified by current educational researchers (Little, 1993): reforms in subject matter (standards, curriculum, and pedagogy), reforms dealing with issues of equity, reforms dealing with school governance, reforms dealing with issues of student assessment, and reforms dealing with the professionalization of teaching. At present, the reform efforts focusing on standards are the most likely to include a professional-development component.

*Systemic change* or *systemic reform* is currently used to describe a good portion of the school-reform efforts. These terms have come to mean different things to different people, organized efforts, associations, and funding agencies.

To assist the scientist in wading through the differences in terminology and connotation, the committee offers some examples of systemic change.

***Example 1:***   Systemic change *is a program initiated by NSF to effect substantial reform in education and permanent change over the long term and includes collaboration among a variety of organizations in state and local school districts.*

An effort funded by the NSF Directorate for Education and Human Resources, the Statewide Systemic Initiatives (SSI), is a competitive-grants program designed to award large grants to individual states to promote statewide systemic reform in science and mathematics education. In the program's first 3 years, NSF awarded 5-year grants of up to $10 million (matching funds are required) to 25 states and Puerto Rico.[1] Through this program, "NSF hopes to encourage more coherent and consistent policies and programs and asks states to identify elements that, taken together, can make a difference in what students know and are able to do" (NSF, 1993, p. 1). States must make a commitment of resources, focus statewide reform efforts, develop a vision of mathematics and science education, involve educators at all levels, and develop a plan for implementing and evaluating results. The oldest programs funded by SSI have been running for only 4 years, and it is too soon to evaluate their effects. The initiative has, however, galvanized interest in science- and mathematics-education reform at the highest political and policy levels in the jurisdictions that have received funds. A new NSF effort, Urban Systemic Initiatives, has recently been initiated to provide funds to large urban centers to support systemic reform.

***Example 2:***   Systemic change *is the implementation of comprehensive curricular frameworks based on standards and the use of these frameworks to improve teacher education, certification, professional development, and recertification, as well as student assessment and classroom instruction.*

The AAAS Project 2061 is a national effort to promote science-education reform. With input from many parts of the science and education communities, the project prepared *Science for All Americans,* which describes what a scientifically literate citizen should know and be able to do. *Benchmarks,* another publication of the project, then described a suggested sequence and age-appropriate order for acquiring this knowledge. Forthcoming "blueprints" will describe the systematic reforms necessary to implement the benchmarks. Another national effort building from this and other projects is the development of national science

---

[1]The first SSI awards were given in FY 1991 to Connecticut, Delaware, Florida, Louisiana, Montana, North Carolina, Ohio, Rhode Island, and South Dakota; recipients in FY 1992 were California, Georgia, Kentucky, Maine, Massachusetts, Michigan, Nebraska, New Mexico, Puerto Rico, Texas, Vermont, and Virginia; recipients in FY 1993 were Arkansas, Colorado, South Carolina, New York, and New Jersey.

education standards for grades K-12. The National Academy of Sciences, through a committee of the National Research Council, has published the National Science Education Standards. The major principles of the standards are that

- All students should have the opportunity to learn science.
- With appropriate opportunities, all students can learn science.
- Students should learn science in ways that reflect the modes of inquiry that scientists use to understand the natural world.
- Learning is an active process that best occurs when students act as individuals who are members of a community of learners.
- The quantity of factual science knowledge that all students are expected to learn needs to be reduced so that students can develop a deeper understanding of science.
- Science content, teaching, and assessment all need to be considered in the context of systemic reform to achieve the goal of science literacy for all.

The support systems for teachers and schools that must be put into place to accomplish that kind of reform require systemic changes in schools and districts and require active participation by scientists. For historical perspective, compare those recommendations with the ones made in 1910 (see Chapter 2 of this report).

*Example 3:* Systemic change *involves a local coalition of scientists, teachers, and administrators committed to professional development of teachers and to provision of methods and infrastructures to support revitalized science instruction for all children in a school or school district.*

The San Francisco City Science Project is systemic reform that has prepared over 100 well-trained teacher-leaders who have been used, with a scientist partner, to conduct workshops and presentations for some 2,000 other K-8 teachers of science. Thus, *every* teacher of science is systematically involved in professional development as part of the overall systemic-reform effort .

Those examples of school-reform efforts based on systemic reform should help scientists to understand different uses of the term and recognize that the professional-development opportunities in their locales can be parts of a larger, systemic effort to improve science education.

## PROFESSIONAL DEVELOPMENT AS A COMPONENT OF SYSTEMIC REFORM

As Hord and others (1987) put it, "the improvements needed in science education and changes required are part of a process, not an event." Professional development is one strategy to be used to support systemic change. Professional development, therefore, is not just a problem to be solved, but a strategy for promoting change. Scientists tend to pose issues as *problems*, not strategies, so they are often ineffective at systemic reform. Sheila Tobias captured this issue by contrasting the thinking of the science and education communities:

> Trained in problem definition and problem solving, scientists inevitably bring the habits of doing science to the problem of reform. Thus, those who would reform science education often frame extremely complex issues in terms they are familiar with, namely, "problems" and "solutions." But reform is not a scientific enterprise. What problem hunting and problem solving may lead to instead is an oversimplification of extremely complex processes and a preference for theoretical, universal solutions over more modest, incremental change. Moreover, having identified one of these "solutions" scientist-reformers may not wish to compromise. Since their thinking is in terms of solutions rather than strategies, their recommendations are not expressed as options; nor are they rooted in the pragmatic, the real, the here and now. They do not offer people in the field (as one person I interviewed put it) any suggestions as to "what we can do tomorrow." [Tobias, 1992, p. 16]

The focus of systemic efforts in science-education reform, and education reform generally, goes beyond the individual teacher; systemic efforts aim to improve the organization of an educational system so that it can function more effectively. Professional-development programs that embrace this approach are linked to larger systemic efforts that aim to improve all components of an educational system—such as teaching, student achievement, curriculum, administrative leadership, and school policies and practice—and to institutionalize changes that have proved to be effective. Particular focus is given to the school life of poor and minority-group students to ensure the improvement of achievement among *all* students. An underlying assumption in this approach is that members of different parts of the system—such as principals, teachers, parents, and university faculty—are included in the planning of the change process from the outset. Their inclusion allows the effort to obtain the massive support it needs by providing stakeholders with a sense of ownership.

Systemic change in science education requires collaboration at all levels of planning and execution, including teachers, scientists, administrators, parents, state and local governments, universities, federal agencies, and students. That ensures that a program is tailored to existing conditions and needs. Professional-development programs for science teachers that embrace the systemic approach are designed to reform how science is taught to all students at all grade levels.

It is most important to recognize that program planners do not have to begin with the whole system of education at once to initiate systemic change. Our pluralistic educational system has enough semiautonomous units that a program can begin with a single school, or a single science department in a large school. By working with all the teachers in that school or department, a program can draw on the resources of local grassroots activities and the efforts of strong individuals. It can then build wider support to expand throughout a school district and beyond. Such systemic professional development differs from individual-teacher professional development in having the initial goal of reaching all the teachers in a unit at once, not just selected individuals.

Some current systemwide efforts began by focusing on all teachers in an elementary school in a hands-on, science-based program of professional development. Ultimately, students engage in learning scientific concepts by doing experiments themselves. Other systemic efforts focus on engaging all teachers in a school's biology department, then expanding to include the entire science department, then the whole school, and eventually the whole school district.

A well-prepared program plan must show direct benefits to the students so that they and their parents will become advocates and must show benefits to the school as a whole, not just individual teachers. Support can be achieved by open participation in planning and a willingness to share the credit so that all involved—students, parents, teachers, scientists, and administrators—feel ownership and are empowered by the new program. Such cooperation takes time to develop and often is difficult to achieve. Although some successful programs have begun as "end runs" around the system, eventually the cooperation of all parties is required for systemwide change.

Several characteristics of professional-development programs have successfully supported systemic change and are in keeping with the characteristics of effective programs described in Chapter 2:

• *There was a substantial commitment to the long-term professional development of all science teachers.* Program developers, administrators, and teachers all recognize that good science teaching at all levels depends on sustained professional development of all teachers.

• *The systemic program evolved gradually.*

• *The program has affected and involved all segments of the educational community.* Existing programs in a school or district are reorganized to support the institutionalization of a new program, and all administrative levels of the school district know about and are involved in the program. The new program is recognized as a regular part of the educational landscape and is protected from the political ups and downs of any school district (for example, the program's implementation becomes a line item in the local school budget).

• *The processes of science are emphasized, in addition to scientific content.* In our experience, the most important reform needed is to change how teachers teach science so that student learning can be improved. We believe that changes in attitudes and teaching strategies can be the most powerful agent for systemic change. Although we acknowledge that scientific content has an essential role in K-12 science education, we believe that content alone cannot drive good teaching. Systemwide change requires both changing how science is taught and involving administrators, teachers, and students in the process of change. That view contrasts markedly with the current K-12 system, in which science is primarily fact-laden and workbook-driven.

• *The school system supports the materials necessary for good science teaching.* Systemic change in science education cannot be accomplished only through professional development. Good science teaching requires good materials for teachers and students and support of the materials by the school district. If individual teachers must arrange for materials, it is less likely that a new curriculum will be taught.

• *Program developers change their ideas to accommodate what has been learned in the process of implementing the program.*

• *School personnel support policies and procedures that encourage curriculum enhancement.* Successful programs have the "buy-in" of teachers, scientists, administrators, parents, and industry.

• *The program works toward becoming self-sustaining and independent of the initial program developers.* When properly constructed, systemic programs can become self-sustaining. If a program has been accepted by the school system and its teachers, administrators, students, and parents, it will be sustained. One clear measure of success of a program is that the program becomes independent of its initiators.

• *Science is coordinated with other disciplines.* Good science teaching will be accomplished when it is connected to other subjects. Science, after all, is a process applied to a particular subject. The process—which includes critical thinking, observation, evaluation, and reproduction—applies well to all subjects.

As in all our descriptions of effective reform programs, the participants must get to know each other and respect each other's varied talents and cultures. The radical description in the accompanying box dramatizes this.

---

### A Success Story of Systemic Change

A high-school principal in a large, deteriorated, inner-city school system beat the odds and created a whole new science-magnet program. Here is how he described the process of that systemic change.

"Our main task in undertaking systemic change was to understand the dominant culture—its formal and informal structures that either facilitate or obstruct progress, and ultimately affect the enterprise. In East Harlem, we adopted a strategy of creative noncompliance, which became creative compliance as we gained control of the system.

"Our first step was the acquisition of knowledge. We lifted a useful metaphor from the scene in *Patton* where old George observes the advance of a tank column. The Germans approach the ambush in the expected order and position. Patton exclaims, 'Rommel, you bastard, I read your book.' Fighting to change bureaucracies may not be as rough as WWII, but increased knowledge will lessen the waiting surprises and frustration.

"We needed to know how the system works, its rules and regulations. Who wrote them? What purpose do they serve? How are they monitored? Is the system designed to monitor paper flow or program effectiveness? Which pressure groups' needs are served? Who are the real decision-makers? Who are the gatekeepers? What issues or actions are most embarrassing to the system? Finding these answers provided some good ways to address the many problems.

"A careful evaluation of our image as perceived by the bureaucracy was essential. Posturing, rhetoric, overemphasis on problems and who might be to blame were avoided. One of the greatest fears is the fear of creating change in the rules accompanied by the risk of rejection of those rules. We always assured the system that we would handle the difficult administrative details.

"We also made good use of the team's social graces. A great deal of business is done at social gatherings and events. Attendance at these events demonstrated our willingness to respect the culture.

"Building political support was an important strategy to assure the status quo we were not alone. We campaigned with elected officials, the private sector, foundations, local community, parents and students, unions, professional groups, and influential decision-makers in the system.

"As we prepared to cast off with our systemic reform, we made sure we were presenting a clear package. The team stayed clear and consistent as it presented its case to would-be supporters. Written and multimedia presentations helped, as well as cultivating the press and television. We found that we did not exist to the community and certain administrative obstructions until appearing in the *New York Times* and on television. When the camera lights go on, remember to stay focused on your goals and remember how this systemic change will affect the children.

"We were careful not to overlook fellow administrators and their needs. When someone wants to change the way you've been running things, the stakes are both personal and professional. We used protocol that seemed least threatening. Other than letters and memos, meetings were the logical choice. Calendars full of meetings are signals of being an important part of the process. This calls not only for respect of the cultural phenomenon but for a strategy to accomplish as much as possible during meetings.

"The temptation is to go to these meetings and just listen. Honing our meeting skills saved time and kept systemic change rolling instead of waiting. We employed premeeting letters, agendas, note-taking, and postmeeting letters. A premeeting conference one-half hour before important meetings helped focus our team on immediate expected outcomes. Often after everyone else went home, we conducted an immediate debriefing, sometimes on site, to communicate the various perspectives team members took away from the event.

"Networking teachers during this process was an integral part of the success of our effort. By having our teachers visit pilot programs with scientists and colleagues from different areas, then giving them time to reflect and digest what they experienced we found a lot more support in our corner from the ground up. At the end of the day, balancing all of these techniques with energy and patience finally paid off."

For scientists, systemic reform has profound effects. Few things are more satisfying than having a role in substantial educational improvement in an entire school district. In addition, scientists benefit by learning about the schools. It is almost impossible for a scientist to be involved in systemic change without examining his or her own assumptions about teachers and reflecting on ways to improve his or her own teaching of science at the undergraduate and graduate levels.

## FOCUSING ON ELEMENTARY SCHOOLS FOR SYSTEMIC CHANGE

There are potential advantages to working with elementary-school teachers to promote systemic change in science education.

• Student and teacher enthusiasm, flexible scheduling, and greater curricular fluidity simplify instructional change at this level. With encouragement from NSF, educators are now placing more emphasis on improving elementary-school science instruction.

• School districts have less investment in science education in the early grades than they do in secondary schools. Moreover, parents and administrators are less concerned about science tests or scores at this level because the children are still years away from college admission.

• Elementary-school teachers have less science background than do middle- and high-school teachers. Although many teachers at this level express a fear of science, once they experience science as a way of knowing about the natural world through inquiry-based activities, many become vocal advocates of science.

• Elementary-school education is more holistic. In most systems, a single teacher is responsible for the education of a specified group of children. Thus, the teacher can integrate science with other areas of the curriculum, rather than treating it as an add-on subject. That is consistent with a previous National Research Council committee's recommendation that "science stories" be integrated into elementary-school language-arts instruction (NRC, 1990).

• Evidence suggests that the elementary-school level is where children make fundamental decisions about what they will pursue later in their educational careers. Elementary school thus provides an opportunity to establish positive attitudes toward science.

• Emphasis on science and its societal implications is important for all students and might be especially important for elementary-school students, who are in the process of forming lifelong attitudes about science (Biological Sciences Curriculum Study, 1978).

• Innovators are finding that educational reform at the secondary level is easier with students who have had 6 years of good elementary science. Well-prepared students and their parents can drive reform in the higher grades. This "trickle-up" effect is caused by the elevation of expectations of students who have been exposed to novel instruction and who then challenge higher-level teachers to update their instructional methods. Thus, focusing instructional change at the elementary-school level can ultimately trickle up to higher education.

## RECOMMENDATIONS

• Although both individual-based and systemic programs can contribute to science-education reform, systemic programs are essential to ensure that professional development supports all teachers and that there is essential programmatic support for high-quality teaching.

• Scientists should first learn about current science-related programs and projects in local schools or school districts that are amenable to scientists' participation. These can include regional programs, such as those funded by NSF, or local projects, such as the Department of Education's Dwight D. Eisenhower State Grants for Science and Mathematics Education.

• Professional-development programs that promote systemic reform must eventually involve all interested parties: teachers, scientists, administrators, parents, colleges and universities, industry, and community organizations. Although a program can originate with any of those parties, scientists, teachers, and administrators must be involved early; other parties can be brought in as the program develops. The adept administrator can help to develop an effective school or district partnership by facilitating school or district communication and support.

• The program must have realistic and well-focused goals to recruit supporters and advocates. It is not realistic to try to do too much at one time. Providing an extensive professional-development program for teachers and developing new curricular materials are challenging tasks. Few projects successfully do both simultaneously. Many excellent curricular materials are available; program planners need not reinvent them (see Appendixes D and F).

• Programs must fit the nature, background, and willingness to change of the potential target audience. Strategies effective for promoting elementary-level science might be less effective with secondary-level teachers.

• Systemic professional-development programs can often be most effective at the elementary-school level, at least at the outset. Elementary-school teachers have more flexibility to incorporate science—particularly hands-on, inquiry-driven investigations—into their teaching.

• Program planners should use national efforts that provide benchmarks or standards for science education as an incentive to promote systemic improvements in local districts and schools. The *National Science Education Standards* and the reports of the American Association for the Advancement of Science Project 2061 are examples.

# 7

# Evaluation of
# Professional-Development Programs

Large amounts of federal and private money are being spent on innovative programs for the professional development of K-12 science teachers, and many people are devoting tremendous amounts of time and energy to this critical component of excellent science education. How do we know whether these resources are productive—whether a program's objectives have been accomplished? We need to be able to determine which programs are working best and which are not, and we need to know whether a program has provided participants with new insights, knowledge, or skills and whether it has led to improved achievement among students. We have few data on the long-term impact of the programs; obtaining objective data on such programs is daunting and expensive. The problem is not new. If we can learn from the past, we should be able to do better in the future.

Much of what we know about the effectiveness of professional-development programs is based on anecdotes and on reports from teachers, principal investigators, and program directors involved with the programs themselves. In our review of professional-development programs, we heard repeatedly that teachers felt empowered by their participation and gained an enhanced sense of professionalism. We also heard that many teachers—particularly elementary-school teachers—felt that they had increased their content knowledge and were more comfortable in using inquiry-based methods of instruction in their classrooms. That kind of subjective information is important and useful, but the overwhelming majority of programs we examined had no formal mechanisms for determining the effectiveness of programs by assessing how students fared after participating in programs in which their teachers participated.

We are concerned about that situation because of the lessons learned in the 1980s. In 1984, the General Accounting Office concluded that although the NSF-sponsored teacher institutes of the 1960s and 1970s had favorable effects on teachers, as measured by attitudinal surveys, there was no empirical evidence to support the contention that the institutes had favorable effects on students. At the time, the costs of evaluation were not allowed in education grants and there might have been a dearth of instruments available to measure effects on students. A decade later, there are still an inadequate number of techniques to measure and evaluate the effects. At a time of federal budget cutbacks, the lack of evidence linking spending to student achievement was used as one excuse for the elimination of science-education programs. Federal appropriations for science education practically disappeared from the political landscape until another "crisis in education" had begun again, this time driven by consensus about science literacy and economic competitiveness rather than national security.

We need to know the effects of professional-development activities on the classroom behavior of teachers, such as the extent to which they incorporate the content and process elements of their training into their classroom teaching. Obviously, we must evaluate student performance—what they know and are able to do as a result of their teachers' professional-development activities. We need to develop measures of the cost effectiveness of various programs on classroom behavior. Ultimately, we need to design ways to collect longitudinal data to measure the effects of professional-development programs for teachers on their students, including how they learn and make decisions beyond high school. Obtaining such data will require perseverance to collect and analyze comparable data over periods of 5-10 years. Funding to support those long-term efforts must also be obtained. But if the barriers can be surmounted, we will gain better insight into how professional development affects teacher and student outcomes over time.

This chapter presents ideas and recommendations for the development of effective evaluation tools that will yield the data we need. The primary question to be answered is, "Has the professional-development program being evaluated helped teachers to create a high-quality learning environment so that the students are doing better in science?" To develop evaluation strategies that answer that primary question, we must know what forms of evaluation are required, who should conduct evaluations, what tools and programs we need to conduct useful evaluations, what levels of funding are needed to conduct useful evaluations, and how the administrative structure supports program evaluation.

## FORMS OF PROGRAM EVALUATION

Program evaluation can take many forms. Not all professional-development programs need to be evaluated in the same way. For example, a lecture series does not require as extensive an evaluation as a program designed to foster systemic reform. In its most general form, however, we believe that evaluation will be most effective if it is designed in the initial planning stages of a program, if it measures the success of a program against its stated goals, and if it continues throughout the life of the program and, for students, beyond.

### Concurrent Design and Evaluation of Professional-Development Programs

If program planners include evaluation in program design, they will find that it will help them to

- Define specific, realistic, important, and measurable program goals.
- Identify scientific content and science-process skills that are appropriate for teachers and their students.
- Choose instructional strategies and followup activities that are consistent with the objectives of the program and reinforce core concepts.
- Establish mechanisms for receiving continuing participant feedback.
- Establish, before the program begins, procedures and instruments for collecting overall program-evaluation data.
- Examine a program's cost effectiveness or efficiency.

The last issue is perplexing because it addresses the age-old problem of "comparing apples and oranges": how can one compare the relatively high cost of a high-school biotechnology program, with its expensive equipment, to the relatively low cost of an elementary-school science program that serves hundreds of teachers? Is the elementary-school science program more cost-efficient simply because it has a lower per-teacher cost?

Table 7.1 shows how the planning of a professional-development program and its evaluation are conceptualized as a seamless process. The sought-after goals of professional-development programs are listed in the first column and are based on the characteristics of effective programs identified in Chapter 2. The remaining columns show the steps toward the goals and what might be evaluated to assess the progress of the program.

### Continuing Evaluation

Continuing evaluation (as contrasted with summary evaluation on completion of a program) can include both informal and formal mechanisms to help program facilitators to identify problems (and successes) during various stages of program implementation. Informal evaluation can be conducted by program staff. Continuing evaluation often uses questionnaires, interviews with participants, or self-reports in the form of journal excerpts; these types of evaluation

TABLE 7.1 Linkage Between Goals and Evaluation of Professional-Development Programs

| Goal | Steps Toward the Goal | Data to Be Collected for Evaluation |
|---|---|---|
| Program should improve teaching and students' learning. | Instruction in the professional-development program will encourage teachers to spend more time on hands-on, inquiry-oriented instruction and to focus on major concepts rather than unconnected facts. Students will improve their understanding of biology, of the nature and methods of science, and of the social and personal implications of biology. | Preprogram and postprogram evaluations of instructional materials and teaching strategies; assessments of students |
| Scientific content should be accurate, and instructional strategies should reflect current research on teaching and learning. | K-12 teachers will receive scientific information that informs their teaching and improves their understanding of biology and receive effective strategies for teaching and learning that are based on current research. | Assessment of accuracy and currency of materials that instructors and participants use; instructional strategies and materials that participants use |
| New partnerships, projects, and networks should be stimulated among participating teachers and between teachers and scientists. | Scientists and teachers will establish long-term collegial relationships that help to improve K-12 science education and teaching at the university level and establish a pattern of involvement of scientists in science education. | Number of cooperative efforts that occur after the formal program; collaboration on new proposals; scientist visits to K-12 classrooms; involvement of K-12 students in summer programs at colleges and universities; involvement of scientists in development of new curricula |
| Opportunities for continued involvement should be provided. | Teachers will receive continuing support to introduce and sustain changes in content and in teaching strategies. | Frequency and quality of followup visits to classrooms; number and types of telephone calls between instructors and participants; number and types of requests for assistance |
| Teachers and other educators should participate in planning and implementing the program's activities. | The professional-development program will meet the needs of teachers and will reflect the reality of their teaching situations on their return to their home institutions. | Number of teachers involved in planning professional-development program; changes in composition of planning team; extent to which teachers' recommendations are reflected in structure of program |

should rely heavily on participants' comments so that appropriate changes can be incorporated into the program. Often, continuing evaluation leads both to better ways to achieve the initial goals and to changes in the goals themselves as perceived needs change. The evolution and improvements in programs that result from observations made during continuing evaluation are desirable, and all the most-effective programs that we studied used it. However, the changes and improvements in programs that result from continuing evaluation complicate long-term evaluation of program effectiveness because it is aiming at a moving target.

## Long-Term Evaluation

Formal evaluation of the impact of an overall program requires long-term strategies for data-gathering and analysis that begin with the program's design and continue throughout the life of the program. Most evaluation stops when a program ends, although it can take years for the impact on students to become apparent. Usually, long-term data are not collected, although their collection might be as simple as tallying the number of science electives taken by students of a teacher in a middle-school program. Such data provide a quick indicator of students' interest in science, which might or might not reflect good science teaching in earlier grades.

We found a lack of overall program evaluations linking teacher participation in professional development with enhancement of teaching skills or student performance. To determine the ultimate impact of a program, long-term evaluation is needed to keep track of program participants and how they incorporate new information and techniques into their classroom activities.

Whether evaluation is intended to be continuing or summary, fundamental questions must be addressed: What are the teachers learning? Is effective pedagogy being modeled in the professional-development sessions? Does the program address "real needs" of teachers? Does the program hold promise of favorably affecting student learning in science? Other questions that one should consider in the evaluation are the following:

- *Is the program built on models of other well-tested programs?* Answers to this question can reveal whether program planners have educated themselves about other professional-development programs around the country rather than inventing new programs from scratch.
- *Does the program engage participants in open discussion about educational practices, reform, curriculum, and policies?* Over the years, educational reforms have been piled on other educational reforms. Veteran teachers have seen them come and go. For strategic reasons or out of skepticism, many teachers wait in silence for each fad to pass so that they can go back to what has worked best for them. Open discussion is a sign of active participation and can reflect a

deep structural change in how schools work (that is, adjustment of a structure to accommodate participating teachers' input).

• *Does the program have or plan to develop a relationship with systemwide initiatives in the region?* Answers to this question will provide evidence about the extent to which a program is complementary to or coordinated with systemwide efforts.

• *Are participants—particularly teachers—being intellectually stimulated and inspired by the program?* Answers to this question might shed light on whether teachers are motivated to participate in other professional-development activities or whether, in the long run, they choose to stay in the field.

• *Who is participating in the program and why?* Answers to this question will reveal whether the program is reaching *all* teachers or only those who are already motivated. Evaluators should also examine the diversity of the participant pool with respect to the age, race, and ethnicity of students taught and teachers' race, social class, work habits, age, teaching experience, and stage of career. Answers to this question might lead to the development of strategies to involve less-motivated teachers in professional-development activities.

• *Does the program result in changes in teachers' teaching practices and in student learning?* Answers to this question require that data be collected that could show changes in teachers' behavior and student performance. Evaluators need to seek creative indicators of these changes. For example, the adoption of hands-on or innovative laboratories could be monitored through records of the purchase of necessary supplies and equipment—assuming that these are being used in the classroom. Changes in lesson plans and laboratory activities might also indicate that teachers have altered their practices, as might videotapes of classroom activities when "before and after" tapes exist.

## EVALUATORS

As noted above, informal, continuing evaluation can be conducted by program staff using questionnaires, interviews with participants, or self-reports in the form of journal excerpts. We found that formal evaluation is usually conducted by principal investigators or program directors. For science-based programs, the principal investigator, hence the evaluator, will probably be a scientist. Special problems face him or her. Scientists are trained to plan careful experiments that generate data to support or refute a hypothesis. In education, objective data are much harder to generate because the variables are harder to identify and control. Scientists are accustomed to having responsibility for the implementation of a program but not for its evaluation. They are unlikely to have training in the evaluation of educational programs. Unlike scientific research, whose product is a peer-reviewed paper, the "product" we are dealing with—an education program—involves human interactions and is not as readily subject to peer review. Scientists therefore must be aware of the complexities inherent in analyzing educational programs. Finally, it is difficult for any principal investigator, whether scientist or science educator, to oversee an *objective* analysis of his or her own program.

Evaluation does not have to be only a means to determine the "success" or "failure" of a program or individuals. If education researchers who are trained in evaluation are involved from the beginning of a program, evaluation can also be a means of conducting research on professional-development programs. Education researchers who serve as evaluators can help to bridge the gap between education research and practice. They can help to design programs that have measurable components. And they can produce overall program reports that highlight difficulties faced during program implementation as a means of letting other program directors know how to improve their programs or avoid mistakes. When evaluation is seen as a means for educating others in the field, program staff might feel that they can be honest in their evaluation of their own programs.

Having an evaluator involved in the planning of the program can help to ensure that program objectives are clear and focused, that the evaluator will begin to think about evaluation strategies and instruments before the program begins, and that the program will include appropriate points for the evaluation of progress and midcourse correction. One warning: As always, balance is necessary. As one increases one's focus on program evaluation, one needs to be careful not to contrive neat evaluations by looking for easily measured outcomes or easily administered tests at the expense of effective program design and implementation.

## EVALUATION TOOLS

In theory, well-designed evaluations of professional-development programs for science-education reform should be based on testable hypotheses. In reality, most current evaluation strategies fall into the category of using "How did you like the course?" questionnaires before teachers have had the chance to try new techniques in the classroom. Instead, long-term followup evaluations of teachers to determine how they are implementing their new knowledge and techniques in the classroom are needed, as are new evaluation instruments that can measure the long-term effects of programs on both teachers and students.

Much research on ways to conduct useful evaluations is still needed. Research could be conducted on existing programs to produce a comprehensive guide to evaluating professional development (including a computer database for ease of access and updating) that would provide program directors and other interested parties with specific examples of effective evaluation techniques and tools. The document could address such issues as measurement of teacher and student conceptual understanding, application of inquiry-based learning, effects of professional-development programs on students (with samples of assessment tools for measuring student outcomes), and change in teaching practices or school reform. The document should include evaluation research being done internationally.

## FUNDING AND ADMINISTRATIVE ISSUES

Most funding agencies and private funders request information about programs' effectiveness, but few provide funds or guidance to conduct full-scale evaluations. Effective evaluation procedures are expensive, and available funding is inadequate for the kinds of evaluation that are necessary to assess the linkages between teacher preparation and student performance. Budgets for programs normally do not include a line item for evaluation. Evaluation of a program's effects will be most valid when time has passed since the program ended. Only then can the impact on students be noted. However, most funding agencies require a grant-program report before an appropriate evaluation time. Funding agencies should allocate more of their resources to support both evaluation of selected existing programs and evaluation research.

NSF previously has placed the responsibility for evaluating programs on principal investigators, most of whom do not have a background in survey or social-science research. NSF's program officers, overwhelmed with large numbers of grants, have little time to provide feedback to grantees about their grants or to follow up on programs. The average tenure of a program officer in the Education and Human Resources Directorate is 2 years, but most grants run for 3 years. Considering that a grant is in preparation, review, and approval for about 9-12 months, it is possible to be assigned to three different program officers over a single grant period. Rarely does an NSF program officer stay long enough to see a round of grants through to completion, much less the next round of proposal submissions as those programs are submitted for renewal. Newer NSF policies recognize the need for outside evaluation.

## RECOMMENDATIONS

• Those involved in professional-development programs should recognize the importance of establishing an evaluation plan from the onset of program design. That process forces a clarity of thinking about program objectives and activities in much the same way that careful planning of one's scientific research forces clarity of thinking about experimental design.

• Every professional-development program should include evaluation mechanisms from the beginning. The evaluation should continue for the life of the program and seek feedback from all participants.

• Because formal long-term evaluation of an entire program requires more extensive analysis than informal evaluation, it is not cost-effective for every program. Instead, we recommend that clusters of similar kinds of programs, such as biotechnology or systemic programs, or all programs in a geographic region be reviewed as a group. The goal is to learn about the net effect of various kinds of programs on teachers and students and to identify strengths, weaknesses, and gaps in content, pedagogy, or geographic distribution.

• Program directors and principal investigators should not necessarily have primary responsibility for long-term evaluation of their own programs; these persons often do not have sufficient background in the methods of social-science and education research and might not be objective about their own programs. Ideally, professional-development programs include a budget item for a qualified evaluator, who should be involved from the onset of program. We concur in previous recommendations to NSF that continuing evaluations (and evaluation specialists) be considered "legitimate uses of project funds" (SRI, 1988).

• Scientists and other program developers should work with colleagues in the social sciences and education to identify experienced program evaluators who can help to plan and participate in overall program evaluation.

• Funding agencies should support more research about effective evaluation methods. NSF should fund the development of a comprehensive guide to evaluating professional development that includes a compendium of educational research and examples of effective evaluation. The task is complex and requires evaluators who have formal training in program evaluation. A recent publication by the Council on Foundations, which includes nine extensive case studies of evaluation projects, is a start in this direction (Johnson, 1993).

# 8

# A Vision of the Future

The committee recognizes that implementing its recommendations will require adequate continued funding, changes in institutional values, and systemic reform at many levels. Nonetheless, our review of programs that are helping teachers to improve science education in many parts of the country makes us optimistic that improvements are possible. This report should help to promote many more such programs. Focusing on empowering teachers in their classrooms and providing scientists with support for involvement in continuing professional development can improve science education for all students. If that happens, teachers, classrooms, and scientists will be different in the future. We describe here our vision of the future.

## A FUTURE TEACHER

Dr. Preston Jordan is a secondary-school teacher in the twenty-first century. He is no longer considered to be a biology or chemistry or even a science teacher, because his professional development has included opportunities to become knowledgeable in at least two major subjects (mathematics and science) and to work with the partnership team at his school, which consists of a humanities–fine arts specialist (from the community), a social-sciences professor (from the local college), a vocational-arts and career counselor (from a local industry), and four aides, two of whom are college undergraduates seriously considering teaching as their future profession. His teaching team is responsible for coordinating the educational activities of a group of ninth-grade students throughout the school year.

As a former research scientist, Dr. Jordan obtained his teaching credential through a special work-study program that enabled him to continue working part-time at a nearby biotechnology laboratory. His preservice experiences were quite similar to those of people who graduated from the regular credential program, in that most of them spent at least one summer and usually part of the school year as interns with one of the local businesses or industries. That enabled them—and Dr. Jordan—to develop some important practical connections to what they would be teaching.

His teaching credential stipulates that he must continue a professional-development program for his entire career. The choice of activities is determined by him and his professional-development counselor (a district employee who works part-time as a student counselor or for a local industry) subject to approval by the district's professional-development coordinator.

The science curriculum, well integrated into the other major subject programs, has been developed from the *National Science Education Standards* and his state's Science Curriculum Framework. The American Association for the Advancement of Science Project 2061 developed some innovative curriculum-implementation models, one of which has been adapted at his school because of its interdisciplinary structure. The Scope, Sequence, and Coordination Project produced by National Science Teachers Association (NSTA), has stimulated the development and dissemination of various integrated science units, some of which he has adapted for use in his classroom.

This summer, because Dr. Jordan will be team-teaching a new integrated unit next year that involves some basic botany concepts, he and his counselor have decided that a special summer institute on Fast Plants would be most appropriate. This program has now developed a network of satellite resource centers throughout the country, and several possibilities are within driving distance.

The 2-week summer institute is wonderful: several well-known botanists from the nearby college and community college have teamed with two experienced secondary-school teachers to present the program. They group-teach the institute and model and provide a variety of effective learning activities, including field trips, that all the participants enjoy. A special provision has been made to help all participants to obtain the necessary equipment and supplies for their classrooms through the sponsorship of the institute and partnership with some local nurseries and florists. Followup activities during the school year will include some classroom visits by the institute staff for both consultation and guest presentations, school-year sessions for continuing opportunities to network and share experiences, and some special laboratory activities and field trips to expand their knowledge base. Next summer, several internships will be available with the nurseries.

Thanks to his summer and school-year professional-development activities, Dr. Jordan has established professional relationships with scientists throughout the region. Several years ago, he took a fascinating earth-science workshop and met a geologist who works at the U.S. Geological Survey. They keep in touch; recently, she provided him with some special topographic maps that helped his students to understand the geology of their area.

Dr. Jordan's district provides 10 professional-development days beyond his normal teaching schedule each year. He may also submit minigrant proposals related to his professional-development activities that will help him to implement what he has learned. Dr. Jordan used three of his days to attend the national convention of NSTA, where he gave a talk on the challenges and rewards of teaching an integrated science curriculum.

Since he joined the district and began his teaching career, Dr. Jordan has been a part of a teacher-support program that was originally developed for new teachers. (His district had the wisdom to see that all teachers, not only beginning teachers, need support.) The support program provides him with two mentors— one at his school and the other at another district school. All teachers have the opportunity to meet regularly during the school year; during these interactions, they may serve as peer coaches or team teachers or merely provide comments as they observe one another teach. Next year, now that Dr. Jordan will have taught for 5 years, he will become a mentor to one of the new teachers recently hired by the district. He is looking forward to expanding the variety of roles played by a truly professional teacher.

## A FUTURE CLASSROOM

Imagine a future classroom. It looks and feels very different from the "old days." There are very thin textbooks with eight or nine basic concepts on two or three topics integrated across mathematics, science, and societal issues. Learning is not book-centered, but centered on information access, management, and use. Each table or learning station has several sets of objects to manipulate to rein-force hands-on, inquiry-based learning. Each learning station also has a modern information-access facility, including computers, Internet access, CD-ROM reader, and satellite feed.

In the classroom of the future,

• Learning takes place in teams of students and is based on themes that are relevant to students and society.
• Teachers show students how to learn with analogies, by posing questions, and by demonstrating methods of finding answers.
• Teachers are linked or partnered with scientists in research facilities or related businesses.
• Students work on actual problems in the business, medical, and research worlds. For example, student teams work with local agencies and companies to examine local problems in transportation, urban water supply, waste disposal, recycling, and new-product development.

- Students carry out both short- and long-term research projects that require integration of science and mathematics. Students write up their observations and interpretations in their personal journals.
- Students gain access to data from the National Institutes of Health, the National Oceanic and Atmospheric Administration, and other agencies to work on real problems with teams from other high schools in other states and countries.
- Students have direct access to the questions being posed by research teams, to their data, and to the teams themselves.
- Students are no longer isolated in the classroom, nor is their education confined to 6 hours per day, 9 months per year. Instead, many options are available, such as year-long classes, evening classes, and work credit related to team involvement in community projects that real address real issues and solve real problems.
- Vocational-biology classes are popular and allow an emphasis on learning job skills needed by laboratory technicians who monitor robotics in laboratory experimentation. Student teams isolate genes in plants, feed into national databases, and help to develop new medications, engineered plants for agriculture, and so on.

## A FUTURE SCIENTIST

Dr. Irene Martinez has just been promoted to associate professor with tenure after 6 years as an assistant professor at a research university that is in the top 20 in extramural funding. She has maintained a continuously funded research program in molecular biology as an assistant professor, but her grants have been supplemented by education funds to support undergraduates and teachers in her laboratory. For 3 years, Dr. Martinez had two high-school teachers working in her laboratory during the summer. They worked most directly with a postdoctoral fellow in the laboratory and participated in regular laboratory-research meetings, presenting their findings to the group. As part of their summer experience, they met weekly with teachers working in other laboratories in the department and discussed their experiences and planned how to translate them into activities in their own classrooms.

During the school year, Dr. Martinez and the students and postdoctoral fellows in her laboratory visited the teachers' classrooms and helped them with their experiments. They also described their own personal background and how they got interested in science. Dr. Martinez's laboratory was "adopted" by the high-school teacher's biology-laboratory class. Because the teacher's school is connected to the nationwide computer network, the students in the classroom can communicate electronically with these scientists, whom they now recognize as "real" people. They can send questions on the network that are posted on a bulletin board in Dr. Martinez's laboratory. Researchers in the laboratory see the questions and help the students to find answers. The answers in turn are posted in the high-school classroom. Laboratory members often debate the appropriate answers to ethical and social questions. They often send pictures, diagrams, or short movies from their university's science library, which contains CD-ROMs and videodisks. Once, when a high-school student inquired about a specific experimental technique, an undergraduate student in the laboratory videotaped herself doing the experiment and forwarded the video over the network.

Dr. Martinez was worried about how much time she was spending in working with the teachers and students, although she and her laboratory found it both rewarding and fun. She was encouraged by her department head to treat this as an important responsibility of all university faculty and to assume that success in her efforts would be rewarded.

As part of Dr. Martinez's record of accomplishment for university promotion to tenure, she described how she had used the education supplements to her research grants. The supplements enabled her to work with the teachers and to provide the computer-network equipment and the training to use it so that they would be able to communicate with the university laboratory.

Dr. Martinez had gotten interested in this technology and in working with the teachers through the university's Center for Science Education. The center provided well-equipped laboratories for high-school teachers and students to work with university faculty in larger groups than could be accommodated in individual laboratories. Half the permanent staff of the center were permanently funded by the university; the remainder were funded by the school district, the state, and a federal grant. Two of the center staff were specialists in education evaluation. Dr. Martinez could not help applying the same rigor to her teaching activities as to designing her experiments, and she wanted to learn which of the activities she conducted with teachers were most effective in helping the students in their classrooms. The staff of the center first helped her to find and analyze the education-research literature on the value of research experiences for teachers. She then decided that she and three other faculty colleagues in her department and six colleagues at a different university would try different kinds of followup activities with the teachers, varying the roles of students, postdoctoral fellows, and faculty in visits and comparing electronic communication with a newsletter and written and telephone contact. Their results suggested that electronic communication worked best because the rapid feedback and somewhat indirect nature increased the comfort of students and led them to ask the questions that they really wanted to have answered, some of which they thought might sound "dumb." Dr. Martinez and her colleagues, with the help of the center staff in analyzing the data from questionnaires and students' standardized testing and hands-on laboratories, published two papers on their findings. They also presented them at the national conventions of the American Society for Cell Biology, and they and the teachers presented a poster at the NSTA national convention.

The paper on the education experiment was regarded by the university's promotion and tenure committee as strong evidence of scholarship in teaching. It recognized that the time spent by Dr. Martinez and members of her laboratory working with high-school teachers and students decreased the number—not the quality—of her publications, but the teaching accomplishments more than compensated for this. It also noted that the education supplements to her research grants made her one of the best-funded assistant professors in her department. The promotion and tenure committee was impressed that Dr. Martinez's experience in using electronic communication with the high-school teachers and students encouraged her to expand the use of electronic communication in her upper-division cell-biology course, whose enrollment had increased to more than 300 students. There she found that electronic communication among the students themselves facilitated their cooperative learning and that they often answered each other's questions before she had a chance to reply.

Dr. Martinez's success has encouraged her faculty colleagues to work with teachers. Their department has now adopted a whole school in their district and is working with teachers and principals to expand electronic communication both within the school and between the school and the university. That has attracted the interest of the English and art departments, which have begun working with other teachers in the school.

## PREPARING FUTURE TEACHERS

Dr. Nahn Daung joined the Upstate University Biology Department 10 years ago as a research geneticist and assistant professor of biology. In addition to the work with his graduate students in the laboratory, he has been teaching the second core course in biology for freshmen every other spring semester. He has found that he enjoys teaching basic conceptual biology because it helps him to translate his own research in the human-genome project into classroom and laboratory activities. It is hard to tell what careers the freshmen will pursue, but because of his love of teaching Dr. Daung has become a mentor for a number of students who plan to become secondary-school science teachers. His goal is to ensure that all future science teachers who pass through his department have worked with a scientist to experience investigative activities in science laboratories. All those students will learn how to design inquiry-based laboratory exercises that can be used in the classroom.

Recently, Dr. Daung has worked with a faculty team in teaching a course for senior science majors who plan to go into teaching. He, a chemist , and a nuclear physicist have been conducting a semester-long seminar in which students from all the sciences re-examine the primary concepts from their undergraduate study and make connections with students who majored in other science fields. During the seminars, he has gotten to know science majors just before they began student teaching. He has kept in touch with several of his beginning teachers through electronic mail and has given several guest presentations for one of them by video conference. In that way, he has been able to show the high-school students what is being done in his laboratory and to engage students in thinking about the kinds of questions that his laboratory is working on.

Dr. Daung also has periodic meetings with the faculty in the school of education. Through a team approach, faculty in the sciences and education work together to develop undergraduate curricula that couple science content and process with pedagogic skills. He enjoys his dual role as researcher-educator. He was most pleased when he was recently appointed to serve on the Science Advisory Board of the State Teacher Credentialing Commission.

# References

AAAS (American Association for the Advancement of Science). 1989. Project 2061: Science for All Americans. Washington, DC: American Association for the Advancement of Science.

AAHE (American Association for Higher Education). Compact Connections, a newsletter of AAHE's Community Compacts for Student Success. Spring 1993.

Alberts, B. M. 1991. Elementary science education in the United States: how scientists can help. Current Biology 1(6):339-341.

Atkin, J. M. 1989. Can educational research keep pace with education reform? Phi Delta Kappan (November):200-205.

Barth, R. S. 1990. Improving Schools from Within: Teachers, Parents and Principals Can Make a Difference. San Francisco, CA: Jossey-Bass.

Blank, R. K., and M. Dalkilic. 1992. State Policies on Science and Mathematics Education. Washington, DC: Council of Chief State School Officers, State Education Assessment Center.

Blank, R. K., and D. Gruebel. 1993. State Indicators of Science and Mathematics Education—1993, State and National Trends: New Indicators from the 1991-92 School Year. Washington, DC: Council of Chief State School Officers, State Education Assessment Center.

Boyer, E. L. 1990. A Special Report. Scholarship Reconsidered: Priorities of the Professoriate. Princeton, NJ: The Carnegie Foundation for the Advancement of Teaching. Available from Princeton University Press, Lawrenceville, N.J.

BSCS (Biological Sciences Curriculum Study). 1978. Guidelines for educational priorities and curricular innovations in human and molecular genetics. BSCS Journal 1(1):20-29.

GAO (General Accounting Office). 1984. New Directions for Federal Programs to Aid Mathematics and Science Teaching. GAO/PEMD-84-4. Washington, DC: U.S. General Accounting Office.

Haycock, K. P. 1990. Partnerships for America's Children. Presentation at the American Association for Higher Education's First National Conference on School/College Collaboration, Chicago, June 17-20, 1990. Pp. 3-11 in Improving Student Achievement Through Partnerships. Washington, DC: American Association for Higher Education.

Hord, S. M., W. C. Rutherford, L. Huling-Austin, and G. E. Hall. 1987. Taking Charge of Change. Alexandria, VA: Association for Supervision and Curriculum Development.

Hurd, P. D. 1961. Biological Education in American Secondary Schools 1890-1960. Washington, DC: American Institute of Biological Sciences.

Hurd, P. D. 1984. Reforming science education: the search for a new vision. Occasional Paper 33. Washington, DC: Council for Basic Education.

Johnson, R. M. 1993. 35 keys to effective evaluating. Foundation News (May/June):16-21. (First published in Evaluation for Foundations: Concepts, Cases Guidelines, and Resources. 1993. Developed for the Council on Foundations. San Francisco, CA: Jossey-Bass.)

Joyce, B., and B. Showers. 1980. Training ourselves to teach: the messages of research. Educational Leadership 37:379-385.

Kennedy, D. 1990. Stanford in its second century. An address to the Stanford community at the Meeting of the Academic Council, April 5, 1990. Stanford University Campus Report (April 11):17-18.

Kober, N. 1993. What we know about science teaching and learning. EDTALK. Washington, DC: Council for Educational Development and Research.

Little, J. W. 1993. Teachers' Professional Development in a Climate of Educational Reform. New York, NY: National Center for Restructuring Education, Schools and Teaching at Teachers College, Columbia University.

Mastain, R. K., ed. 1991. The NASDTEC Manual 1991: Manual on Certification and Preparation of Education Personnel in the United States. A report from the National Association of State Directors of Teacher Education and Certification (NASDTEC). Dubuque, IA: Kendall/Hunt Publishing.

Mechling, K.R., C. H. Stedman, and K. M. Donnelan. 1982. An NSTA report: preparing and certifying science teachers. Science and Children (October):9-14.

NRC (National Research Council). 1990. Fulfilling the Promise: Biology Education in the Nation's Schools. Washington, DC: National Academy Press.

NRC (National Research Council). 1996. National Science Education Standards. Washington, DC: National Academy Press.

Nelson, B. H., I. R. Weiss, and L. E. Conway. 1992. Science and Mathematics Education Briefing Book. Vol. III. A report from Horizon Research Inc. Chapel Hill, NC: Horizon Research Inc. (Available from the National Science Teachers Association, Alexandria, VA.)

NSTA (National Science Teachers Association). 1992-1993. Standards for the preparation & certification of teachers of science, K-12. In NSTA Handbook. Arlington, VA: National Science Teachers Association.

Raizen, S. A., and A. M. Michelsohn, eds. 1994. The Future of Science in Elementary School: Educating Prospective Teachers. A report from the National Center for Improving Science Education. San Francisco, CA: Jossey-Bass.

Roth, K. J. 1989. Science education: it's not enough to 'do' or 'relate.' American Educator (Winter):16-22, 47-48.

SRI International. 1988. An Approach to Assessing Initiatives in Science Education. Summary Report: Recommendations to the National Science Foundation prepared by M. S. Knapp, P. M. Shields, M. St. John, A. A. Zucker, and M. S. Stearns for the National Science Foundation. Menlo, CA: SRI International.

Tierney, D. S. 1988. Teaching content through a multicultural lens: a social studies case study. Journal of Educational Issues of Language Minority Students, A journal of a teacher training program at Boise State University. Summer:15-21.

Tobias, S. 1992. Revitalizing Undergraduate Science: Why Some Things Work and Most Don't. Tucson, AZ: Research Corporation.

Yager, R. E., and E. Zehr. 1985. Science education in U.S. graduate institutions during two decades. Science Education 69(2):163-169.

# Appendixes

# APPENDIX A

# Professional-Development Programs that Responded to the Committee's Request for Information, Organized by Geographic Location[1]

## ARIZONA

**1. Science in Action**
**Tucson Unified School District; University of Arizona**
**Contact: Gail Paulin, Tucson, (520) 617-7052, FAX: (520) 617-7051,**
**Internet: gpaulin@ccit.arizona.edu**

Cosponsored by the Tucson Unified School District and the University of Arizona, Science in Action brings together K-6 science teachers and university scientists to develop hands-on science activities for K-6 classrooms. The objectives of the program are to familiarize teachers with local research resources, to encourage collaboration among teachers and scientists, to help teachers foster enthusiasm for science among their students, and to improve student achievement in science. With funding from the Howard Hughes Medical Institute, the program familiarizes participants with Science in Action concepts and materials

---

[1]Information about almost 200 programs was collected by the committee in 1992 and 1993, and the information was used to assess the characteristics of effective professional-development programs. Appendix A was updated in late 1995. Some of the original programs that had been examined and then listed in this appendix had ended; descriptions of these programs have been removed. Several original programs had changed scope to some extent; these are designated with asterisks (*) to indicate that they are not now exactly as they were when the committee reviewed them. Some entirely new programs were identified during the updating; they are designated with double asterisks (**).

through 5 days of workshops, discussions, demonstrations, and lectures. In addition, participants practice implementing program concepts in a 3-day teaching practicum with area students. Teachers are encouraged to present the material in thematic or interdisciplinary units; to emphasize mathematical, social, and technical applications; and to include the arts when possible. In light of the high numbers of limited-English-proficient students in Tucson who speak Spanish as a first language, the program provides Spanish translations of all materials.

**2. Science Update Series and Research/Technology Tours**
**Arizona Alliance for Mathematics, Science and Technology Education**
**Contact: Charles Hoyt, Phoenix, (602) 943-9332, FAX: (602) 589-2716,**
**Internet: n/a**

For 6 years, the Arizona Alliance for Mathematics, Science and Technology Education has offered a Science Update Series to K-12 teachers. Funded by local education agencies, the program offers hands-on training to teachers in science, mathematics, and technology. The presenters include research scientists, technologists, professors, and members of various professional societies. The series is made up of lectures, discussions, and laboratory activities and runs between 8 hours and 32 hours. Program goals are to update the participants' knowledge of mathematics, science, and technology and to improve their strategies for teaching these subjects. A new biotechnology training session for elementary- and junior-high-school teachers runs from 1 to 5 days. The alliance also sponsors Research/ Technology Tours, which take about 150 grade 6-12 teachers to various research sites. Tours include 1-day visits to the University of Arizona laboratories, where teachers are updated on current laboratory research and technology. On returning to their classrooms, teachers are expected to present their new knowledge to their students and to encourage them to use the information in their development of laboratory and science-fair projects.

## CALIFORNIA

**3. City Science Program, Science and Health Education Partnership**
**University of California-San Francisco; San Francisco Unified School**
**District**
**Contact: Liesl Chatman, San Francisco, (415) 476-0337, FAX: (415) 476-9926, Internet: liesl@itsa.ucsf.edu**

With support from the National Science Foundation, the Science and Health Education Partnership has developed a K-5 hands-on science curriculum that is being implemented throughout the San Francisco public schools. Over a 4-year period, the project aims to familiarize K-5 teachers with the City Science curriculum through 1-month summer sessions and monthly Saturday meetings throughout the academic year. During these sessions, master teachers and scientists work together to provide model teaching experiences for participants. Program goals include providing participants with the background and skills they need to facilitate City Science activities in cooperative groups, to couple hands-on science with hands-on assessment, and to integrate science with writing, reading, and mathematics. Participants work with a team of lead teachers to provide inservice training to noninstitute teachers. In addition, they are expected to work closely with principals to monitor the implementation of the science curriculum.

**4. Exploratorium Teacher Institute**
**The Exploratorium**
**Contact: Karen Mendelow, San Francisco, (415) 561-0313, FAX: (415) 561-0307, Internet: karenm@exploratorium.edu**

The Exploratorium Teacher Institute provides middle-school and high-school teachers with 4 weeks of science and mathematics learning with Exploratorium exhibits and staff. Activities include hands-on experiences with exhibit apparatus and small-group discussions about how to use experiential learning in their classrooms. Participants build models of the exhibits that can be transported to their classrooms. Discussion topics, which often reflect the Science Framework for California Public Schools, include physical sciences, life sciences, and mathematics. Subjects investigated are vision, light, hearing, sound, genetics, mathematics, ecology, plant growth, electricity, magnetism, thermodynamics, and weather. Program facilitators develop workshops on the ideas and needs voiced by participating teachers, including the specific needs of teachers who work with limited-English-speaking students. As followup, the program offers four Saturday discussions during the academic year, which are open to all institute alumni. Formal program evaluations are an integral part of the program.

**5. San Francisco Zoological Gardens**
**Contact: Diane Demee-Benoit, San Francisco, (415) 753-7073, FAX: (415) 681-2039, Internet: n/a**

Motivated by the belief that teachers' skills and confidence in conservation education can affect student attitudes toward the environment, the San Francisco Zoo has expanded its role in classroom science education to include teacher programs. Through workshops, the program demonstrates exemplary hands-on science teaching that cuts across scientific disciplines. The workshops, developed for multicultural audiences, last 7 hours and include the following topics: endangered species, rain forests, wetlands, applied ecology, and insects in the classroom. A shorter version of the workshop on rain forests is also presented at area conferences. The program aims to bridge formal and informal education, to align science instruction with the new Science Framework for California Public Schools, and to give teachers an active role in improving science education.

**6. Teacher Education in Biology**
**San Francisco State University**
**Contact: Lane Conn, San Francisco, (415) 338-7872, FAX: (415) 338-2295, Internet: lconn@sfsu.edu**

The Teacher Education in Biology program offers an array of opportunities in biology, biotechnology, and bioethics. Organized by scientists, social scientists, and science teachers, activities include a 10-day laboratory workshop at one of four sites in California, a 3-day summer symposium, and several 2-day academic year followup meetings. Program goals are to familiarize participants with new teaching strategies, leadership skills, current issues in science-education reform and biology research, the Science Framework for California Public Schools, opportunities for networking with teachers and scientists, and hands-on activities for the classroom. Program participants include California middle- and high-school science teachers, district science coordinators, and university teacher-education faculty. Teachers receive stipends of $60/day and classroom resources.

**7. California Science Project**
**University of California**
**Contact: Rollie Otto, Berkeley, (510) 486-5325, FAX: (916) 754-8086, Internet: rjotto@lvl.gov**

The California Science Project (CSP) was initiated in 1989 with funds from the Intersegmental Education Budget of the University of California, which administers the program on behalf of California's teachers. A 17-member advisory committee is composed of representatives from all the major science-education segments of California, including higher education (the Association of Independent California Colleges and Universities, the California Community Colleges, the California Postsecondary Education Commission, California State University, and the University of California), K-12 teachers, the national laboratories, and the Industry Education Council of California. CSP has a broad mandate to provide staff-development opportunities to teachers of science in grades K-14, building on models of the California Writing Project and the California Mathematics Project. Campuses in the University of California system compete for funds to conduct professional-development programs for teachers. Current CSP programs and sites are California Science Project of Inland Northern California, at California State University, Chico, with Butte College and Shasta College; Sacramento Area Science Project, at California State University, Sacramento and the University of California, Davis; Bay Area Science Project, at the University of California, Berkeley;  Central Valley Science Project, at California State University, Fresno, with Fresno Pacific College; South Coast Science Project, at the University of California, Santa Barbara; USC/LAUSD Science Project, at the University of Southern California; the UCLA Science Project, at the University of California, Los Angeles with the Los Angeles Educational Partnership; Orange County Science Education Network, at the University of California, Irvine with several community colleges and Chapman College; Inland Area Science Project, at the University of California, Riverside and California State University, San Bernardino;  CSP of San Diego and Imperial Counties, at the University of California, San Diego and San Diego State University; and Central Coastal Area Science Project, at the University of California, Santa Cruz.

**\*\*8.  Evolution and the Nature of Science Institute**
**San Jose State University; Indiana University**
**Contact:  Jean Beard, San Jose, CA, (408) 924-4870, or Craig Nelson,**
**Bloomington, IN, (612) 855-1345, FAX:  (408) 924-4840, Internet:**
**beard@biomail.sjsu.edu**

Three National Science Foundation grants to the same co-principal investigators have supported 3-week residential institutes (ENSI) for 30 high-school biology teachers for 6 years (1989-1995), have supported additional preparation (LTPP) of 38 institute graduates for four summers (1991-1994), and have partially supported 36 two-week satellite institutes for up to 20 teachers (1992-1995) taught by pairs of specially prepared institute alumni.  The current grant will support additional satellites (SENSI) beginning in summer 1996 at sites from Ohio to California.  The summer institutes and two academic-year followup sessions (fall and spring) are designed to update participants' knowledge of the nature of science, general organic evolution, and human evolution and to help them integrate these topics into their teaching.  Teachers are encouraged to apply in teams from schools, school districts, or geographic regions so as to have colleagues to work with after the summer.  The institutes consist of curriculum-development activities, lectures, seminars, demonstration, discussions, hands-on activities and field work.  Participants are assigned to apply some of their new knowledge in teaching, monitor their experiences, and report back to the group at followup sessions.  A more-complete explanation of the ENSI/SENSI program content and philosophy has been accepted for publication in the *American Biology Teacher* and is tentatively titled "Better Biology Teaching by Emphasizing Evolution and the Nature of Science."

**9.  AIMS Instructional Leadership Program**
**AIMS Education Foundation**
**Contact:  Arthur Wiebe, Fresno, (209) 255-4094, FAX:  (209) 255-6396,**
**Internet:  aimsed@fresno.edu**

The AIMS (Activities Integrating Math and Science) Education Foundation, an educational nonprofit organization, has provided hands-on leadership training to over 80,000 teachers in 46 states. Since 1986, AIMS facilitators, who are predominantly classroom teachers with 7 weeks of special training, have implemented 1-week staff-development programs for K-8 teachers. Through hands-on workshops, discussions, demonstrations, and lectures, AIMS informs participants about learning theory, science and mathematics content, and teaching strategies that are consistent with the guidelines of the American Association for the Advancement of Science Project 2061, National Research Council standards, and National Council of Teachers of Mathematics standards. The goals of the program are to enable participants to implement a hands-on, integrated mathematics-science program in their classrooms and to foster the leadership skills needed to share with their colleagues. The project is intended to improve student achievement in mathematics and science and to encourage networking among teachers. The program is funded primarily by local education agencies. Former participants often serve as instructors for related 1-day and 1-week workshops.

**10. Central Valley Science Project**
**School of Education, California State University, Fresno**
**Contact: James E. Marshall, Fresno, (209) 278-0239, FAX: (209) 278-0404, Internet: jamesm@zimmer.csufresno.edu**

A primary goal of this project is to encourage teachers to assume science-education leadership roles in their schools, in their districts, or at the state level. Through networking activities and a 14-day residential summer institute in the mountains, the project aims to provide high-quality professional development for teachers, establish an active science-education network in the Central Valley, and promote community participation in science education. Ultimately, the project aims to improve the education of K-12 students, who will benefit from the efforts of better-informed, qualified, and motivated teachers.

**11. Schools and Colleges for Advancing the Teaching of Science**
**California State University, Sacramento**
**Contact: Tom Smithson, Sacramento, (916) 278-5487, FAX: (916) 278-6664, Internet: scats@csus.edu**

Schools and Colleges for Advancing the Teaching of Science (SCATS) is an alliance of grade K-12 teachers, university and community-college faculty, and local industrial scientists and engineers who work to improve science education in the Sacramento area public and private schools. For 11 years, SCATS has offered grant programs, workshops, seminars, dinner meetings, field trips, and networking opportunities to science educators in the Sacramento region. SCATS projects cover a wide range of disciplines, including chemistry, biology, physics, earth science, astronomy, meteorology, pedagogy, and computer science. Underlying each initiative is a belief in the importance of developing professional-enrichment activities that join educators from all sectors of the community.

**12. Amgen Inc. Lab Kit**
**Contact: Hugh Nelson, Newbury Park, (805) 498-8663, FAX: (805) 499-3549, Internet: n/a**

In 1991, Amgen Inc., a biotechnology pharmaceutical company, developed a Lab Kit to educate area teachers about gene splicing and complex procedures used in extended laboratory experiments. With assistance from a local school district, Amgen integrated the Lab Kit into the curricula of 20 high schools during the 1994-1995 school year, reaching a total of 75 teachers and 2,500 students. Amgen has also sponsored a school lecture series and a teacher-intern program.

**13. Industry Initiatives for Science and Math Education-San Francisco Bay Area**
**Lawrence Hall of Science; University of California, Berkeley**
**Contact: Marie Earl, Santa Clara, (408) 496-5340, FAX: (408) 496-5333, Internet: mlearl@aol.com**

IISME's core program, the Summer Fellowship Program, provides San Francisco Bay Area science, mathematics, and computer-science teachers with mentored, paid summer jobs at high-technology companies, government agencies, and university laboratories. There is year-round assistance to teachers as they strive to meet their commitment to translating their summer experiences into updated and enriched classroom instruction. Summer meetings, peer coaching, resource-brokering, academic-year workshops, small grants, and an electronic network are among the services provided to teachers. Each summer, 80-90 scientists and engineers work side by side with IISME teachers on technical assignments. Many of these industry-school relationships continue after the summer, as mentors host students at their worksites, make classroom presentations or attend career fairs, donate surplus equipment or supplies, or provide advice to curriculum committees. Funding from the National Science Foundation enabled the Triangle Coalition for Science and Technology Education and IISME to work together to replicate the summer-fellowship-program model nationally. IISME's Summer Fellowship Program has been recognized by the U.S. Department of Education as a model program helping the nation to achieve the national education Goals 2000.

**\*14. NSF-Advances in Biological Science/Institutionalizing Student Research Projects**
**Center for Cancer and Developmental Biology, California State University, Northridge**
**Contact: Steven Oppenheimer, Northridge, (818) 885-3336, FAX: (818) 885-2034, Internet: n/a**

For 10 years, the Center for Cancer and Developmental Biology at California State University-Northridge has offered an inservice program to area teachers. With funding from the National Science Foundation, the Howard Hughes Medical Institute, the Urban Community Service Program, and the Joseph Drown Foundation, the center provides lectures, laboratories, curriculum-development activities, and discussions addressing cutting-edge issues in biology. Program facilitators have developed participant materials into biology and life-science curriculum guides for the Los Angeles Unified School District that have also been distributed nationally. Recent emphasis has been on training teachers to incorporate student research projects into their curricula in the hope that abstracts of student projects would be published in the *Journal of Student Research Abstracts*.

**\*15. Science Programs for Teachers Grades Kindergarten through College**
**Center X, UCLA Graduate School of Education**
**Contact: Janet Thornber, Los Angeles, (310) 825-1109, FAX: (310) 206-5369, Internet: thornber@gse.ucla.edu**

The professional-development arm of Center X offers programs for science teachers of all grade levels. It currently houses the UCLA Science Project, a component of the California Subject Matter Projects; UCLA Project Issues (Integrated Systems for Studying Urban Environmental Science); and a professional-development program of workshops available to all schools in Los Angeles County. Programs focus on urban science and promote strategies that make science accessible to all students, whatever their backgrounds. Programs offer intensive institutes during the summer and school year and model constructivist approaches to teaching and learning. Teacher participants attend interactive seminars with faculty and experts in the field; perform field studies, mini-investigations, and self-guided city explorations; see models of effective pedagogy; and compile constructivist teaching units for their own classrooms.

**16. TOPS**
**Occidental College**
**Contact: April Mazzeo, Los Angeles, (213) 259-2892, FAX: (213) 341-4912, Internet: amazzeo@oxy.edu**

With funding from the National Science Foundation, Occidental College's Departments of Biology, Chemistry, and Education offer a 2-week summer institute and a "van laboratory" service to high-school teachers. The program, TOPS (Teachers + Occidental = Partnership in Science), aims to provide high-school teachers with advanced scientific instrumentation for hands-on integrated laboratory experiences in line with the state's new Science Framework for California Public Schools. The summer institute, held at Occidental's laboratories, involves participants in experiments in molecular biology and analytical chemistry as applied to life science. Followup is provided by a TOPS resource teacher who travels with the "van laboratory" to participants' classrooms, providing the equipment that they need to carry out the experiments. Each institute is limited to 30 chemistry and biology teachers, who each receive a $400 stipend for their participation. Preference is given to teams of biology and chemistry teachers who apply from the same school.

**17. The Caltech Precollege Science Initiative**
**California Institute of Technology**
**Contact: Jim Bower, Pasadena, (818) 395-3222, FAX: (818) 440-0865,**
**Internet: j.bower@capsi.caltech.edu**

The Caltech Precollege Science Initiative (CAPSI) supports a number of coordinated reform efforts in precollege science education. These efforts focus on encouraging inquiry and discovery in the learning process, on promoting the active participation of underrepresented student populations, on fostering cooperation between scientists and educators, and on encouraging teachers to participate fully in the process of education reform. A primary goal is to provide materials and methods for improving science education that can be applied across the nation. The CAPSI effort began with an emphasis on the needs of elementary-school children and has more recently begun a wide-ranging set of programs. The elementary-school science program, originally dubbed Project SEED, is now the districtwide science program of the Pasadena Unified School District. As a result of its success, work has started on expanding the elementary-school program to the middle grades and on the establishment of models for the continuing professional development of teachers. CAPSI also has initiated the Pasadena Center for Improving Elementary Science Education through a partnership with the Pasadena Unified School District and support from the National Science Foundation. This program is designed to support other urban school districts in California that seek to introduce or enhance high-quality hands-on science instruction based on the Pasadena model. Other CAPSI programs include the development and pilot testing of an inquiry-based undergraduate science course for preservice teachers and the creation of computer simulations to complement students' hands-on experiences.

**18. UCI Summer Science Institute and Affiliated Programs**
**University of California, Irvine**
**Contact: Ann Miller, Irvine, (714) 824-6390, FAX: (714) 824-7621,**
**Internet: amiller@uci.edu**

Since 1982, University of California, Irvine (UCI) science faculty, industrial representatives, and experienced teachers have served as instructors in a summer institute for K-12 teachers. With support from southern California business and industry, the National Science Foundation, and the California State Department of Education, the program aims to upgrade  participants' teaching skills and expand their knowledge in biology, physical science, earth science, chemistry, biotechnology, and other subjects. Stipends are available for participating teachers. UCI also offers programs that facilitate the development of K-12 science-leadership teams in Orange County.

**\*19. Program for Teacher Enhancement in Science and Technology**
**University of California, San Diego**
**Contact: Melanie Dean, La Jolla, (619) 534-8587, FAX: (619) 534-7483,**
**Internet: melanie_dean@unexpost.ucsd.edu**

The Program for Teacher Enhancement in Science and Technology (PTEST) offers programs in science and technology for K-12 teachers. Current PTEST programs are the following. The Supercomputer Teacher Enhancement Program (STEP) consists of a 3-week summer institute and six academic-year followup meetings each year for 3 years; STEP prepares high-school teachers to incorporate the basics of supercomputing and computational science into their physics, chemistry, biology, and earth-science classrooms. The Science Teacher Enhancement and Enrichment Project (STEEP) consists of 3-week summer programs that emphasize science content, pedagogy, and leadership training; the goals of the program are to upgrade the science-content background and science-teaching methods of K-6 teachers, to provide teams of teachers with leadership training and staff-development skills, to develop teacher leaders to implement an enrichment program for underserved students, and to develop teacher leaders to implement parent and community involvement in science education. The National City School District Science Systemic Teacher Enhancement Project (NSSTE) is intended to bring about a systemic science-education reform effort in a small school district. The California Science Project for San Diego and Imperial Counties (CSP) is funded by the president's office of the University of California; its primary purpose is to develop a cadre of K-12 teacher leaders in science who will model effective science teaching for culturally and linguistically diverse students and function as leaders in their schools and districts to disseminate effective practices to their peers.

## COLORADO

**20. Adventures in Science**
**Adams District Twelve-Five Star Schools**
**Contact:  Nancy Kellogg, Northglenn, (303) 894-2144, FAX:  n/a, Internet: n/a**

Adventures in Science was an inservice program that offered a menu of professional-development opportunities for teachers from September to May. Through presentations by exemplary scientists and teachers, workshops on content and pedagogy, and networking, teachers learned about cutting-edge scientific research and broadened their repertoire of hands-on activities for the classroom.  The program, which reached hundreds of K-12 teachers in a 4-year period, was funded by Eisenhower Mathematics and Science Education State Grant funds and a small registration fee paid by the teachers.  The program is no longer active.

**\*\*21.  Colorado College-Integrated Sciences Teacher Enhancement Program**
**Colorado College**
**Contact:  Paul Kuerbis, Colorado Springs, (719) 389-6726, FAX:  (719) 634-4180, Internet:  pkuerbis@cc.colorado.edu**

The purpose of the Colorado College-Integrated Sciences Teacher Enhancement Program (CC-ISTEP) is to initiate and establish long-term collaboration among Colorado College scientists, mathematicians, science and mathematics educators and local and regional science and mathematics educators.  CC-ISTEP will result in theme- or issue-based summer institutes through which teacher-participants (middle level) will improve their science-content understanding and instructional skills and will result in long-term changes in participants' teaching behavior through sound implementation efforts.  CC-ISTEP builds on, refines, expands, and institutionalizes CO-STEP, the Colorado Science Teacher Enhancement Program, by putting into practice a graduate-degree program, the Master of Arts in Teaching Integrated Natural Sciences (MAT-INS).

**22.  Keystone Science School Teacher Institutes**
**Keystone Science School**
**Contact:  Chris Minor, Keystone, (970) 468-5824, FAX:  (970) 468-7769, Internet:  tkckss@keystone.org**

The Keystone Science School (KSS) provides residential field science programs for teachers and their students throughout the school year, using the Central Rocky Mountain ecosystems as an outdoor classroom.  Specializing in field programs that augment and enhance the National and Colorado State Science

Standards, these programs are a one-of-a-kind hands-on experience for students and teachers. Additionally, KSS offers nationally renowned summer teacher-training programs for middle- and high-school teachers. Key Issues, a 1-week program, provides a framework for investigating an environmental issue with students at the middle-school level. Keys to Science is a 2-week program for high-school biology teachers in cellular and molecular biology. Both teacher programs provide resource liaisons and on-line followup, connecting teachers— locally, regionally, and nationally—to one another, other educators, and the world.

**23. Project Learn**
**National Center for Atmospheric Research**
**Contact: Carol McLaren, Boulder, (303) 497-1172, FAX: (303) 497-8610,**
**Internet: cmclaren@ncar.ucar.edu**

Project Learn provides 55 middle- and junior-high-school science teachers with experiential training at the National Center for Atmospheric Research (NCAR) in Boulder, Colorado. Through three consecutive summers, workshops at NCAR are on atmospheric dynamics, ozone, and cycles of the earth and atmosphere and their impact on climate change. The program aims to improve the participants' understanding of atmospheric sciences, related mathematics- and science-teaching methods, and laboratory work. With funding from the National Science Foundation, the workshops bring in teachers from eight school districts in California, Colorado, North Carolina, and Texas. The project targets teachers of students from ethnic and minority groups who have been traditionally underrepresented in the sciences.

**24. Hughes/NIH Research for Teachers**
**College of Natural Sciences, Colorado State University**
**Contact: C.W. Miller, Fort Collins, (970) 491-7842, FAX: (970) 491-7569,**
**Internet: cmiller@vines.colostate.edu**

The Research for Teachers program provides Colorado middle- and high-school, science teachers with 7 weeks of summer research activities in the laboratories of life-science faculty at Colorado State University. The first week is spent in a 40-hour workshop where participants are exposed to current trends and issues in molecular-biology research techniques. As followup, participants are asked to write scientific reports and give oral presentations of their research experiences. The grants provide six graduate credits and stipends of $3,600.

**25. Earth Systems Education Program**
**University of Northern Colorado; Ohio State University**
**Contact: William H. Hoyt, Greeley, (303) 351-2487, FAX: (303) 351-1269,**
**Internet: bhoyt@dijkstra.univnorthco.edu**

The Earth Systems Education (ESE) Program addresses concerns about how science is presented to K-12 students. It provides a rationale and framework for developing integrated science programs having as their conceptual focus the earth system. The ESE Program, with centers at Ohio State University and the University of Northern Colorado, assists teachers to develop curriculum, instructional approaches, and assessment procedures that address the National Standards for Science Education developed by the National Research Council. Several school systems in central Ohio, Colorado, Florida, and New York have developed such approaches with the assistance of the ESE centers. Teachers incorporating the ESE approach find that their students' interest in science increases because they develop a deeper understanding of science methods and the cooperative skills necessary in the workplace. A publication titled *Science Is a Study of Earth: A Resource Guide for Science Curriculum Restructure* is also available.

## CONNECTICUT

### 26. The Natural Guard Amphibian Training Program
**Contact: Diana Edmonds, New Haven, (203) 787-0229, FAX: same, Internet: n/a**

In collaboration with the National Undersea Research Center of the University of Connecticut at Avery Point, The Natural Guard (TNG) began its Amphibian Training Program 5 years ago. Every week, TNG, an environmental organization, holds four in-school classes for about 120 seventh- and eighth-graders and their teachers and conducts three after-school programs. The program serves a population that is about 98% blacks and 2% Latino and involves participants in hands-on science activities, field trips, and laboratory experiences.

### 27. Yale-New Haven Teachers Institute
**Yale University; New Haven Public Schools**
**Contact: James Vivian, New Haven, (203) 432-1080, FAX: (203) 432-1084, Internet: ynhti@yale.edu or http://www.cis.yale.edu/ynhti**

The Yale-New Haven Teachers Institute, an educational partnership between Yale University and the New Haven Public Schools, was designed to strengthen teaching and learning in all disciplines. Since 1979, the institute has provided science-related inservice activities to improve teacher preparation, heighten teacher expectations of students, and encourage teachers to remain in New Haven's urban school district. Through the institute, Yale faculty members and local teachers meet collegially in a wide array of activities, including lectures, seminars, curriculum-unit writing, research, discussion and individual fellow-faculty meetings. Each participating teacher becomes an institute fellow and prepares a curriculum unit to teach during the next academic year. In general, teachers identify the subjects to be addressed by the institute. On successful completion of the institute, fellows receive an honorarium of $1,000 and four continuing-education units. The program targets teachers of students who are underrepresented in the sciences.

## 28. SMART
**Central Research Division, Pfizer Inc.**
**Contact: Kathi Morianos, Groton, (203) 441-5983, FAX: (203) 441-5982, Internet: n/a**

Sponsored by all divisions of Pfizer Inc., SMART (Science and Math Are Really Terrific!) is a school-business partnership that includes a professional-development program for middle-school teachers. SMART workshops, which have involved teachers from 11 schools throughout Connecticut and Rhode Island, introduce hands-on activities and classroom materials developed by Pfizer scientists. The program also provides teachers with summer employment opportunities, a speakers bureau, on-site tours of Pfizer, and opportunities to observe Pfizer scientists and academic consultants. Program goals include improving science and mathematics teaching in grades 5-8, increasing the range of teaching strategies among workshop participants, improving outcomes among mathematics and science students, networking teachers with scientists and with each other, and developing curricular materials.

## 29. Statewide Biotechnology Workshops
**Pfizer Inc.; National Association of Biology Teachers; Project for Improving Mastery of Math and Science at Wesleyan University**
**Contact: Richard Hinman, Groton, (203) 441-4541, FAX: (203) 441-5728, Internet: n/a**

Pfizer Central Research has collaborated with the National Association of Biology Teachers to develop a source book of laboratory exercises in recombinant DNA technology for use in middle- and high-school classrooms. After carrying out a trial teaching of the source book, a group of Connecticut teachers formed a committee under the auspices of the PIMMS program of Wesleyan University to organize workshops for teachers throughout Connecticut. These workshops, sponsored by Pfizer Inc., are held three times per year at industrial sites where genetic engineering is practiced. As followup, Pfizer technical staff make themselves available for classroom visits as requested by participants. The goals of the program are to introduce cutting-edge technology in modern biology to middle- and high-school teachers and to lessen the public anxiety that often surrounds the use of this technology by involving future citizens at an early age.

**30. SMARTNET 2000**
**Sacred Heart University**
**Contact: Bette J. DelGiorno, (203) 255-8394, FAX: (203) 255-8247,**
**Internet: dlgiorno@smartnet.org**

SMARTNET 2000 is a staff-development program for teacher enhancement in precollege science and mathematics education in Connecticut. The program is a collaborative effort between Sacred Heart University, Fairfield Public Schools, area school districts, and community resources. The partnerships extend a staff-development model throughout the state and affect about 5,000 K-12 teachers of science and mathematics and their supervisors in 67 towns.

## DISTRICT OF COLUMBIA

**31. American Chemical Society Inservice Programs**
**American Chemical Society**
**Contact: Janet Boese, Washington, DC, (202) 872-4076, FAX: (202) 833-7732, Internet: jmb97@acs.org**

The American Chemical Society (ACS) aims to improve the expertise of K-12 science teachers through a variety of national and local inservice programs. Doing Chemistry, funded in 1989 by the National Science Foundation (NSF), was a 1-year project established to train teachers in the use of videodisks for chemistry experiments, to disseminate ACS-developed materials, to encourage the use of hands-on chemistry experiments in the classroom, to expand participants' range of teaching strategies, and to improve student outcomes in chemistry. Chemistry in the Community (ChemCom), a year-long course for college-bound high-school students, was developed by ACS between 1988 and 1990 to highlight the role of chemistry in everyday life. A third edition is now being prepared. With funding from NSF, ACS has held workshops to train teachers in the philosophy, teaching strategies, and content of this course and to introduce issues of small-group learning and assessment. ACS facilitates continuing communication among ChemCom users through a nationwide directory, a newsletter, and a project that sponsors local ChemCom clubs. Operation Chemistry is a national teacher-training program. In 3.5-week workshops at the University of Wisconsin-Oshkosh and at Purdue University, the program provides 36 teams of teacher-educators with the skills to conduct chemistry workshops for upper elementary-school and middle-school teachers in their regions. FACETS (NSF-funded) is a 6th-, 7th-, and 8th-grade integrated science curriculum. Teacher

training will be available to support this program.  A *Program Summaries* booklet is available free on request, as is a free subscription to *Chemunity News*, the
newsletter of the Education Division.

**32.  Proyecto Futuro**
**American Association for the Advancement of Science**
**Contact:  Edward Gonzalez, Washington, DC, (202) 326-6670, FAX:  (202)**
**371-9849, Internet:  egonzale@aaas.org**

Proyecto Futuro works with teachers, principals, school-council members, and
parents to bring about excellence in K-8 mathematics and science education for
Hispanic children.  The program provides curricular materials, training, and technical support for schools and teachers, and it provides specific strategies for
parents to encourage their children in mathematics and science.

**\*\*33.  Project Alliance**
**American Association for the Advancement of Science**
**Contact:  Betty Calinger, Washington, DC, (202) 326-6629, FAX: (202)**
**371-9849, Internet:  bcalinge@aaas.org**

Sponsored by the National Science Foundation, Project Alliance involves interdisciplinary teams of middle-school teachers and administrators in a 2-year program that covers two summers and academic years.  The program is designed to
increase knowledge of science, mathematics, and computer technologies, as well
as pedagogical content.  In the first academic year, teams produce, pilot, and
refine an integrated curriculum unit in their schools; and in the second year, they
disseminate to other teachers the process for developing an integrated curriculum
and team approach to teaching.  The teams work with scientist-engineer partners
and school administrators throughout the program.

**34.  Borrowed Time**
**Environmental Education Associates, Inc.**
**Contact:  Elizabeth Curwen, Washington, DC, (202) 296-4572, FAX:  (202)**
**452-9370, Internet:  72540.3332@compuserve.com**

Developed by Environmental Education Associates, Inc., Borrowed Time is both
a curriculum and a workshop designed to help grade 7-12 teachers include complex waste-management issues in their classroom teaching.  Borrowed Time
includes demonstrations and classroom activities focusing on source reduction,
recycling, waste-to-energy incineration, and landfill disposal of municipal solid
waste.  Through workshops, Borrowed Time reaches about 1,000 teachers each
year. Participants receive take-home kits, lesson plans, and other materials to
help implement Borrowed Time activities and apply the materials to other disci-

plines, including earth science, biology, physics, chemistry, ecology, home economics, social science, and economics.

## 35. Department of Biochemistry and Molecular Biology
## School of Medicine, Georgetown University
**Contact: Jack G. Chirikjian, Washington, DC, (202) 687-2160, FAX: (202) 687-2232, Internet: n/a**

The Department of Biochemistry and Molecular Biology of the Georgetown University's School of Medicine offers a variety of educational opportunities to biology and chemistry teachers in secondary schools and community and 4-year colleges. Among them are graduate-level workshops on biotechnology and shorter introductory courses on hands-on laboratory experiences, held at sites across the country. Reaching hundreds of participants each year, the department aims to provide teachers with the background and skills they need to integrate biotechnology concepts and activities into their classrooms. In a collaboration with an industrial partner, 100 college, high-school, and middle-school experiments have been developed.

## 36. Educational Research and Dissemination Program
## American Federation of Teachers
**Contact: Deanna Woods, Washington, DC, (202) 879-4495, FAX: (202) 879-4537, Internet: deannawds@aol.com**

Through the Educational Research and Dissemination Program, the American Federation of Teachers (AFT) brings K-12 teachers into active discussions addressing aspects of practice and research in teaching. The AFT program, which is in various stages of institutionalization in school districts nationwide, aims to provide motivating, continuing professional-development opportunities for teachers.

## 37. National Science Education Leadership Initiative
## National Science Resources Center
**Contact: Leslie Benton, Washington, DC, (202) 287-2063, FAX: (202) 287-2070, Internet: lbenton@nas.edu**

To catalyze the systemic reform of science education in local school districts throughout the country, the National Science Resources Center (NSRC) is conducting the National Science Education Leadership Initiative as a part of its Outreach program. A major component of the initiative is national and regional NSRC Science Education Leadership Institutes. Each institute prepares leadership teams of superintendents, curriculum specialists, teachers, and scientists to design and implement hands-on science programs for their school districts.

Through presentations, discussions, and workshops, teams assess their knowledge of the characteristics of effective science learning and teaching; develop a working knowledge of the infrastructure that is needed to support a high-quality science program; become familiar with national and regional resources that can inform their efforts; prepare strategic plans for reforming their districts' science programs; and communicate how they will anticipate technical assistance. Teams are selected through an application process. The Smithsonian Institution and the National Academy of Sciences operate NSRC to improve the teaching of science for all children in the nation's school districts. NSRC collects and disseminates information about exemplary science-teaching resources, develops innovative science-curriculum materials, and sponsors outreach activities to develop and sustain hands-on science programs. Sponsors of NSRC programs include the National Science Foundation, the U.S. Department of Education, and several major corporations and foundations.

**38. Integrating Mathematics and Science with Language Instruction**
**Center for Applied Linguistics**
**Contact: Deborah Short, Washington, DC, (202) 429-9292, FAX: (202) 659-5641, Internet: debbie@cal.org**

The Center for Applied Linguistics (CAL) is dedicated to improving the education of limited-English-proficient (LEP) students. CAL conducts professional-development workshops, institutes, and long-term projects to foster collaborative efforts among K-12 language, mathematics, and science teachers. The professional-development objectives are to sensitize mathematics and science teachers to the language-development needs and processes of LEP students and to help teachers modify their instructional practices to maximize student comprehension and success. Through the professional-development activities, CAL aims to supply teachers with strategies to prepare curricula, materials, and techniques needed to address the challenges faced by LEP students in acquiring mathematics- or science-related language and concepts.

**39. Teacher Educator's Network**
**Association of Science-Technology Centers**
**Contact: Andrea Anderson, Washington, DC, (202) 783-7200, FAX: (202) 783-7207, Internet: aanderson@astc.org**

The Association of Science-Technology Centers (ASTC) is an organization of museums and related institutions dedicated to increasing public understanding and appreciation of science and technology. One of ASTC's many goals is to help museums broaden and diversify their audiences and serve as educational resources for their communities. ASTC operates a Teacher Educator's Network in which museum staff who work with schools come together to share ideas and resources. The network also provides inservice activities directly to teachers. Network goals are to improve museum services for teachers, to encourage teacher educators at science centers to continue refining their craft, to facilitate the replication of successful practices in the field, and to disseminate strategies for minority-group, female, and physically challenged students. Specifically, the network offers seminars, institutes, funding information, and reports on exemplary programs that focus on scientific content, teaching methods, and equity issues.

**40.  Teaching Materials**
**American Plastics Council**
**Contact:  Paula Cox, Washington, DC, (202) 371-5305 or (800) 2-HELP-90, FAX:  (202) 371-5679, Internet:  http://www.plasticsresource.com**

The American Plastics Council offers teachers materials on resource management and the benefits of plastics.  Materials available include the Hands on Plastics Kit, the How to Set Up a School Recycling Program guide, and activity booklets specific to grades K-3, 4-6, and 7-12.  Other materials are also available.

**41.  Population Education Workshops**
**Zero Population Growth, Inc.**
**Contact:  Pamela Wasserman, Washington, DC, (202) 332-2200, FAX:  (202) 332-2302, Internet:  zpgpoped@igc.apc.org**

Since 1975, Zero Population Growth, Inc. (ZPG) has conducted population-education workshops for K-12 science and social-studies teachers across the country. Through presentations and hands-on activities, ZPG aims to illustrate how population studies can be integrated into classroom curricula and related to students' experiences. Activities also include games, quizzes, simulations, and films. Each participant receives resources, including data sheets and bibliographies, and followup support through telephone calls and newsletters.  ZPG implements workshops at events sponsored by university teacher-education programs, local and state education agencies, and science, social-studies, and environmental-education conferences.  The program has an extensive evaluation component.

**42.  Project Atmosphere**
**American Meteorological Society**
**Contact:  Ira Geer, Washington, DC, (202) 466-5728, FAX:  (202) 466-5729, Internet:  n/a**

With funding from the National Science Foundation, the American Meteorological Society has initiated Project Atmosphere, a major teacher-education program. Through a wide range of professional opportunities, the program aims to improve the content knowledge of over 10,000 K-12 teachers per year through peer-training sessions using project-developed instructional and course materials.

**\*\*43. Maury Project**
**American Meteorological Society**
**Contact: Ira Geer, Washington, DC, (202) 466-5728, FAX: (202) 466-5729, Internet: n/a**

With funding form the National Science Foundation, the American Meteorological Society has initiated the Maury Project, a major teacher-education program. Through a wide range of professional opportunities, the program aims to improve the content knowledge of over 2,000 K-12 teachers per year through peer-training sessions using project-developed instructional resource materials.

## FLORIDA

**44. Coastal Ecology**
**Rookery Bay National Estuarine Research Reserve, Department of Natural Resources**
**Contact: Ginger Hinchcliff, Naples, (813) 775-8845, FAX: ( 813) 775-7606, Internet: n/a**

Coastal Ecology is a teacher inservice workshop designed to familiarize participants with local coastal resources. Through 8 days of hands-on experiences, lectures, laboratories, and field studies, participants learn about water quality, coastal habitats, endangered species, fish, and invertebrates. Facilitated by education and research staff of the Rookery Bay National Estuarine Research Reserve, the program provides the use of boats and biological sampling equipment to explore tropical hammocks, barrier islands, mangrove forests, and seagrass beds. Teachers participate in research (e.g., a mangrove-restoration site). In addition, they are expected use their knowledge to develop curricular materials for their classrooms. The program involves 15 teachers in public or private schools.

## GEORGIA

**45. Field Trips and Collections**
**Fernbank Science Center**
**Contact: Fred Sherberger, Atlanta, (404) 378-4311, FAX: (404) 370-1336, Internet: gfs001@sol1.solinet.net**

Fernbank Science Center, a part of the DeKalb County, GA school system, supports and supplements the K-12 county science curriculum. During this course, teachers produce "proper" plant and insect collections for use with their students. Discussion and demonstration of techniques to collect, preserve, identify, and use the specimens are integrated throughout the actual preparations, and several local field trips to a variety of habitat types are used to gather specimens. Lesson plans to be shared with all participants are required followup.

**46. Molecular Biology of DNA**
**Department of Biology, Valdosta State College**
**Contact: Dennis Bogyo, Valdosta, (912) 333-5759, FAX: (912) 333-7389,**
**Internet: n/a**

Molecular Biology of DNA was a 15-day summer course offered at Valdosta State College. Through sessions on nucleic acid isolation, DNA characterization, DNA "fingerprinting," the use of restriction enzymes, mapping of DNA plasmids, and transformation of bacterial cells, the course provided 24 high-school teachers per year with opportunities to enhance their knowledge of molecular biology. The program also aimed to help teachers integrate theories and scientific applications into their high-school science curricula. Funded by the National Science Foundation, the course combined intensive morning lectures devoted to modern molecular biology theory with afternoons of hands-on laboratory experiences.

## ILLINOIS

**47. Teachers Academy for Mathematics and Science**
**Contact: Lourdes Monteagudo, Chicago, (312) 808-0100, FAX: (312) 808-0103, Internet: eallen@teacher.depaul.edu**

The Teachers Academy for Mathematics and Science is an independent, not-for-profit organization devoted to the reform of mathematics and science teaching and learning in Chicago's public schools. A key premise of the academy is that teachers are the agents of change and that schools are the units of change. Academy staff assist teachers in improving their content knowledge, pedagogical skills, and the use of alternative assessment strategies. Programs also engage school administrators, parents, and community leaders in fostering and supporting the whole-school changes needed to enhance student learning. The use of educational technologies is emphasized as an increasingly important tool in curriculum development, selection, and adaptation. The academy works closely with universities, community colleges, museums, and other education reformers. This systemic "retooling" process guides schools in using job-embedded professional development to re-create themselves as true learning organizations. The academy's 3-year-long, intensive intervention is a demonstrably successful model for improving student achievement.

**48. University of Chicago Summer Seminar**
**University of Chicago**
**Contact: Malka Moscona, Chicago, (312) 702-1713, FAX: (312) 702-2254,**
**Internet:**
**m-moscona@uchicago.edu**

For 7 years, the University of Chicago has held a summer seminar on biology for Chicago public-school teachers. In 70 hours of instruction, the seminar provides review of basic concepts and processes in developmental biology and genetics, lectures and discussions on current research, informal group discussions, hands-on laboratory activities, and computer instruction. The goals of the program are to facilitate communication among science-teachers and scientists and to update teachers' knowledge of biology, stimulate them to be life-long learners, and increase their range of teaching strategies. Program evaluations, made up of questionnaires and informal communication, indicate that the program has led to the establishment of a network of teachers working to improve biology teaching in the Chicago public schools.

**49. Collaborative Outreach Education**
**Chicago Botanic Garden**
**Contact: Alan Rossman, Glencoe, (708) 835-8224, FAX: (708) 835-4484,**
**Internet: tamstree@orian.depaul.edu**

The Chicago Botanic Garden offers inservice training to K-12 teachers in botany and environmental science. Over 800 teachers each year receive 30 hours of training in the program. The goal of the training is to integrate science and pedagogy through experiences that highlight inquiry-based activities, experimentation, and the acquisition of subject-matter knowledge.

**50. Footlocker Program in Biotechnology**
**University of Illinois-Urbana-Champaign**
**Contact: George Kieffer, Urbana, (217) 333-0438, FAX: (217) 244-1224,**
**Internet: georgeki@uiuc.edu**

With funding from the Howard Hughes Medical Institute, the School of Life Sciences at the University of Illinois at Urbana-Champaign has a continuing program for educating teachers and, through them, their students in molecular biology and biotechnology. The program includes summer institutes for high-school and community-college science teachers on the University of Illinois campus, academic-year courses and 2-day workshops in Chicago and other cities, presentations at teachers' conferences, and the distribution of Footlockers that contain the equipment and supplies needed for genetics experiments to be performed in individual classrooms.

**\*\*51. The Prairie Flower Program for Middle School Science**
**University of Illinois-Urbana-Champaign**
**Contact: George Kieffer, Urbana, (217) 333-0438, FAX: (217) 244-1224,**
**Internet: georgeki@uiuc.edu**

The name "Prairie Flowers" is meant to convey the image of science education blooming on the prairie of east central Illinois. Funded by the Howard Hughes Medical Institute, the program has two major goals: networking isolated rural teachers into a virtual community and promoting hands-on, minds-on science through the use of teacher-prepared science kits. Month-long summer workshops and academic-year meetings are conducted for teachers in the use of the latest computer educational technology and approaches to teaching hands-on science. The "community" is formed by providing each participant with a laptop computer, software, and dialup access to the Internet through the School of Life Sciences at the university. Science kits covering a range of topics usually taught in middle-school science courses are also prepared by teachers during these workshops. Teachers have free access to the use of the kits in their classrooms.

**52. Illinois Rivers Project**
**Southern Illinois University**
**Contact: Robert Williams, Edwardsville, (618) 692-3788, FAX: (618) 692-3359, Internet: rivers@siue.edu**

The Illinois Rivers Project was established in 1990 as a pilot water-quality monitoring program for high-school teachers along the Mississippi and lower Illinois rivers. The program, which now reaches teachers throughout the United States, engages science, social-studies, mathematics, and English teachers and students in the collection and analysis of data and publication of ideas about their rivers. Program activities—including hands-on workshops, seminars, demonstrations, computer instruction, and creative-writing projects—provide an interdisciplinary approach to the study of science. SOILED NET, a telecommunication network, links participants and project staff to Internet. Funding from the National Science Foundation has also been used to develop the Rivers Curriculum, which fosters the development and dissemination of "rivers" curricula addressing concepts in geography, geology, chemistry, biology, language arts, and mathematics. Additional units on zebra mussels have also been developed.

**\*\*53. Illinois Middle School Groundwater Project**
**Southern Illinois University**
**Contact: Robert Williams, Edwardsville, (618) 692-3788, FAX: (618) 692-3359, Internet: rwillia@siue.edu**

The Illinois Middle School Groundwater Project was established in 1993 through a grant from the W.K. Kellogg Foundation to bring groundwater education to selected counties in Illinois. A unique aspect of the project is cooperation between the many state agencies, local organizations, and schools to provide groundwater information and hands-on water-testing experiences. Agencies supporting the project in the schools are the Illinois Department of Natural Resources and Environmental Protection Agency, the Illinois Farm Bureau, the Illinois Section of the American Water Works Association, soil and water conservation districts, county health departments, regional education offices, well drillers, and other interested persons and environmental groups. A middle-school curriculum unit, $H_2O$ Below, and an easy-to-assemble kit have been developed. During the teaching of the unit, students and parents produce a well history and conduct five chemical tests. Groundwater models are made available through agency support and are an essential part of the teaching unit.

## INDIANA

### 54. Central Indiana Biology Teachers Focus Group
**Indiana University-Purdue University at Indianapolis**
**Contact: Florence Juillerat, Indianapolis, (317) 274-3789, FAX: (317) 274-2846, Internet: n/a**

The focus group, sponsored by the Biology Department of the Indiana University-Purdue University at Indianapolis, consists of teachers in the Indianapolis metropolitan area who meet once a month to address a wide range of issues. Activities, designed by the participants, include discussions on student laboratories, subject-matter research, instructional technology, interdisciplinary classroom approaches, and local environmental issues. In addition, the participants facilitate equipment exchanges. To encourage networking, the group distributes a monthly two-page newsletter to biology teachers in area private and public schools.

### 55. Warren Science Institute
**Warren Central High School**
**Contact: Linda Bayne, Indianapolis, (317) 894-3323, FAX: (317) 899-6842, Internet: n/a**

The Warren Science Institute is made up of four components: Teachers Teaching Teachers, a peer-teaching program practicum for K-12 teachers; Cadet Teaching, which provides science experiences for secondary-school and elementary-school students; P.A.C.T.S. (Parents and Children for Terrific Science), which involves parents, students, and teachers collaboratively in science activities; and Outreach in Science, a forum for teachers to share information about their science-teaching experiences. Program goals are to reduce anxiety around the teaching of science;

to encourage the use of a thematic, integrated curriculum in the classroom; and to foster creativity in science teaching. The program involves about 65 teachers each year in lectures, demonstrations, workshops, discussions, computer instruction, and field work.

## 56. Agronomy High School Teacher Internship
**Department of Agronomy, Purdue University**
**Contact: J.J. Volenec, (317) 494-8071, West Lafayette, FAX: (317) 496-1368, Internet: jvolenec@dept.agry.purdue.edu**

Purdue University's Department of Agronomy offers an 8-week summer internship program in plant, soil, and environmental sciences to high-school teachers. The internship provides each participant with an in-depth laboratory experience in the workplace of an agronomic scientist. In addition, each intern is assigned a mentor with experience in crop- or soil-science education who can model the techniques needed for incorporating agriscience concepts into classroom activities. During the practicum, interns develop their own classroom exercises, which are reviewed by program staff and collated for dissemination. As followup, the program supports participant attendance at national meetings of the American Society of Agronomy, the Soil Science Society of America, and the Crop Science Society.

## 57. Inservice Programs for Biology Teachers
**Department of Biological Sciences, Purdue University**
**Contact: Isadore Julian, West Lafayette, (317) 494 4983, FAX: (317) 494-0876, Internet: ijulian@bilbo.bio.purdue.edu**

Since 1990, with support from the Howard Hughes Medical Institute and the Indiana Department of Education, the Department of Biological Sciences of Purdue University has offered summer institutes for high-school biology teachers in Indiana. The goals of these outreach efforts have been to inform teachers about current issues in biology and to introduce them to laboratory experiences in molecular biology and the College Board's advanced-placement biology program. There are also weekend workshops and institutes for high-school biology teachers during the school year.

## **58. Evolution and the Nature of Science Institutes
**Indiana University; San Jose State University**
**Contact: Craig Nelson, Bloomington, IN, (612) 855-1345, or Jean Beard, San Jose, CA, (408) 924-4870, FAX: (408) 924-4840, Internet: beard@biomail.sjsu.edu**

Three National Science Foundation grants to the same co-principal investigators have supported 3-week residential institutes (ENSI) for 30 high-school biology teachers for 6 years (1989-1995), have supported additional preparation (LTPP) of 38 institute graduates for four summers (1991-1994), and have partially supported 36 two-week satellite institutes for up to 20 teachers (1992-1995) taught by pairs of specially prepared institute alumni. The current grant will support additional satellites (SENSI) beginning in summer 1996 at sites from Ohio to California. The summer institutes and two academic-year followup sessions (fall and spring) are designed to update participants' knowledge of the nature of science, general organic evolution, and human evolution and to help them integrate these topics into their teaching. Teachers are encouraged to apply in teams from schools, school districts, or geographic regions so as to have colleagues to work with after the summer. The institutes consist of curriculum-development activities, lectures, seminars, demonstration, discussions, hands-on activities and field work. Participants are assigned to apply some of their new knowledge in teaching, monitor their experiences, and report back to the group at followup sessions. A more-complete explanation of the ENSI/SENSI program content and philosophy has been accepted for publication in the *American Biology Teacher* and is tentatively titled "Better Biology Teaching by Emphasizing Evolution and the Nature of Science."

## 59. Project Genethics
**Department of Biology, Ball State University**
**Contact:  Jon R. Hendrix, Muncie, (317) 285-8840, FAX:  (317) 285-1624, Internet:  01jrhendrix@bsu.edu**

Since 1978, Project Genethics has involved 510 secondary-school biology teachers in 2-week summer workshops on human genetics and bioethical decision-making and 228 teachers in 4-week on-campus workshops. Through lectures, seminars, and workshops, the project informs participants about concepts in contemporary genetics and human genetics, reproductive technology, social sciences and laws as they apply to human genetics, and bioethical decision-making. Project Genethics strives to improve student outcomes in secondary-school life-science classrooms. The project also provides a newsletter and an 800 telephone line to facilitate communication among participants. In addition, the program includes leadership training so that participants can run similar workshops in their own schools. The program assesses teacher growth and secondary-school student achievement through a continuing-evaluation component. The project is funded primarily by the National Science Foundation.

## IOWA

**60. Iowa Chautauqua Program**
**Science Education Center, University of Iowa**
**Contact: P. Maxwell Dass, Iowa City, (319) 335-3578, FAX: (319) 335-1188, Internet: pdass@blue.weeg.uiowa.edu**

The Iowa Chautauqua Program (ICP) strives to empower science teachers to make science more meaningful and useful for their students. Program participants partake in a 3-week summer workshop and two 3-day academic-year workshops to develop and assess units that match those of the Science, Technology, Society (STS) reform effort. Selected teachers are invited to attend an additional Leadership Institute, which allows them to become part of the ICP staff. Program goals include improving teachers' confidence in science teaching; encouraging teachers to foster creativity, problem-solving abilities, and an understanding of scientific concepts among their students; and developing teachers as leaders in science-education reform. Program facilitators use a comprehensive assessment method to evaluate effectiveness of both teachers and their students. Since 1983, the network of ICP participants has grown to 3,000. ICP also fosters alliances among educators, students, parents, business leaders, government officials, and other community members to improve science education locally. The U.S. Department of Education has validated the ICP as a model inservice program to be disseminated throughout the nation through the National Diffusion Network (NDN).

## KANSAS

**61. Genetics Education Network (GENE)**
**Department of Physics, Department of Biochemistry, and Division of Biology, Kansas State University**
**Contact: Thomas R. Manney, Manhattan, (913) 532-6789, FAX: (913) 532-6806, Internet: tmanney@ksuvm.ksu.edu**

With funding from the National Science Foundation and the Howard Hughes Medical Institute, the GENE Project promotes training, networking, and logistical support for middle- and high-school life-science and biology teachers. The program promotes classroom use of research organisms, especially Baker's yeast, flour beetles, and rapid cycling plants (e.g., Wisconsin Fast Plants). Basic activities and open-ended experiments have been developed through collaboration between research scientists and classroom teachers. Concepts focus on genetics and genetics-environment interactions. Simple qualitative and quantitative experiments with yeast enable students to monitor the biological consequences of solar ultraviolet radiation and the effects of ozone depletion. A Classroom Guide to Yeast Experiments, including videotapes and computer software, is designed to serve both teachers and their students. A 1-week workshop for workshop leaders will be held on the Kansas State University campus in June 1996. Participating teachers will be trained to give workshops in their school districts during the 1996 school year. Logistical support will be provided by the GENE staff.

**62. Kansas Environmental Monitoring Network**
**Olathe East High School**
**Contact: Brad Williamson, Olathe, (913) 780-7120, FAX: n/a, Internet:**
**bwilliam@ksuvm.ksu.edu**

The Kansas Environmental Monitoring Network (KEMNET) is a network of students and teachers who participate in research processes of environmental monitoring at sites throughout Kansas via telephone and computer interactions. Network membership is available to schools across the state. Modeled after TERC's Global Laboratory Program, KEMNET aims to involve teachers in the learning of science by *doing* science. Program goals include fostering an appreciation of science research and inquiry-based science instruction, encouraging communication between teachers and scientists, improving student outcomes, and developing curricular materials. KEMNET has evolved into related projects, such as the Monarch Watch, which involves students and teachers from three countries in monitoring the migration of the monarch butterfly.

**63. MASTERS Project**
**Department of Curriculum and Instruction, University of Kansas**
**Contact: Lelon Capps, Lawrence, (913) 864-9669, FAX: (913) 864-5076,**
**Internet: capps@kuhub.cc.ukan.edu**

The MASTERS (Math And Science Teachers for Reservation Schools) Project, a National Science Foundation teacher-enhancement program, ran from 1988 until 1994. It provided mathematics and science training to over 200 teachers from across the nation who worked with American Indian students. Emphasis was placed on integrating American Indian culture with the science and mathematics curriculum. Teachers attended an 8-week summer session and were supported by site visits throughout the school year. The project is not currently funded, but the publications *Earth's Caretakers: Native American Lessons* and *Signs of Traditions: Native American Lessons* are available for a nominal fee. The two books include profiles of American Indians who use science and mathematics in their everyday lives interwoven with lesson plans that are appropriate for K-8.

**64. Teacher inservice programs**
**University of Kansas Museum of Natural History**
**Contact: Jama Gabbert, Lawrence, (913) 864-4540, FAX: (913) 864-5335,**
**Internet: jama@falcon.cc.ukans.edu**

The University of Kansas Museum of Natural History offers inservice programs in the form of hands-on workshops, seminars, and lectures to teachers in the Kaw Valley Service Council. The objectives of the programs are to increase teachers' factual knowledge about science, to help teachers become comfortable teaching science, and to provide information about how to use the museum as an educational resource.

## KENTUCKY

**65. Outreach Center for Science and Health Career Opportunities**
**University of Kentucky Chandler Medical Center**
**Contact: Don Frazier, Lexington, (606) 323-5418, FAX: (606) 257-6439,**
**Internet: n/a**

The Outreach Center offers summer workshops for middle- and high-school science and biology teachers. Motivated by the belief that teacher enthusiasm and innovation attract students to the discipline, the workshop facilitators are devoted to developing and sustaining positive attitudes toward science. Workshops include lectures, laboratories, and discussions about how teachers can be more innovative, given limited resources and facilities. All workshops and related efforts emphasize the importance of improving communication between students, middle- and high-school teachers, and university faculty.

## MAINE

**66. Partnership for Science Education**
**Department of Biology, Colby College**
**Contact: Jay Labov, Waterville, (207) 872-3329, FAX: (207) 872-3555,**
**Internet: jblabov@colby.edu**

Over a 6-year period, the Natural Sciences Division of Colby College has developed a series of outreach programs in the sciences and mathematics for K-12 teachers in four local school districts. As volunteers, Colby scientists visit classrooms, respond to teachers' inquiries, host field trips to Colby science facilities, or lend equipment to the schools. With a grant from the Maine Department of Education under the Eisenhower Mathematics and Science Education State Grant, Colby established small teams of pre-K through grade 7 teachers and members of the Colby science faculty. A total of 47 participants have worked in 14 teams to address self-selected topics, including anatomy, environmental science, rocks and minerals, properties of matter, genetics, and physical sciences. The partnership also received a 6-year grant from the Howard Hughes Medical Institute to expand outreach programs to local schools targeting persons from groups traditionally underrepresented in the sciences. This grant has resulted in the establishment of a science-equipment lending library and a program in which local high schools hire a full-time, certified science teacher to release up to five teachers each semester to take courses in science and mathematics at Colby.

**67. Wells National Estuarine Research Reserve's DEPTHS (Discovering Ecology: Pathways to Science)**
**Wells National Estuarine Research Reserve**
**Contact:  Rick Kaye-Schiess, Wells, (207) 646-1555, FAX:  (207) 646-2930, Internet:  mewells@alice.terc.edu**

The Wells National Estuarine Research Reserve has both on-site and outreach programming. Teachers wishing to visit the site can either participate in a guided program for fourth-graders and special groups or design their own programming in consultation with reserve staff. As part of its outreach program, Wells Reserve has designed a K-8 scope and sequence curriculum on ecology, drawing its examples from coastal systems within the Gulf of Maine. Teaching kits have been developed with instructional materials ranging from big books and posters to breaks and dialysis tubing. The program is designed to involve the entire teaching staff of a school over a 3-week period. The program is introduced with a half-day or full-day workshop and ends with a 2-hour followup. The curriculum has been formally adopted by four school districts. It is annually placed in 12 schools in the Gulf of Maine region. More than 200 teachers have been involved in creating and evaluating this program.

## MARYLAND

**68. ASCB Summer Teacher Research Fellowship Program**
**American Society for Cell Biology**
**Contact:  Robert Bloodgood, Charlottesville, (804) 924-1739, FAX:  (804) 982-3912 or (301) 530-7139, Internet:  ddoyle@ascb.faseb.org**

The American Society for Cell Biology (ASCB) offers 8- to 10-week summer research fellowships for middle-, junior-high, and senior-high-school teachers in the laboratories of individual ASCB members. The goals of the program are to update teachers on modern research equipment and information about cell biology; to develop linkages between public schools, colleges, and universities; and to encourage a greater number of female and minority-group students to make career choices related to science.

**69. "Hands-on" Workshops and Short Courses in Biotechnology**
**EDVOTEK**
**Contact: Mark Chirikjian, Bethesda, (301) 251-5990, FAX: (301) 340-0582, Internet: edvotek@aol.com**

With funding from the National Science Foundation, Georgetown University, and other sources, EDVOTEK has offered a hands-on science program in new technology to K-12 teachers. For 5 years, the program has acquainted teachers with background information and skills needed for teaching laboratories. In addition, program activities that include workshops, lectures, demonstrations, and discussion sessions illustrate how new information in biotechnology can be incorporated into current biology curricula. The primary program goals are to update participants' knowledge of biotechnology and to assist them in improving student achievement in science.

**70. High-School Science Teacher Summer Research Fellowships**
**American Society for Biochemistry and Molecular Biology**
**Contact: Peter Farnham, Bethesda, (301) 530-7147, FAX: (301) 571-1824, Internet: pfarnha@asbmb.faseb.org**

Implemented by the American Society for Biochemistry and Molecular Biology (ASBMB) Committee on Education Affairs, the High-School Science Teacher Summer Research Fellowships program places high-school teachers of biology and chemistry in the biochemistry laboratories of individual ASBMB members for 8-10 weeks of hands-on activities. The goal of the program is to update teachers about the latest research and techniques in the fields of biology and biochemistry. Teachers receive $5,000 for the summer.

**71. High School Teachers Internship in Immunology**
**American Association of Immunologists**
**Contact: David Scott, Bethesda, (301) 517-0335, FAX: (301) 517-0344, Internet: scottd@hlsun.red-cross.org**

Initiated by the Education Committee and the Minority-Affairs Committee of the American Association of Immunologists (AAI), the High School Teachers Internship in Immunology has offered internships to high-school teachers since 1989. The internship objectives are to provide high-school teachers with hands-on experiences in immunology laboratories, to increase the amount and quality of immunology taught in high schools, to improve teachers' scientific knowledge, and to develop instructional materials for classroom use. The program also aims to foster continuing professional relationships among local scientists and high-school teachers. Scientists are encouraged to involve themselves in community and school activities so that they can educate the public about immunology, the scientific process, and the need for basic research. Finally, through improved materials and classroom teaching, the program hopes to encourage students to pursue scientific careers. Funded primarily by AAI, the program has established internships across the nation. In addition, AAI offers several comprehensive lesson guides, including *Warlord's Revenge—Can You Dig It?* and *Food Forensics: A Case of Mistaken Identity*, developed by program interns.

**72. Science Alliance**
**National Institutes of Health**
**Contact: Anne Baur, Bethesda, (301) 402-2827, FAX: (301) 402-3034,**
**Internet: n/a**

Science Alliance is a partnership between several elementary-school classroom teachers in Montgomery County and the District of Columbia and National Institutes of Health scientists. The underlying conviction of the Science Alliance is that partnerships between scientists and teachers promote an atmosphere of professional support for teachers and that this atmosphere helps them to create classrooms in which science learning can flourish. At the heart of the alliance is a communication network available to all participating schools. The network is made up of meetings, telephone conversations, faxes, and the electronic Science Alliance Bulletin Board system.

**73. Biology Teachers' Field Ecology Skills Development Project**
**Appalachian Environmental Laboratory**
**Contact: John Slocomb, Frostburg, (301) 689-3115, FAX: (301) 698-8518,**
**Internet: slocomb@ael.umd.edu**

In 1989, the Appalachian Environmental Laboratory (AEL), one of three laboratories that make up the University of Maryland System's Center for Environmental and Estuarine Studies, held an inservice program for high-school teachers in the Allegany County, Maryland, public schools. The Biology Teachers' Field Ecology Skills Development Project drew on AEL staff and area resource people to introduce teachers to the concepts, skills, equipment, and laboratory techniques of field ecology study. The overall program goals were to encourage teachers to use the outdoors as their classroom and thereby to increase student excitement about the biological sciences. Funding for the program came from an Eisenhower Mathematics and Science Education State Grant.

**74. Chesapeake Bay National Estuarine Research Reserve**
**Tidewater Administration, State of Maryland Department of Natural**
**Resources**
**Contact:  Kathleen Buppert, Annapolis, (410) 974-3382, FAX:  (410) 974-**
**2833, Internet:  n/a**

Funded by the sanctuaries and reserves division of the National Oceanic and
Atmospheric Administration and the Maryland Department of Natural Resources,
the Chesapeake Bay National Estuarine Research Reserve is one of 22 research
reserves established to protect estuarine areas for research, education, and monitoring; education and outreach events; technical workshops, marsh cleanups;
"estuary talks"; duck-banding demonstrations; and marsh hikes.

**75.  Fall and spring conferences**
**Maryland Association of Biology Teachers**
**Contact:  Paul Hummer, Frederick, (301) 696-3853, FAX:  (301) 694-7653,**
**Internet:  pjhummer@aol.com**

The Maryland Association of Biology Teachers (MABT) has been providing
hands-on workshops and instant-update sessions for biology and life-science
teachers in Maryland since 1934.  MABT holds two large conferences and various 1-day workshops throughout the year.  Every few years, the association
surveys its members to find out what they would like to address at the
association's two conferences.

**76.  Outdoor Education Program**
**Anne Arundel County Public Schools**
**Contact: Russell Heyde, Millersville, (410) 222-3822, FAX:  (410) 222-3826,**
**Internet:  n/a**

The Outdoor Education Program of Anne Arundel County public schools offers
courses to teachers to improve their content skills in environmental education.
There is an extensive evaluation at the completion of each course, which is used
to make decisions for the design of new courses.  Each year, about 250 classroom
teachers participate in for-credit and noncredit courses offered by the program.
Of the participants, 70% are elementary-school teachers and 30% secondary-
school teachers.

**77.  Ecology of the Chesapeake Watershed: Authentic Applications for**
**Science and Mathematics Instruction**
**Center for Environmental and Estuarine Studies**
**Contact:  Wayne H. Bell, Cambridge, (410) 228-9250, ext. 608, FAX:  (410)**
**228-3843, Internet:  bell@hpel.umd.edu**

This program is offered to middle- and high-school science and mathematics teachers and is offered every other summer (resuming in 1997) as a 2-week, intensive workshop that travels to various locations across the Chesapeake watershed. Participants earn 3 graduate credits. This program is funded by the Maryland Higher Education Commission and the Chesapeake Bay Trust. The goals of the project are for teachers to learn first-hand the ecological principles that affect environmental problems in each region of the Chesapeake Bay watershed, to develop authentic applications of environmental principles and calculations to enrich science and mathematics instruction in their schools in response to the Maryland Science Performance Assessment Program and Maryland's Environmental Education Bylaw, and to contribute to a new resource book that identifies environmental issues and places across the state that can be used as authentic examples for mathematics and science teaching.

## MASSACHUSETTS

**78. Biotechnology For Teachers**
**New England Science Center**
**Contact: Duke Dawson, Worcester, (508) 791-9211, FAX: (508) 752-6879, Internet: n/a**

The New England Science Center engages K-12 teachers and people from industry, academe, and science museums in activities that promote increased awareness of biotechnology and its applications for everyday use. Activities include lectures, laboratory tours, hands-on activities, and curriculum development. Programs range from week-long summer institutes focusing on laboratory skills to one-time inservice sessions. Developed to reduce apprehension about the teaching of biotechnology, the center offers its services to 60-80 self-selected teachers each year. Followup efforts include reunions, classroom visits by scientists, networking opportunities for teachers and scientists, seminars, and the dissemination of educational materials.

**79. Consortium for the Improvement of Math and Science Teaching**
**North Adams State College**
**Contact: Edward A. Filiault, North Adams, (413) 662-5537, FAX: (413) 662-5010, Internet: efiliaul@nasc.mass.edu**

The Consortium for the Improvement of Math and Science Teaching, a division of the Educators' Resource Center at North Adams State College, is a collaborative effort among all Berkshire County and several Franklin County school districts, a 4-year college, and two community colleges. The consortium's overall goals are to consolidate the region's funding from Eisenhower Mathematics and

Science Education State Grants designated for teacher inservice programs and to maximize the use of local resources in a rural area among schools, colleges and businesses. The consortium aims to develop professional networks, enhance teacher abilities to work with students of varied skill levels, and improve mathematics and science instruction at all educational levels. It has also been a leader in providing professional-development opportunities for both school districts and individual teachers to assist them in meeting the requirements of education reform and the demands of recertification, using a combination of college faculty and experienced presenters.

**80. Five College/Public School Partnership**
**Five Colleges Inc.**
**Contact: Mary Alice Wilson, Amherst, (413) 256-8316, FAX: (413) 256-0249, Internet: mwilson@k12.o.t.umass.edu**

The Five College/Public School Partnership was formed in 1984 to facilitate communication and resource-sharing between the members of the Five Colleges consortium (Amherst, Hampshire, Mount Holyoke, and Smith Colleges and the University of Massachusetts at Amherst) and the 43 school systems in western Massachusetts. Partnership activities are planned by committees of school and college faculty who work in a common discipline. Services include conferences and seminars, summer institutes, summer research fellowships, a data bank of projects designed to strengthen public education through collaboration, publications, and a telecommunications network. Major partnership goals are to update school faculty on recent research; to introduce all participants to underused resources in area institutions; to provide opportunities for collegial discussions among school and college faculty, museum staff, and industry representatives; and to improve the teaching abilities of participating college faculty and increase their knowledge about K-12 schools.

**81. Greater Boston Biology Teachers Group**
**Contact: Hazel Schroeder, Shrewsbury, (508) 845-4641, FAX: (508) 842-8512, Internet: n/a**

The Greater Boston Biology Teachers Group is an informal gathering of K-12 life-science teachers who meet once a month throughout the year. The group, which has been meeting for 25 years, gathers at high schools in the greater Boston area to share ideas, resources, new activities, and approaches to biology teaching. The yearly fee is $10 per person, which covers costs of mailings and other materials. The group provides professional fellowship to about 100 members.

**82. CityLab**
**School of Medicine and School of Education, Boston University**
**Contact: Connie Phillips, Boston, (617) 638-5622, FAX: (617) 638-5621,**
**Internet: cphilli@acs.bu.edu**

CityLab is a biotechnology learning laboratory for high school and middle school students and teachers at the Boston University School of Medicine. CityLab is supported by grants from the National Institutes of Health (SEPA) and the Howard Hughes Medical Institute. The aim of CityLab is to provide access to state-of-the-art laboratory facilities and curriculum in biotechnology otherwise unavailable to most school systems. Teachers bring their students to CityLab where they are challenged to solve problems by applying the same techniques and concepts of genetics and molecular biology used in modern biotechnology laboratories today. More than 6,000 students have participated in hands-on, discovery oriented investigations at CityLab. Over 500 teachers have attended workshops.

**83. Museum Institute for Teaching Science**
**MITS, Inc.**
**Contact: Emily Wade, Boston, (617) 695-9771, FAX: same, Internet:**
**mits@usa1.com**

The MITS mission is to improve the teaching of science and mathematics at the elementary-school level using the resources available in museums, aquariums, arboretums, nature centers, etc. MITS offers 2-week summer workshops in seven regions of Massachusetts with room for 360 teachers. MITS became a 501(c)3 corporation in 1992 after 6 years of providing teacher workshops and distributing a teacher's resource publication. MITS continues to publish *Science Is Elementary* (SIE) on a subscription basis as a quarterly resource magazine for K-6 teachers providing background information and hands-on activities on specific science-education topics. Before 1992, MITS was funded mostly by grants from the National Science Foundation. It is now funded by a combination of contracts, grants, and donations from the Massachusetts Cultural Council, the Massachusetts Department of Education, foundations, corporations, and individuals.

**\*\*84. Neuroscience Program for High-School Science Teachers**
**Minority Faculty Development Program, Harvard Medical School**
**Contact: Joan Y. Reede, Boston, (617) 432-2413, FAX: (617) 432-3834,**
**Internet: jreede@warren.med.harvard.edu**

The Minority Faculty Development Program at Harvard Medical School (HMS) strives to improve the scientific literacy of high-school students, particularly nonwhite students, and to encourage them to think more ambitiously about their futures, including the pursuit of biomedical careers. To that end, the Teacher Institute in the Neurosciences (TIN) emphasizes enhancing scientific knowledge, introducing new teaching approaches and materials, and the development of new curriculum and the creation of new materials and resources for teaching neurosciences in high schools in innovative ways. Working with high-school and middle-school teachers, TIN works with basic neuroscience content, provides practice experience in the problem-based case-study method, and introduces new hands-on curricular materials on neuroscience. Teachers participate in a week-long summer workshop and in research seminars and activities during the academic year. Teacher fellows are provided with classroom kits, which include a video-taped "case," and receive academic support from HMS faculty throughout their affiliation with the Institute. Institute objectives include dissemination of a neuroscience high-school curriculum with hands-on experiments and teacher kits; creation of a team of teachers (from two urban school districts) trained in the use of the neuroscience curriculum and the case-study, problem-based pedagogical approach; and furthering partnership between Harvard faculty and secondary schools.

## 85. People and Animals:  United for Health
**Massachusetts Society for Medical Research**
**Contact:  Boston, (617) 891-4544, FAX:  (617) 893-7934, Internet: debra@msmr.terranet.com**

*People and Animals: United for Health* is a comprehensive reference manual on current topics in the biological sciences. The complete package consists of a reference manual for teachers, a set of 180 slides, a discussion guide, a timeline poster, and a compendium of critical- and creative-thinking activities designed for use with each of the topics. The reference manual is supported through bimonthly teacher-training workshops held at the Massachusetts Society for Medical Research (MSMR) headquarters and throughout Massachusetts. The workshops generally cover 8-10 of the 12 units, including an intensive session on critical- and creative-thinking exercises. To date, the MSMR has trained well over 1,500 teachers in the tristate area (Massachusetts, New Hampshire, and Rhode Island).

## 86. Project for Products, Processes, and Technology in the Elementary School Curriculum
**Biology Department, Simmons College**
**Contact:  Sandra Williams, Boston, (617) 521-2667, FAX:  (617) 521-3199, Internet:  swilliams@vmsvax.simmons.edu**

Project For Products, Processes, and Technology in the Elementary School Curriculum is designed to improve science education in elementary schools by facilitating collaborative efforts among teachers, science coordinators, principals, and representatives of local industry. The program consists of three summer workshops in which participants learn about hands-on science, critique newly developed Product-Process-Technology curriculum modules, develop new curriculum, and prepare an industry-school collaborative plan for implementation in their own districts. Participants reconvene for 3 days during the next summer to discuss the implementation of their district plans and to find ways to continue the industry-school collaboration.

### 87. Introduction to Biotechnology and Cancer and Immunology
### Education Development Center
**Contact: Jackie Miller, Newton, (617) 969-7100, ext. 438, FAX: (617) 965-6325, Internet: jackiem@edc.org**

With funding from the Bay State Skills Corporation, the Education Development Center (EDC) has conducted summer workshops for middle- and secondary-school biology teachers. The goal of the workshops is to assist teachers in integrating biotechnology into existing curriculum, as opposed to presenting it as an add-on subject. So that these concepts can be introduced in the teaching environments of the participants, the workshops, conducted by a team of teachers and scientists, have been held in high-school biology laboratories. In response to requests, EDC has also developed a second workshop, Cancer and Immunology, that helps teachers explore issues in cancer and immunology without using expensive equipment or hazardous materials. Through workshops, lectures, and discussion, the program draws connections between classroom experiences and current issues in health and medicine. It aims to increase participants' range of teaching strategies, to help teachers network with each other, and to improve student outcomes in middle- and secondary-school biology.

### 88. Master of Arts in Teaching Education
### Department of Education, Tufts University
**Contact: Robert Guertin, Medford, (617) 627-3106, FAX: (617) 627-3901, Internet: rguertin@pearl.tufts.edu**

The Tufts University teacher-preparation program has certified several teachers of biology, physics, and mathematics in the last several years. Program officers expect to increase the number of K-12 teachers that they reach through programs established at the Dudley Wright Center for Science Education, the Center for Science and Mathematics Teaching, and the Department of Child Study. All are dedicated to integrating science education into elementary-school teacher-preparation programs.

**89. Laboratory Safety Workshop**
**Contact: James Kaufman, Natick, (508) 647-1900, FAX: (508) 647-0062,**
**Internet: jkaufman@curry.edu**

In 15 years, the Laboratory Safety Workshop has provided safety-training opportunities for over 25,000 science teachers at the elementary and secondary levels. Workshops review fundamental safety issues and assist teachers in bettering their laboratory-safety programs. Through workshop demonstrations and the distribution of two newsletters, *Safety Is Elementary* and *Speaking of Safety*, facilitators offer examples of hands-on activities that teachers can use in their classrooms. Followup services include equipment loans, continuing seminars, the dissemination of program materials, and networking opportunities.

**90. The "Current Students/Future Scientists and Engineers" Program**
**Clark Science Center, Smith College**
**Contact: Casey Clark, Northhampton, (413) 585-3804, FAX: (413) 585-3786, Internet: cclark@science.smith.edu**

Smith College inaugurated a program in 1983 to address the decline in the number of students who were preparing for careers in the scientific and technical fields. The year-long program begins with a 3-day workshop and is directed at junior- and senior-high-school science and mathematics teachers and guidance counselors. The "Current Students/Future Scientists and Engineers" Program is designed to help teachers and counselors develop and implement programs within their schools that will encourage students of all abilities, especially young women and minority-group members, to continue their studies and explore career options in science and mathematics. Through panel presentations with successful women in science and engineering, hands-on laboratory sessions led by Smith College faculty and undergraduates, and interactive workshops on the influences of sex bias and other constraints that have discouraged women and members of minority groups from pursuing science, they have immersed workshop participants in the world of engineering and technology. The participants receive free room and board and a variable number of continuing-education credits.

## MICHIGAN

**91. Teacher inservice programs**
**Division of Science Education, Michigan State University**
**Contact: Clarence Suelter, East Lansing, (517) 432-1490, FAX: (517) 432-2175, Internet: suelter@msu.edu**

The Michigan State University (MSU) Division of Science Education, housed in the College of Natural Science, offers a range of programs to K-12 science teachers that can be applied toward a master of science in biological or physical science for teachers with secondary credentials and a master of arts for K-8 certified teachers. Program goals vary but each strives to share MSU and local resources with area teachers, in addition to giving each participant a solid foundation in the sciences. The program offerings for secondary-school teachers include Frontiers in Biological Science, Frontiers in Physical Science, and summer courses in chemistry, earth science, physics, environmental and behavioral biology, and cellular and molecular biology. Offerings for elementary-school certified teachers of science include Energy and Matter; Everyday Physics; Rocks, Minerals and Fossils; Weather and Space Science; Cells and Organisms; and Interrelationships of Organisms. Opportunities for teachers to research and develop independent projects on campus are also available.

### 92. Hands-on science workshops
### Science Department, Lansing Community College
**Contact: Jeannine Stanaway or Christel Marschall, Lansing, (517) 483-1092, FAX : (517)483-9649, Internet: alex@alpha.lansing.cc.mi.us**

The Science Department at Lansing Community College, through its Teacher Education Project, offers inquiry-based workshops for K-6 teachers. The goals of these workshops are to help teachers become more confident about their knowledge of fundamental concepts in biology, chemistry, geoscience, and physics and to encourage them to integrate process-oriented activities and student investigations into their classroom instruction. Workshop leaders demonstrate research-based teaching strategies and provide ready-made materials for classroom use, which reflect the new science objectives of the Michigan Department of Education. In addition, each teacher receives $100 worth of science equipment, which is used in science investigations. The workshops, open to teachers in the Lansing School District and nine neighboring counties, reach 300 teachers each year through six 12-hour sessions—three during the school year and three in the summer.

### 93. Young Entomologists' Society, Inc.
**Contact: Gary Dunn, Lansing, (517) 887-0499, FAX: same, Internet: n/a**

Since 1965, the Young Entomologists' Society, Inc., has offered programs for schools, clubs, day-care centers, camps, and science and nature centers. In cooperation with school districts, the society has also offered teacher-inservice programs for 6 years. These programs cover a wide range of topics, including insect anatomy, life cycles, and diversity; related educational games and puzzles; endangered species; observing, studying, and collecting insects and spiders; and attracting butterflies and hummingbirds. The organizers are available to design special programs to meet the needs of individual groups. The workshops are interactive and involve hands-on activities, discussions, and demonstrations. The goals are to provide teachers with innovative activities for the classroom, to improve teachers' knowledge of insects and other arthropods, and to encourage the incorporation of insect studies in classroom instruction.

**94. ScienceGrasp**
**Kalamazoo College**
**Contact:  Paul Olexia, Kalamazoo, (616) 337-7013, FAX: (616) 337-7251,**
**Internet:  polexia@kzoo.edu**

The ScienceGrasp program, a teacher-training workshop for science-shy elementary-school teachers to increase their confidence and skills in teaching hands-on science, is sponsored by Kalamazoo College (Kalamazoo, MI) with funding support by the Upjohn Company Foundation and program support by the National Science Teachers Association (NSTA), Delta Education, Inc., and Disney's Hyperion Books for Children. The program consists of 12 teachers, selected each spring from applications distributed by NSTA and printed in the December or January issues of *Science & Children*, who come to Kalamazoo for a 1-week intensive workshop—all expenses paid. Topics covered include chemistry, physics, biology, outdoor education, and other subjects that include mathematics-science integration at the elementary level. The outreach program includeds publication of a book of hands-on activities, with one chapter written by each participant; the book is distributed at no charge at the NSTA national conference. Workshop participants can order up to $1,000 worth of hands-on materials during the next school year at no cost. The program began in 1990, and more than 100 teachers have completed the workshop. In 1992, the Council for Elementary Science International recognized ScienceGrasp with its Advocate Award. Many alumni of the program have broken their "science-shy" limitation and have become presenters at state, regional, and national NSTA conferences.

**95. Summer Institutes in Science**
**Wayne State University**
**Contact:  David Njus, Detroit, (313) 577-3105, FAX:  (313) 577-6891,**
**Internet:  hhmi@sun.science.wayne.edu**

With funding from the Howard Hughes Medical Institute, the Wayne State College of Science has offered summer science institutes to high-school science teachers. The institutes are designed to acquaint science teachers with recent developments in their fields and to provide them with material for immediate incorporation into their curricula. An institute includes laboratory exercises and demonstrations that can be used in 1-hour class periods and modestly equipped laboratories. The intent is to assist teachers in using a hands-on approach in their science courses and in getting their students to learn by discovery. Each institute, limited to 20 teachers, offers participants 3 semester-hours of graduate credit and waivers of tuition, laboratory, and registration fees. Textbooks and other course materials are provided.

**\*\*96.  Laboratory Apparatus Bank**
**Wayne State University**
**Contact:  David Njus, Detroit, (313) 577-3105, FAX:  (313) 577-6891,**
**Internet:  hhmi@sun.science.wayne.edu**

The Wayne State University Laboratory Apparatus Bank lends scientific laboratory equipment at no cost for use in high-school classrooms.  Equipment for this program was purchased with financial support from the Howard Hughes Medical Institute and the Community Foundation for Southeastern Michigan.  The objective of the program is to establish a pool of shared laboratory equipment enabling individual schools to expand dramatically the hands-on scientific experiences available to their students.  Available equipment, which may be borrowed for 1-week periods, includes spectrophotometers, electrophoresis units, and environmental-analysis kits.

## MINNESOTA

**97.  A Multidimensional Program to Enhance Subject Matter Competency of and Improve Collaboration among Teachers of Grades 5-12**
**Gustuvas Adolphus College**
**Contact:  Myron Anderson, St. Peter, (507) 933-7327, FAX:  (507) 933-6285, Internet:  myron@gac.edu**

With support from the National Science Foundation, this program served directly 27 different teachers of grades 5-12 in rural Minnesota in each of 3 years.  Each attended a 4-week summer workshop in either earth, life, or physical science and was involved in a followup inservice program during the next academic year. The nine participants in each workshop were divided into three cooperative learning groups consisting of a teacher from middle school, junior high school, and senior high school.  Assisting in the program were three master teachers each year, called guest instructors, who were selected from a national pool of applicants.  They were on leave from their home schools for the entire year.  They worked with Gustavus faculty in their own workshops and had primary responsibility for conducting the inservice program that followed.  Additionally, each taught at the introductory college level.  Three Gustavus undergraduate students who were preparing to become science teachers also assisted during the summer workshops.

**98. Sci-Link**
**University of Minnesota; North Carolina State University**
**Contact: Harriett Stubbs, Raleigh, NC (919) 515-3311, FAX: (919) 515-3593, Internet: sci-link@ncsu.edu or http://www2.ncsu.edu/ncsu/cep/SCI-LINK/SCI-LINK_HP.html**

Sci-Link consists of two components. First, it brings together scientists and elementary-, middle-, junior-high-, and senior-high-school teachers in workshops of various lengths. The goal of each workshop is to provide a forum for integrating current scientific research into curricula and teaching practices. Workshop participants develop classroom applications based on a cooperative-learning approach, review current educational materials, and produce new classroom activities. Topics include acid rain, ozone, carbon dioxide warming and global-climate change, and other environmental issues of concern. Second, Sci-Link creates networks of participating teachers in North Carolina and Minnesota with scientists in their own areas. The goal of this effort is to increase participants' knowledge about the personnel, facilities, and research available at surrounding universities and federal and state agencies.

**99. Teacher Enhancement in Applied Soil Ecology**
**Mankato State University**
**Contact: John Frey, Mankato, (507) 389-2908, FAX: (507) 389-2788, Internet: jfrey@vax1.mankato.msus.edu**

The 5-week workshop involves middle- and junior-high-school teachers in individualized hands-on research experience in applied soil ecology. Lectures on current topics and sessions on laboratory techniques provide the necessary background. Participants, whose attendance is based on a selective process, receive a $300/week stipend, full meal expenses, and private housing. Teachers translate their workshop experiences into classroom activities during weekly team writing sessions. The program aims to reverse the decline in student interest in science—a problem that project officers believe begins in middle school.

## MISSOURI

**100. Biotechnology Education Project**
**Mathematics and Science Education Center**
**Contact: Paul Markovits, St. Louis, (314) 516-5650, FAX: (314) 516-5342, Internet: spmarko@slvaxa.umsl.edu**

Funded by the Monsanto Company Fund and the National Science Foundation, the Mathematics and Science Education Center (MSEC) in 1987 developed the Biotechnology Education Project. Led by teams of teachers, researchers, and education specialists, the program provides training opportunities for grade 5-12 teachers. The goals of the project are to upgrade teachers' knowledge of biotechnology and to familiarize them with new methods for teaching this topic, to improve the quality of teaching in the life sciences, to better student outcomes, to encourage teachers to introduce basic concepts of biotechnology to students in grades 5 and 6, to stimulate professional development of teachers by involving them actively in the writing of curricula, and to provide a school-industry-university model for development and dissemination of curriculum materials. The program is a joint effort of the research scientists and science-education specialists at the Monsanto Company, Washington University, the University of Missouri-St. Louis, Principia College, and Southern Illinois University at Edwardsville, local and national teachers, and the staff of MSEC. MSEC coordinates the dissemination and revision of materials.

## 101. Ecology for Teachers
**Missouri Botanical Garden**
**Contact: Barbara Addelson, St. Louis, (314) 577-5139, FAX: (314) 577-9592, Internet: baddelso@ridgway.mobot.org**

The Education Division of the Missouri Botanical Garden sponsors an ecology and environmental-science course for grade K-6 teachers. The program involves up to 25 teachers, selected from regional public and private schools, in 60 hours of instruction. Activities include demonstrations, field work, and a wide range of hands-on activities. The goal of the program is to increase participants' knowledge in ecology and environmental education while expanding their repertoire of strategies for developing and implementing curriculum in their classrooms. Other workshops available are Ecology Through Inquiry, Field Methods in Ecological Investigation, and Ecology of Aquatic Environments.

## 102. Molecular Biology: The Gene Revolution
**Mathematics and Science Education Center; Washington University**
**Contact: Cynthia Moore, St. Louis, (314) 935-4550, FAX: (314) 935-4432, Internet:**
**moore@biodec.wustl.edu**

The Mathematics and Science Education Center (MSEC), in collaboration with Washington University (WU), will hold a 3-week lecture-laboratory summer course on molecular biology and biotechnology for secondary-school science teachers. Molecular Biology: The Gene Revolution will focus on basic techniques of gene cloning and analysis with applications to human genetics. Teachers will work with WU and MSEC faculty to become familiar with materials from a DNA-science course developed by the DNA Learning Center at Cold Spring Harbor Laboratory. They will also develop strategies for using these materials in their classrooms. Funding from the Howard Hughes Medical Institute allows WU and MSEC to offer the course free of charge to the teachers, with supplies and use of an equipment-loan program. In addition, participants will receive 4 hours of graduate credit from WU. During alternate summers, WU offers a similar course for middle-school teachers, "The Molecular Basis of Life." This course focuses on background information and hands-on activities. MSEC provide K-12 science and mathematics teachers with other innovative programs in science, mathematics, and environmental education.

**103. Molecular Biology for Teachers**
**Biomedical Sciences Department, Southwest Missouri State University**
**Contact: Harley Mortensen, Springfield, (417) 836-5603, FAX: (417) 836-5588, Internet: hem439f@vma.smsu.edu**

Since 1988, the Biomedical Sciences Department of Southwest Missouri State University has held a summer program on molecular biology for teachers. This 1-month program provides participants with 3 hours of graduate credit through extensive hands-on laboratory activities and lectures addressing theoretical aspects of molecular biology. The program is funded by Eisenhower Mathematics and Science Education State Grants and the National Science Foundation and is coordinated by the chair of the Biomedical Sciences Department, a local high-school biology teacher, and the district science-curriculum coordinator.

## NEW JERSEY

**104. Biology-Teacher Summer Grant Program**
**Hoffmann-La Roche Inc.; New Jersey Science Supervisors Association**
**Contact: Marjorie Ford, Nutley, (201) 562-2186, FAX: (201) 562-2999, Internet: n/a**

With funding from Hoffmann-La Roche, the New Jersey Science Supervisors Association has given biology teachers $5,000 cash awards to conduct research with experienced research scientists at a Hoffmann-La Roche laboratory. The goals are to enable teachers to use state-of-the-art laboratory equipment and to update their own curricula with current scientific information. Three teachers are selected each summer for an 8-week program of hands-on experience in modern research technology. The program is designed to renew enthusiasm for the teaching of biology, to encourage teachers to link concepts and theory to everyday application for students, and to give teachers exposure to the kinds of skills that students need to go into industry and to the kinds of jobs that can be found there. The teachers also receive grants to purchase equipment for their classroom laboratories.

**105.  Ciba-Geigy Partnership in Science**
**Pharmaceuticals Division/Research Department, Ciba-Geigy Corporation**
**Contact:  Elizabeth O'Byrne, Summit, (908) 277-4692, FAX:  (908) 277-**
**2577, Internet:  eob%ussu02@ussu.ciba.com**

Ciba-Geigy scientists work with science faculty from neighboring schools to design activities that enhance and enrich the school curriculum.  The partnership gives students opportunities to meet researchers and to experience hands-on investigations.  The program addresses topics in biology, chemistry, environmental science, and physics.  The partnership also provides speakers to discuss ethical use of animals in research on request from students and civic groups.

**106.  The Consortium for Educational Equity**
**Rutgers University**
**Contact:  Arlene Chasek, New Brunswick, (908) 445-2071, FAX:  (908)**
**445-0027, Internet:  chasek@gandalf.rutgers.edu**

The Consortium for Educational Equity's mission is to promote the full achievement of all students, especially targeting the concerns and effects of sex, race, national origin, language, culture, socioeconomic status, and disability.  Current focuses are parental involvement, cooperative learning, multicultural education, reducing ethnic and racial tensions, and eliminating sexual harassment.  Rutgers Family Science is a family-involvement program that fosters curiosity and helps parents and teachers work with children to channel that curiosity in productive ways.  The focus is experiential in order for children and their parents to learn science and problem-solve together; it stresses the process of scientific thinking, rather than specific content.  During a 4-day workshop at Rutgers University, elementary-school teachers are trained in all the Rutgers Family Science workshop techniques and the hands-on activities and experiments, including strategies that specifically promote the participation of girls and ethnic and racial-minority children and parents.  Teachers then return to their schools to lead and facilitate a series of six classes after school hours with families.

**107.  National Leadership Program for Teachers**
**Woodrow Wilson National Fellowship Foundation**
**Contact:  Dale S. Koepp, Princeton, (609) 452-7007, FAX:  (609) 452-0066,**
**Internet:  geri@wwnff.org**

Begun in 1982, the National Leadership Program for Teachers (NLPT), which has reached over 85,000 teachers, is best understood as a cluster of professional-development programs for precollege teachers.  The program, which encourages teachers to see themselves as life-long learners and as professionals, focuses on content-driven institutes that are rooted in the premise that the most-effective professional development is achieved by *teachers teaching teachers.*  There are two phases in the yearly NLPT program cycle.  Month-long summer residential institutes (called core institutes) in Princeton, NJ, bring together seasoned teachers from across the country for institutes in mathematics and science; participants learn new content from experts and scholars in the field and then apply their own expertise and experience as teachers to the task of developing classroom strategies that translate that content into effective hands-on/minds-on learning experiences for middle- and high-school students.  One-week Teacher OutReaCH (TORCH) institutes at local sites nationwide aim to disseminate the content and methodology developed at the core institutes.  TORCH institutes are led by teams of teachers from the core institute who have developed a condensed 1-week version of the program, which they take to sites easily accessible to local teachers.  TORCH institutes are hosted by colleges and universities, school districts, and local education agencies, which often provide opportunities for earning graduate credit or continuing-education units for participation in the program.

## NEW YORK

**108.  Biotechnology Institute**
**Department of Biology, University of Rochester**
**Contact:  Paul Marquis, Rochester, (716) 276-1674, FAX:  (716) 473-9573,**
**Internet:  mutansst@aol.com**

Since 1983, the Biotechnology Institute has offered 2-week, graduate-level courses to high-school teachers in genetic engineering, immunology, microbiology, or ecology.  The courses, which admit up to 20 teachers selected on a competitive basis, focus on biology as an investigative discipline and include an extensive laboratory component.  Among the institute's primary goals are to improve participants' content knowledge, to improve student outcomes in the participants' classrooms, and to encourage networking among the high-school teachers themselves.

**109.  Cornell Institute for Biology Teachers (CIBT)**
**Division of Biological Sciences, Cornell University**
**Contact:  Peter Bruns, Ithaca, (607) 255-5042, FAX:  (607) 254-4916,**
**Internet:  pjb4@cornell.edu**

Funded by the Howard Hughes Medical Institute and the New York State Center for Advanced Technology in Biotechnology at Cornell, the Cornell University Division of Biological Sciences sponsors an institute for teachers to improve high-school biology instruction. On the Ithaca campus, the program consists of a 3-week summer institute and three full-day sessions during the next year.  During the summer institute, teachers participate in lectures, laboratories, and demonstrations to enhance teacher knowledge of contemporary biology; visits to Cornell facilities to promote contacts with Cornell faculty; lessons on the use of computers for communication and planning course work; and hands-on experience with a set of laboratory exercises designed and tested for use in high-school classrooms. Participants receive a stipend, academic credit, a room, a supply budget for their school, a Macintosh computer with modem and software, and a free subscription to the CIBT electronic network. During the academic year, the teachers are visited in their classrooms by a CIBT extension agent and are supported for a set of equipment-intensive laboratories by supplies and equipment from a lending library. CIBT also presents workshops at a variety of locations during the year. To target underrepresented minority populations, the program includes inner-city and rural schools in New York and a satellite group of inner-city schools in Cleveland, Ohio. A continuing goal of the program is to foster communication among institute staff, Cornell faculty, and participating teachers through computer communication and the formation of regional groups.

## 110. DNA Science Workshop
**Leadership Institute in Human and Molecular Genetics; DNA Learning Center of Cold Spring Harbor Laboratory**
**Contact: David Micklos, Cold Spring Harbor, (516) 367-7240, FAX: (516) 367-3043, Internet: miklos@cshl.org**

Developed in 1985 and supported by the National Science Foundation (NSF) since 1987, the DNA Science Workshop has been taken by 2,300 high-school biology teachers nationwide. The 50-hour training program consists of a 5-day summer workshop and a 1.5-day winter followup. Hands-on experimentation and analysis make up 80% of the training experience. Using equipment identical with that found in research laboratories, participants perform nine experiments that introduce modern methods for producing and analyzing recombinant-DNA molecules. The Leadership Institute in Human and Molecular Genetics was developed in 1993 with NSF support and provides intensive training for outstanding biology teachers nationwide who have already implemented units in molecular genetics and have proven networking abilities. The 20-day institute is held at the DNA Learning Center and includes advanced experimentation, computer applications, instructional pedagogy, and leadership skills. The Genetics as a Model for Whole Learning in Science program involves six Long Island school districts committed to the systematic introduction of genetics modules in elementary- and middle-school classes. The goal is to train classroom teachers, who usually have backgrounds in reading and language arts, to use genetics as a way to link science with more familiar disciplines, such as mathematics, geography, and the humanities. Each school district receives 100 hours of consultation by DNA Learning Center staff. The program involves 27 faculty and 1,000 students at 15 elementary and middle schools.

**111. The Elementary Science Training and Education Center**
**Contact: Douglas Seager, Newark, (315) 331-5763, FAX: (315) 331-2016,**
**Internet: n/a**

The Elementary Science Training and Education Center offers extensive support services in science and mathematics to K-8 teachers in the 25 school districts of the Wayne-Finger Lakes Board of Cooperative Educational Services. To enhance teaching and learning in science and mathematics the services are designed to increase teacher confidence and background related to science skills, physical science, life science, environmental science, and problem-solving in mathematics. Comprehensive services include formal workshops, school-based meetings and classroom visits, information-gathering and distribution, coordination of K-12 mentoring activities, and "whatever we can do to help." This center produces and distributes over 60 different K-8 science and mathematics kits, prepares classroom teachers to operate a portable planetarium, offers a graduate-credit course from an accredited university, and facilitates two annual science-teachers conferences.

**112. Inservice Teacher Enhancement Program in Biology**
**Elmira College**
**Contact: P. Y. Bouthyette, Elmira, (607) 735-1856, FAX: n/a, Internet:**
**n/a**

With funding from a Dwight D. Eisenhower Mathematics and Science Education State Grant, Elmira College brings together 25 local high-school biology teachers for a 2-week summer workshop. The goals of the program are to strengthen high-school biology curricula at the participants' schools and to develop an experimental approach to biology. The summer institute and followup sessions during the academic year emphasize cooperative learning, deductive reasoning, and experimental science.

**113. Summer Teacher Inservice Programs**
**State University College-Potsdam**
**Contact: Charles Mlynarczyk, Potsdam, (315) 267-2525, FAX: (315) 267-4802, Internet: mlynarhc@potsdam.edu**

Serving teachers from local middle and junior high schools in the Potsdam area, the summer teacher inservice workshops aim to help teachers upgrade their knowledge about science issues and science-teaching strategies and to work toward an improved understanding of the New York state science frameworks. The projects provides a 2-week summer workshop and a 1-day demonstration meeting during the next school year.

**114. Statewide Biology Mentor Network to Provide Inservice Biology Teacher Training**
**Finger Lakes Community College; SUNY**
Contact: Lee Drake, Canandaigua, (716) 394-3500, ext. 322, FAX: (716) 394-5005, Internet: drakela@snyflcc.fingerlakes.edu

The goal of the Mentor Network is to improve and expand the instructional and assessment skills of 3,000 New York state biology teachers. The emphasis is on promoting learner-centered classrooms through staff-development activities and resource expansion to achieve the conceptual changes necessary to support instructional and assessment reforms. The network provides training for coordinating mentors who develop workshop and classroom materials and train regional mentors. Regional mentors, in turn, provide funded workshops for local biology teachers. These local workshops have been attended by about 1,100 teachers per year in 1992-1995. Funding is provided by a Dwight D. Eisenhower Mathematics and Science Education State Grant.

**115. Statewide Program for Preparing New Teachers of Regents Biology**
**Syracuse University**
Contact: Marvin Druger, Syracuse, (315) 443-9150, FAX: (315) 443-1142, Internet: druger@sued.syr.edu

With funding from an Eisenhower Mathematics and Science Education State Grant, Syracuse University brings together a group of first-year regents biology teachers for a 10-day summer institute. The institute, taught primarily by a team of experienced regents biology teachers, also involves university scientists giving presentations on current biological research. Participants return to the Syracuse campus for two weekend seminars during the academic year for a content update by a scientist and to discuss classroom problems.

**116. Summer Research Program for Secondary School Science Teachers**
**Columbia University**
Contact: Jay Dubner, New York, (212) 305-6899, FAX: (212) 305-5775, Internet: jd109@columbia.edu

Columbia University provides two consecutive summers of laboratory research experiences for New York City science teachers in cell biology, chemistry, physics, genetics, immunology, molecular biology, microbiology, neurobiology, parasitology, cellular physiology, toxicology, ecology, and earth sciences. The teachers, who are selected competitively, receive a $6,000 stipend each summer for their participation and $1,000 for classroom materials and supplies. The primary goal of the program is to provide science teachers with sustained hands-on experiences in scientific research so that they can better understand scientific concepts and discovery and transmit to their students and fellow teachers a feeling for the practice of science. The laboratory experience provides teachers with accurate and timely information for their students about prerequisites for entering careers in science, about the types of skills needed to succeed in science, and about the many career opportunities available in the sciences.

## 117. Ventures in Education
**Contact: Phyllis McCabe, New York, (212) 696-5717, FAX: (212) 696-5726, Internet: 75000.1654@compuserve.com**

Founded in 1990 by the Josiah Macy, Jr. Foundation, Ventures in Education is an independent, nonprofit corporation that works with schools and school districts to revitalize education for minority-group and disadvantaged K-12 students. Its mission is to lift the academic performance of such youngsters and encourage them to pursue careers in science and the health professions. Ventures works with schools in western Alabama, the Delta region of Arkansas, New York City, the District of Columbia, and the Navajo Reservation (in Arizona, New Mexico, and Utah). Ventures collaborates with teachers and administrators to establish high course standards and higher expectations for all students; it helps district leadership and teachers develop plans for curricular and instructional improvements. All sites emphasize student-centered instructional techniques, such as problem-based learning, hands-on instruction, Socratic questioning, and use of the seminar and independent study. An ancillary service provided by Ventures for underrepresented minority-group students around the country (i.e., not only those in Ventures schools) is the Macy Minorities in Medicine (MIM) Program, which is designed to increase the number of students pursuing careers in medicine and the biomedical sciences. Candidates for MIM are selected according to their performance on the PSAT.

## 118. Urban Ecology Seminar
**Pace University**
**Contact: Angelo Spillo, Pleasantville, (914) 773-3789, FAX: (914) 773-3337, Internet: spillo@pacevm.dac.pace.edu**

Funded by an Eisenhower Mathematics and Science Education State Grant, Pace University's campus in Pleasantville, New York, offers a 1-week summer session and a 1-day followup workshop to 17 New York City elementary-school teachers. During the program, teachers become familiar with strategies for teaching urban ecology. In addition, they develop curriculum materials for use in their own classrooms and for dissemination among their home school districts.

**119. Watershed Watch Teacher Workshops**
**Institute of Ecosystem Studies**
**Contact: Kass Hogan, Millbrook, (914) 677-5358, FAX: (914) 677-6455,**
**Internet: kh1254@cnsvax.albany.edu**

Watershed Watch workshops began in the fall of 1991 as 3- to 5-day inservice activities for teachers implementing curricula that involve middle-school students in monitoring water quality and land-water interactions. Teacher-workshop topics and activities include overviews of aquatic ecology and watershed research by Institute of Ecosystem Studies scientists, field work with a scientist, experimenting with cooperative learning techniques for science classes, experiencing exemplary lessons, and introduction to professionals in water-land management.

**120. Eco-Inquiry Teacher Workshops**
**Institute of Ecosystem Studies**
**Contact: Kass Hogan, Millbrook, (914) 677-5358, FAX: (914) 677-6455,**
**Internet: kh1254@cnsvax.albany.edu**

Eco-Inquiry is an ecology curriculum for the upper elementary-school and middle-school grades. It is divided into three modules that engage students in problem-solving activities. Since 1988, the Institute of Ecosystem Studies has held 1- to 5-day workshops to introduce teachers to the ecology curriculum and to encourage its use in the classroom. Workshop topics and activities include field work with a scientist, learning and practicing Eco-Inquiry hands-on activities, analyzing students' ecology misconceptions, reflecting on instructional and evaluation strategies, experiencing cooperative learning, and using writing as a tool for teaching science. Workshops are held at schools and science centers around the country. The Eco-Inquiry teacher's guide is available from Kendall/Hunt publishers at 1-800-228-0810.

**\*\*121. Schoolyard Ecology for Elementary School Teachers Workshops**
**Institute of Ecosystem Studies**
**Contact: Alan Berkowitz, Millbrook, (914) 677-5358, FAX: (914) 677-6455, Internet: 74301.1575@compuserve.com**

Schoolyard Ecology for Elementary School Teachers (SYEFEST) is a project of the Institute of Ecosystem Studies in Millbrook, New York. The Ecological Society of America is an active supporter, and funds were provided by the National Science Foundation in 1994. SYEFEST is a nationwide program, with 15 teams (a practicing teacher and a professional ecologist) each working with 10-15 local teachers. SYEFEST workshops aim to give teachers a positive experience doing ecological studies in their own schoolyards through hands-on investigations and direct engagement in the process of science. Teachers participate in an introductory meeting, a 2-week summer institute, and 3 days of workshops during the school year. Shorter programs are available at some sites. During the summer institutes, participants do ecological research in schoolyard habitats, reflect on the process of scientific inquiry, create activities for their students, plan for integrating the new activities into their overall curriculum, and develop authentic assessments of student learning in schoolyard ecology.

**122. Project Leadership**
**York College-CUNY**
**Contact: Jack Schlein, Jamaica, (718) 262-2716, FAX: (718) 262-2652,**
**Internet: schlein@ycvax.york.cuny.edu**

In 1987-1990, with funding from the National Science Foundation, Project Leadership offered summer institutes and academic-year workshops to high-school biology teachers in the New York metropolitan area. Activities included lectures, seminars, demonstrations, hands-on workshops, and computer instruction. The primary program goals were to familiarize participants with up-to-date curricula, teaching methods, and research and equipment in biology, chemistry, physics, earth science, and mathematics. Other goals included improving student outcomes, encouraging teachers to form networks with scientists and each other, and involving participants in developing curricular materials. Project participation was selective, with priority given to minority-group teachers and teachers from predominantly minority-group classrooms.

**\*\*123. NASA-Math, Science, Technology Awards Program (MASTAP)**
**York College-CUNY**
**Contact: Jack Schlein, Jamaica, (718) 262-2716, FAX: (718) 262-2652,**
**Internet: schlein@ycvax.york.cuny.edu**

This program uses a 3-year grant to increase the number of minority-group undergraduates choosing teaching careers in mathematics, science, and technology and to improve the quality of the teaching of those subjects in middle schools. The grant totals $527,000 and runs through the 1997-1998 academic year.

**\*\*124. Project STEPPS (Science Teacher Enhancement Program in**
**Physical Science)**
**York College-CUNY**
**Contact: Jack Schlein, Jamaica, (718) 262-2716, FAX: (718) 262-2652,**
**Internet: schlein@ycvax.york.cuny.edu**

The N.Y. State Dwight D. Eisenhower award to York College has been granted for the last 4 years. The title of the program is Project STEPPS (Science Teacher

Enhancement Program in Physical Science). The goal is to improve the teaching of physical sciences in elementary school, primarily grades 4-6. A total of 100 teachers have been through the program to date. It is funded at about $40,000 per year.

## NORTH CAROLINA

**125. Biotech Inservice**
**Cabisco Biotechnology, a branch of the Carolina Biological Supply Company**
**Contact: Ray Gladden, Burlington, (910) 538-6320, FAX: (910) 222-1926, Internet: caroscidna@aol.com**

Biotech Inservice offers inservice training on request by teachers at the high-school, community-college, and college levels in DNA restriction-enzyme analysis, transformation of *E. coli* with an antibiotic-resistant plasmid, and plasmid isolation from bacteria carrying an antibiotic-resistant gene. In addition, an equipment-loan program is available for participating teachers.

**126. Secondary Education Project**
**North Carolina Biotechnology Center**
**Contact: Lynn Elwell, Kathleen Kennedy, or Adrianne Massey, Research Triangle Park, (919) 541-9366, FAX: (919) 549-9710, Internet: n/a**

Through its Secondary Education Project, the North Carolina Biotechnology Center aims to inform North Carolina's middle-school, high-school, and community-college science teachers about the science applications and issues of biotechnology. The center's introductory and advanced biotechnology workshops update teachers on such topics as general biotechnology, restriction-enzyme analysis, human genetics, genetic engineering of microbes and plants, and bioethical issues. Instructors base their workshops on the center's textbook, *Teaching Basic Biotechnology,* which will be published in 1996 by ASM Press. This text is available to all participants on completion of the program with a semiannual newsletter. In addition, the center provides participants with lesson plans, audiovisual aids, laboratory equipment, and other supplies needed to implement biotechnology curricula in the classroom. The project's ultimate goal is to increase student awareness of biotechnology by informing classroom teachers of current developments and issues in the field.

**\*127. Teacher Inservice Programs**
**Natural Science Center of Greensboro**
**Contact: Rick Betton, Greensboro, (910) 288-3769, FAX: (910) 288-0545, Internet: n/a**

The Natural Science Center of Greensboro offers different programs for teachers during the course of a year. Primary objectives of the program are to improve participants' content knowledge, to increase their range of teaching strategies, and to improve student outcomes. The workshops provide participants with hands-on activities, lectures, demonstrations, and discussions.

**128. Partnership for Minority Advancement in the Biomolecular Sciences**
**University of North Carolina at Chapel Hill**
**Contact: Walter E. Bollenbacher, Chapel Hill, (919) 962-2289, FAX:**
**(919) 962-5815, Internet: wbollenb@email.unc.edu**

The Partnership for Minority Advancement in the Biomolecular Sciences was established at the University of North Carolina at Chapel Hill (UNC-CH) in 1989 and renewed in 1994 to attract underrepresented minority-group students into science careers. The partnership is an alliance between seven North Carolina historically minority-group universities (HMUs) and UNC-CH. One component of the program is under development: summer biomolecular workshops for North Carolina high-school biology teachers held at regional HMUs. Teachers will be able to commute to their local HMU and will receive a stipend. Workshop content will be hands-on laboratories in the biomolecular sciences, which will translate directly into the high-school classroom.

**129. Project Learning Tree**
**Center for Math and Science, University of North Carolina at Chapel Hill**
**Contact: Lin Dunbar-Frye, Chapel Hill, (919) 966-5922, FAX: (919) 962-**
**0588, Internet: ladunbar@email.unc.edu**

Project Learning Tree is a multidisciplinary, hands-on environmental-education program that aims to encourage greater understanding, awareness, and appreciation of natural resources. With funding from various sources, the center has offered 2- to 3-day programs for about 500 mathematics and science teachers in North Carolina over the last 8 years. Program activities include hands-on workshops, lectures, seminars, discussion, and fieldwork.

**130. UNC Mathematics and Science Education Network**
**University of North Carolina at Chapel Hill**
**Contact: Gerry Madrazo, Chapel Hill, (919) 966-3256, FAX: (919) 962-**
**1316, Internet: gmadrazo@email.unc.edu**

The Mathematics and Science Education Network was formed in 1984 by the North Carolina General Assembly to improve the quality of mathematics and science education in North Carolina. The network's central coordinating office is at the University of North Carolina (UNC) at Chapel Hill. There are 10 network centers on UNC-system campuses across the state.  The mission is to improve mathematics and science education in North Carolina by increasing the quality and size of the teaching base in mathematics and science and by increasing the number of students who graduate from high school prepared to pursue careers requiring mathematics and science education.  The network's major components are K-12 professional development, a precollege program for minority-group and female students in grades 6-12, and applied research.  Because the centers are spread across the state, this structure allows for building responsive relationships at regional and local levels with teachers, schools, school districts, and businesses.  Over the last 10 years, the network has provided a total of 57,850 teachers with 2,924 professional-development programs, and over 70 schools across the state now participate in the precollege program.

## 131.  Sci-Link
**North Carolina State University; University of Minnesota**
**Contact:  Harriett Stubbs, Raleigh, (919) 515-3311, FAX: (919) 515-3593,**
**Internet:  sci-link@ncsu.edu or http://www2.ncsu.edu/ncsu/cep/SCI-LINK/**
**SCI-LINK_HP.html**

Sci-Link consists of two components.  First, it brings together scientists and elementary-, middle-, junior-high-, and senior-high-school teachers in workshops of various lengths.  The goal of each workshop is to provide a forum for integrating current scientific research into curricula and teaching practices.  Workshop participants develop classroom applications based on a cooperative-learning approach, review current educational materials, and produce new classroom activities.  Topics include acid rain, ozone, carbon dioxide warming and global-climate change, and other environmental issues of concern.  Second, Sci-Link creates networks of participating teachers in North Carolina and Minnesota with scientists in their own areas.  The goal of this effort is to increase participants' knowledge about the personnel, facilities, and research available at surrounding universities and federal and state agencies.

## 132.  Rural Science Initiative
**North Carolina School of Science and Mathematics**
**Contact:  Sally Adkin, Durham, (919) 286-3366, FAX:  (919) 286-5960,**
**Internet:  adkin@odie.ncssm.edu**

The North Carolina School of Science and Mathematics (NCSSM) offers a summer workshop to North Carolina's high-school science teachers working in rural areas who wish to sponsor or direct student research in science.  The workshop is devoted to learning and reviewing laboratory skills, investigative strategies, experimental design, and data analysis.  As a leader in providing educational course work on North Carolina's information highway, the workshop is now provided at several broadcast sites in rural regions of the state. Participants receive a $1,000 grant for equipment, supplies, or other expenses in support of student science research. They are also encouraged to stay in touch with the workshop instructors throughout the year and to participate in a symposium focusing on the students' research. The cost of the initiative is underwritten by a grant from a local foundation, which allows NCSSM to offer the session at no cost to the participants. Teachers and students receive stipends for participating in the program.

## OHIO

**133. Earth Systems Education Program**
**Ohio State University; University of Northern Colorado**
**Contact: Roseanne Fortner, Columbus, (614) 292- 1078, FAX: (614) 292-7812, Internet: fortner.2@osu.edu**

The Earth Systems Education (ESE) Program addresses concerns about how science is presented to K-12 students. It provides a rationale and framework for developing integrated science programs having as their conceptual focus the earth system. The ESE Program, with centers at Ohio State University and the University of Northern Colorado, assists teachers to develop curriculum, instructional approaches, and assessment procedures that address the National Standards for Science Education developed by the National Research Council. Several school systems in central Ohio, Colorado, Florida, and New York have developed such approaches with the assistance of the ESE centers. Teachers incorporating the ESE approach find that their students' interest in science increases because they develop a deeper understanding of science methods and the cooperative skills necessary in the workplace. A publication titled *Science Is a Study of Earth: A Resource Guide for Science Curriculum Restructure* is also available.

**134. Ohio Energy Workshop for Teachers**
**School of Natural Resources, Ohio State University**
**Contact: Robert Roth, Columbus, (614) 292-2265, FAX: (614) 292-7432, Internet: roth.3@osu.edu**

Sponsored by the Columbus Southern Power Company, the Ohio State University School of Natural Resources offers the Ohio Energy Workshop for Teachers of grades 6-12. The 2-week workshop provides participants with information on current energy technologies and methods of incorporating energy and environmental studies into classroom curricula. During the workshop, teachers meet with energy specialists from industry, academe, and government agencies who address environmental issues, energy economics, power production, and energy issues peculiar to Ohio. The workshop objectives are to provide opportunities for teachers that improve their understanding of Ohio energy sources, production, and use and to help them develop energy-related activities for the classroom. Participants, who receive graduate credit for the course, prepare study units that are relevant to their own classrooms. They are expected to present the units to teachers in their local school districts.

**135. Science Alliance**
**Cincinnati Museum of Natural History; Hoechst Marion Roussel**
**Contact: Kani Meyer, Cincinnati, (513) 287-7020, ext. 7065, FAX: (513) 287-7029, Internet: n/a**

Seven years ago, the Cincinnati Museum of Natural History joined in partnership with Hoechst Marion Roussel to form the Science Alliance to increase science literacy among grade 6-8 students. Working with teachers through workshops and networking, the alliance provides ideas, tools, and materials for hands-on activities. The goal of the alliance is to help teachers foster excitement about science among their students. The program reaches about 450 teachers each year.

**136. Science Inservice Committee**
**Miami Valley Laboratories, Procter & Gamble Co.; American Chemical Society**
**Contact: Richard Sunberg, Cincinnati, (513) 627-2230, FAX: (513) 627-1045, Internet: n/a**

The Science Inservice Committee is made up of employees of Procter & Gamble and members of the American Chemical Society who are dedicated to demonstrating the excitement of teaching and learning chemistry. Concerned with improving science education in elementary and secondary schools, members provide demonstrations for local teachers, develop chemistry-enrichment courses and career presentations, offer laboratory tours, and arrange donations of laboratory equipment to area schools.

**137. Hands-on Science in Trotwood**
**Department of Biological Sciences, Wright State University; Trotwood-Madison School District**
**Contact: Joyce Corban, Dayton, (513) 873-2699, FAX: (513) 873-3068, Internet: jcorban@desire.wright.edu**

Hands-On Science in Trotwood is a partnership between Wright State University and the Trotwood-Madison School District. The program results from a 3-year project funded by the National Science Foundation (NSF). The program successfully developed a new life-science and physical-science curriculum for the school system that includes hands-on activities, increased student literacy, and improvement of student problem-solving abilities. The program offered K-6 teachers year-round teacher-training and retraining opportunities that introduced strategies for developing discovery-based, rather than memory-based, lesson plans. In addition, the program provided each of the six elementary schools with full sets of modern, grade-appropriate teaching tools from GEMS, AIM, FOSS, and others. The program also funded dozens of field trips for hundreds of children, allowing them opportunities to visit museums, zoos, laboratories, and other science-related sites. The NSF-funded component of the program ended in summer 1994. However, the partnership between Wright State University and Trotwood-Madison schools continues and grows. Students continue to learn science from hands-on activities, taught by teachers motivated to use discovery-based techniques.

## 138. The MAT in the Biological Sciences
**Miami University**
**Contact: Robert G. Sherman, Oxford, (513) 529-6327, FAX: (513) 529-6900, Internet: n/a**

The MAT (Master of Arts in Teaching) in the Biological Sciences program operates with funding from the Howard Hughes Medical Institute and Miami University in Oxford, Ohio. The program offers courses and workshops primarily in the summer for high-school biology teachers. The offerings include lectures, laboratories, and field work focusing on biology content. The program is designed to update and broaden participants' content knowledge.

## 139. Petals & Wings: Natural and Environmental Make-It Take-It Workshop
**Lourdes College; the Toledo Botanical Garden; the University of Toledo**
**Contact: Sister Rosine Sobczak, Sylvania, (419) 885-3211, ext. 200, FAX: (419) 882-3786, Internet: n/a**

The Petals & Wings: Natural and Environmental Make-It Take-It Workshop for elementary-school teachers is a collaborative effort between Lourdes College, the Toledo Botanical Garden, and the University of Toledo. Workshop goals are to improve content knowledge, to foster new teaching strategies in line with the Ohio Science Model, to help teachers to network with each other, to develop curricular materials, to sensitize participants to issues that encourage better stewardship of the earth, and to introduce an interdisciplinary approach to teaching mathematics, science, and social studies. With funding from the Eisenhower Program and other grant providers and sponsorship by local organizations, the workshops of the last 5 years have attracted over 1,000 teachers/year locally from 90 school districts throughout Ohio; nationally from Georgia, Missouri, Wiscon-

sin, Massachusetts, Nevada, Michigan, and Indiana; and internationally from
Moscow, Russia.

## OREGON

**140. Estuary Study Program and Estuary Net**
**Oregon South Slough National Estuarine Research Reserve**
**Contact: Tom Gaskill, Charleston, (503) 888-5558, FAX: (503) 888-5559,**
**Internet: tgaskill@ednet1.osl.or.gov**

The Estuary Study Program has available four manuals and a reading guide for
grade 4-6, middle-school (on-site), and high-school (on-site and in-class) audiences. The overall program goals are to help teachers to relay knowledge about
estuaries to students—why estuaries are important and how they change because
of natural processes and human use. Teacher trainings are held on site before the
programs. Estuary Net is a new high-school curriculum designed around estuarine water-quality monitoring, research, and use of a telecommunication system.

**141. Industry Initiatives for Sciences and Math Education Oregon**
**Business-Education Compact**
**Contact: Pat Moore, Beaverton, (503) 627-5505, FAX: (503) 627-5533,**
**Internet: n/a**

Industry Initiatives for Sciences and Math Education (IISME) Oregon, operated
under the auspices of the Business-Education Compact, has offered internships at
research and industry sites to K-16 teachers since 1991. The program provides
paid mentor-directed work-site activities, opportunities to participate in an electronic network, and curriculum-development activities. To support participants,
the program also offers continuing networking opportunities for mentors and
teachers, continuing materials support, equipment loans, and classroom visits by
mentors. IISME Oregon is affiliated with the Oregon Graduate Institute and
Portland State University and is funded primarily by corporations, individuals,
and local education agencies. Coordinators have received additional funds to
replicate the program at other sites throughout Oregon.

**142. Marine Education/Sea Grant**
**Hatfield Marine Science Center**
**Contact: Vicki Osis, Newport, (503) 867-0257, FAX: (503) 867-0320,**
**Internet: osisv@ccmail.orst.edu**

The Marine Education/Sea Grant program at the Hatfield Marine Science Center
has involved teachers in marine-science field work and hands-on activities for
over 20 years. The program goals are to familiarize participants with marine-

science and general-science concepts. The program also aims to encourage the teaching of marine science in school districts throughout Oregon.

## PENNSYLVANIA

**143. Bullfrog Films, Inc.**
**Contact: Sieglinde Abromaitis, Oley, (800) 543-3764, FAX: (610) 370-1978, Internet: bullfrog@igc.apc.org**

Bullfrog Films, Inc. offers audiovisual materials for use in teacher inservice programs. A highlight of the materials is a film called, *The Great Horseshoe Crab Field Trip,* which outlines the benefits and mechanics of field trips. In the film, a teacher working at a school in the Harlem neighborhood of New York City makes learning about the biology of horseshoe crabs and the scientific method an exciting experience for his class of seventh-graders. The film offers insights on the benefits of a hands-on approach to learning and how to make the most of an educational field trip.

**144. Commonwealth Partnership**
**Franklin and Marshall College**
**Contact: Ellen Trout or Nancy Rogers, Lancaster, (717) 392-3403, FAX: (717) 399-4518, Internet: cwp_ert@admin.fandm.edu**

Established in 1985, the Commonwealth Partnership is a consortium of 12 independent colleges and universities in Pennsylvania. It seeks to advance and enrich precollege curriculum and instruction by linking teachers in Pennsylvania and surrounding states with each other and with college faculty. Motivation for the partnership's programs stems from the enthusiastic response given its *What We Expect: A Statement on Preparing for College*, issued in 1983. The partnership's latest project, IMAST (Integrated Mathematics and Science Teaching), is focused on the integration of these two subjects through the development of curriculum projects. Modeled on the processes used by mathematicians and scientists, these projects are problem-centered, inquiry-based, and articulated through all grade levels. The goals are to increase student interest and achievement in mathematics and science. IMAST expands the partnership's collaborative experience in two important ways: the inclusion of elementary-school teachers for the first time and the integration of two subjects. The program also continues the partnership's concentration on science. Members of the Commonwealth Partnership are Allegheny College, Bryn Mawr College, Bucknell University, Carnegie Mellon University, Chatham College, Dickinson College, Franklin and Marshall College, Gettysburg College, Haverford College, Lafayette College, Lehigh University, and Swarthmore College.

**145. Neurobiology and Behavior**
**Bryn Mawr College**
**Contact:  Paul Grobstein, Bryn Mawr, (610) 526-5098, FAX:  (610) 526-**
**5086, Internet:  pgrobste@brynmawr.edu or http://**
**serendip.brynmawr.edu**

During the summers of 1990, 1993, 1994, and 1995, Bryn Mawr College offered
2-week Brain and Behavior Institutes for teachers from Philadelphia schools.
The goal of the institutes, which were funded by the Howard Hughes Medical
Institute, was to provide teachers with a review of present understandings of
behavior in terms of nervous-system function and to involve teachers in discussion of the relevance of such material both for science curricula and for precollege
education generally. Participants in the institutes, scheduled to be offered again in
1996 and 1997, have formed a resource group, Brain/Behavior Link, and work
with college faculty during the year on a variety of curriculum-development and
exchange programs.

**146.  Leadership Institute in Science-Technology-Society Education**
**Pennsylvania State University; West Virginia University**
**Contact:  Peter Rubba, University Park, (814) 863-2937, FAX:  (814) 863-**
**7602, Internet:  par4@psuvm.psu.edu**

In August 1991, the National Science Foundation awarded a grant to Pennsylvania State University and West Virginia University to develop and support a cadre
of science-technology-society (STS) teacher-leaders in rural central Pennsylvania and northern West Virginia middle and junior high schools.  The two universities developed a 3-week Leadership Institute in Science-Technology-Society
Education at the University Park Campus of Pennsylvania State University.
Through a combination of lectures, discussions, demonstrations, and hands-on
activities, 30 participants addressed the sources and effects of global warming
and developed curriculum units for their classrooms.  In addition, they tried to
identify the components of STS instruction that led students to take action on
STS issues (acid rain, global warming, waste management, and species extinction).  The project ended in July 1995.

**147.  Pennsylvania Science Teacher Education Program**
**Center for Science and Technology Education**
**Contact:  Blake Andres, Clarion, (814) 782-6301, FAX:  (814) 782-6453,**
**Internet:  7142.1422@compuserve.com**

The Pennsylvania Science Teacher Education Program (PA STEP) was developed by the Pennsylvania Higher Education Assistance Agency to improve sci-

ence, mathematics, and technology education for all public-, private-, and parochial-school students in Pennsylvania. Headquartered in Shippenville, PA STEP served the needs of science and mathematics teachers across the state, as expressed by teachers themselves. PA STEP offered 40 graduate-level courses, tuition-free, to elementary- and secondary-school science teachers, as well as courses for elementary-school principal-teacher teams. Its began in 1983-1984, and over 13,000 teachers and administrators participated. The program ended September 1995.

**148. Pocono Environmental Education Center**
**Contact: John Padalino, Dingmans Ferry, (717) 828-2319, FAX: (717)**
**828-9695, Internet: jackpeec@aol.com**

The Pocono Environmental Education Center (PEEC) is a private, nonprofit organization that offers residential programs designed to educate participants about the environment. In cooperation with the National Park Service, PEEC holds 65 inservice workshops for K-12 teachers each year. The workshops aim to foster awareness of and concern for the environment through formal and informal educational experiences. In addition, the programs introduce participants to hands-on science-teaching methods, science curricula, and microcomputer-based laboratories. Among the teacher workshops offered in 1992 were Microchemistry Workshop, Science Olympiad Institute, Ten-Minute Field Trips, Environmental Concerns, and Improving School Climate Through Outdoor Environmental Education. PEEC is affiliated with the National Network for Environmental Education.

**149. Research Scientist Precollege Educator Partnership**
**School of Medicine, Temple University**
**Contact: N.P. Willett, Philadelphia, (215) 707-4905, FAX: (215) 707-7788,**
**Internet: willettn@astro.ocis.temple.edu**

The project matches K-12 science teachers in the Delaware Valley with university faculty to engage in 7-week summer sessions of lectures and in-depth research experiences. The objectives of the partnership are to improve the quality of K-12 education in biological and biomedical sciences; to improve the general level of science literacy of precollege teachers; to interest young people, especially women and minority-group members, in careers in the biological sciences and science education; and to improve the public perception of science, science teachers, and research scientists by illuminating the processes and accomplishments of science. During the summer, participants are expected to construct a teaching module that they take back to their schools. Participants receive a $4,000 stipend. A total of 38 modules have been developed and field tested.

**\*\*150. Biomedical Workshops for Precollege Educators**
**School of Medicine, Temple University**
**Contact: N.P. Willett, Philadelphia, (215) 707-4905, FAX: (215) 707-7788,**
**Internet: willettn@astro.ocis.temple.edu**

This program is a continuation of previous workshops held at Temple to develop and test teaching modules. Key features of the program include a lending library of small equipment and supplies and a voice-mail support system. Scientific subject matter presented includes concepts related to cell biology, genetics, microbiology, and molecular biology and development of an edible-cell structure featuring the stages of mitosis.

## TENNESSEE

**151. Naturalist and Educator Weeks**
**Great Smoky Mountains Institute at Tremont**
**Contact: Ken Voorhis or Nancy Condon, Townsend, (423) 448-6709, FAX:**
**(423) 448-9250, Internet: nancy_condon@smokiesnha.org**

Naturalist and Educator Weeks is a residential program addressing environmental education in the Great Smoky Mountains National Park. The program objectives are to expose K-12 teachers to current techniques and materials in environmental education and to familiarize them with the flora and fauna of the southern Appalachians through hands-on explorations. The program, which offers a number of scholarships to participants each year, is available for graduate credit.

## TEXAS

**152. CORD Applications in Biology/Chemistry, A Contextual Approach to Laboratory Science**
**Center for Occupational Research and Development**
**Contact: Jim Cockerill, Waco, (800) 972-2766, FAX: (817) 772-8972,**
**Internet: abcstaff@cord.org**

With funding and direction from a consortium of 46 state education agencies and the U.S. Department of Education, the Center for Occupational Research and Development (CORD) has developed a set of classroom-tested materials, CORD Applications in Biology/Chemistry (ABC), to be woven into existing science courses or taught as a stand-alone course. Developed by science and vocational teachers and CORD staff, the materials integrate biology and chemistry and present science in the context of major life issues: work, home, society, and the environment. The course objective is to involve students in hands-on learning activities that relate scientific principles to occupational, social, and personal issues. Consortium-member states provide various teacher-training opportunities to assist in the implementation of ABC materials. In Texas, CORD has a training center to house teacher workshops, train-the-trainer workshops, laboratories, and conferences. CORD also provides assistance to states in staff development and course implementation.

**153. Microbiology for Elementary Teachers, Microbiology Instruction for Middle Schools, and Microbiology Instruction for Secondary Schools**
**University of Texas Health Science Center**
**Contact:  Joan Ratner, San Antonio, (210) 567-3913, FAX:  (210) 567-6612, Internet:  n/a**

Through hands-on activities, institutes, and workshops, the University of Texas at San Antonio Alliance for Education illustrated how experiments can be used to teach biological and physical concepts to elementary-school students and how microbiology can be introduced at the middle-school level. The programs' goals were to enhance the knowledge, enthusiasm, and confidence of K-12 teachers in microbiology, biology, and physical science; expand their range of teaching strategies; improve student outcomes; encourage networking among scientists and teachers; and transfer science resources from the university to public schools. Program evaluations suggested an increase in knowledge among participating teachers and their students. Minority-group teachers and teachers of minority-group students were actively recruited. The Microbiology Instruction for Middle Schools program drew 94% of its teacher participants from classrooms of minority-group students. Funding for these programs was provided by the National Science Foundation, the Carnegie Corporation of New York, the Texas Coordinating Board, Eisenhower Mathematics and Science Education State Grants, and other sources.

**154. Museum Family Science**
**The Witte Museum of History, Science, and Humanities**
**Contact:  Marty Gonzalez, San Antonio, (210) 820-2181, FAX:  (210) 820-2187, Internet:  n/a**

Museum Family Science was a joint effort of the University of Texas at San Antonio Alliance for Education and the now-transformed San Antonio Museum Association. The program was designed to involve children, parents, and teachers in learning experiences that improve critical thinking skills. Program participants were selected from schools with high proportions of minority-group and lower-socioeconomic populations; participating teachers were selected from the minority groups represented. Funded by a grant from the National Science Foundation, the program aimed to interest students and their families in continuing science activities at home, in school, and in related community organizations. The materials are still available from the contact listed above. The Witte Museum is planning on opening the Science Treehouse in spring of 1997. It will have demonstration areas, a rooftop classroom, a below-groundlevel aquifer exhibit and special treehouse exhibition, and experimental space.

**155. Project MECCA**
**The Witte Museum of History, Science, and Humanities**
**Contact: Marty Gonzalez, San Antonio, (210) 820-2181, FAX: (210) 820-2187, Internet: n/a**

Project MECCA (Minority Education Collaborative for Children and Adults) aimed to motivate minority-group children's scientific thinking, to develop teacher skills for guiding children's scientific inquiry, and to assess children's growth in scientific observation and inferential thinking. In 1988, the program added a new goal: to design, develop, test, publish, and disseminate curriculum based on the model of the initial program. In addition, a component focused on parental involvement to introduce families to informal science-education programs at community resource centers. Project MECCA curriculum resources to grades 2-5 teachers are still available.

**156. Science Partners for Houston**
**Center for Education, Rice University; Houston Independent School District**
**Contact: Elnora Harcombe, Houston, (713) 285-5139, FAX: (713) 285-5459, Internet: nonie@ruf.rice.edu**

In collaboration with the Houston Independent School District and the Houston corporate-science community, the Center for Education at Rice University has established Science Partners for Houston. Dedicated to supporting laboratory-based science education in classrooms throughout Houston, the program has developed an interactive resource network that links middle-school teachers, Rice University faculty, and practicing scientists. In addition, the program has set up a Model Science Laboratory at an inner-city middle school, which acts as a site for various activities. Among other efforts, the project offers a scholarship program for eight middle-school science teachers to attend a Teacher Leadership Residency Program each year. Through seminars with Rice University faculty and area scientists, the residency program aims to help teachers to update their knowledge of science research, evaluate and develop science curricula, and present the teaching of science as an inquiry-based, constructivist process for student understanding in their classrooms. In addition, the laboratory offers evening and weekend opportunities, which have been taken advantage of by over 450 urban science teachers who instruct about 40,000 students each year.

**157. Harris County Alliance for Science, Mathematics and Technology Education**
**Baylor College of Medicine; Harris County Department of Education**
**Contact: Barbara Tharp, Houston, (713) 798-8200, FAX: (713) 798-8201, Internet: btharp@bcm.tmc.edu**

With funding from the National Science Foundation, Baylor College of Medicine and the Harris County (Texas) Department of Education have joined as partners to promote sustainable improvement in integrated science, mathematics, and technology education for all students in 15 Houston-area elementary schools. This goal will be accomplished by involving participating district and school administrators, teachers, and parents in the enhancement of science, mathematics, and technology education in the 15 targeted schools; training three two-teacher teams (six teachers) from each school each year to serve as lead teachers through participation in an intensive 4-week integrated science, mathematics, and technology institute for three consecutive summers and through workshops held during the school year (two per year); sponsoring school-year inservice sessions for all teachers in the targeted schools to be conducted by program participants; and providing the teacher teams with additional activities and guidance during the school year to increase the probability of success in achieving sustained improvement in integrated instruction. The program is projected to result in the professional development of 216 teachers.

**\*\*158. My Health, My World**
**Baylor College of Medicine**
**Contact: Barbara Tharp, Houston, (713) 798-8200, FAX: (713) 798-8201, Internet: btharp@bcm.tmc.edu**

Funded by the U.S. Department of Health and Human Services in 1994, My Health, My World is a curriculum-materials development project that targets elementary-school children in three learning environments: classroom, home, and community. The overall goal of the project is to promote a deeper understanding of environmental-health science concepts while conveying the excitement of "doing science" to students in grades K-4. This goal will be realized through the development of three instructional units developed by a team of scientists, educators, and science-education writers and editors, in close collaboration with active environmental-health researchers and other specialists. Each unit will consist of a science adventure story (in Spanish and English), a teachers' guide to accompanying classroom activities, and a colorful minimagazine (in Spanish and English) with appealing games and activities, which students will take home.

**\*\*159. Houston Science Education Partnership (BrainLink)**
**Baylor College of Medicine; Harris County Medical Society**
**Contact: Barbara Tharp, Houston, (713) 798-8200, FAX: (713) 798-8201,**
**Internet: btharp@bcm.tmc.edu**

The *BrainLink*[SM] project, a partnership of Baylor College of Medicine and the Harris County Medical Society, is an innovative science-education program targeted for three learning environments: classroom, home, and museum settings. Funded by the National Institutes of Health, *BrainLink*[SM] creates educational materials and activities that present the latest factual information about the brain and behavior and convey the excitement of "doing" science to teachers, parents, and elementary- to middle-school students. Workshops are held locally and nationally to assist teachers in using *BrainLink*[SM] materials. A national dissemination network established in 1994 supports additional *BrainLink*[SM] centers at Boston University School of Medicine, the University of California at San Francisco School of Medicine, and the University of Kentucky College of Medicine.

## UTAH

**160. Light From Life: Science in the Dark**
**Center for Integrated Science Education, University of Utah**
**Contact: Joe Andrade, Salt Lake City, (801) 581-4379, FAX: (801) 585-5361, Internet: joe.andrade@m.cc.utah.edu**

Designed for teachers who are insecure about teaching science, Light From Life: Science in the Dark uses bioluminescence (light produced by animals and plants) to familiarize K-12 teachers with principles of biology, chemistry, physics, and environmental sciences. The project provides inservice workshops for teachers, demonstrations and discussions, classroom visits by scientists, and networking opportunities. All participants receive materials for hands-on inquiry and discovery experiences and kits to take back to their classrooms. About 50 teachers participate in the program each year.

**161. National Energy Foundation**
**Contact: Edward Dalton, Salt Lake City, (801) 539-1406, FAX: (810) 539-1451, Internet: nef@xmission.com**

Since 1976, the National Energy Foundation (NEF) has offered teacher and student training programs in energy, natural resources, and K-12 environmental education. With support from corporations, government agencies, and the education community, NEF has involved over 55,000 teachers in workshops and field experiences to help to increase their energy-related knowledge, improve their teaching strategies and practices, and encourage sharing and networking. More recently, NEF has developed the NEF Academy, whereby teachers can earn university graduate credit for implementation of NEF programs. Many schools have incorporated NEF materials and practices into district guides and achievement programs. NEF continues to create innovative materials and programs to support and enrich education.

## VERMONT

### 162. GrowLab Regional Trainings
**National Gardening Association**
**Contact: Karen Reinhardt, Burlington, (802) 863-1308, FAX: (802) 863-5962, Internet: karen@nga.mhs.compuserve.com**

With funding from the National Science Foundation, the National Gardening Association held 15 training workshops to familiarize teachers with the GrowLab curriculum, a K-8 program that encourages the use of plants in the classroom. The goals of the training workshops were to develop the participants' cognitive and experiential understanding of the GrowLab curriculum and to assist them in determining helpful support structures for teachers in their own areas. Since the completion of the training workshops, program coordinators have offered followup support to participants who offer inservice activities in their local areas. Followup services include technical assistance and dissemination of GrowLab materials.

### 163. Inservice Teacher Workshops
**Vermont Institute of Natural Science**
**Contact: Jenna Guarino, Woodstock, (802) 457-2779, ext. 113, FAX: (802) 457- 4861, Internet: n/a**

The Vermont Institute of Natural Science (VINS) has offered professional-development programs for K-12 teachers for over 20 years. Focusing on natural history, these programs provide teachers with hands-on learning experiences, easy-to-use activities, and other resources for use with their students. Through workshops and field work, the programs aim to increase participants' knowledge of natural history, improve their repertoire of classroom activities, enhance student learning, develop and compile curricular materials, and help teachers to network with each other. Participants are encouraged to use VINS as a resource throughout their teaching careers.

## VIRGINIA

**164. Virginia Bay Team**
**Virginia Institute of Marine Science; College of William and Mary**
**Contact:  Lee Larkin, Gloucester Point, (804) 642-7172, FAX:  (804) 642-7161, Internet:  larkin@vims.edu**

The Bay Team Program was organized in 1985 to assist K-12 teachers in teaching about Virginia's marine and estuarine resources.  Two experienced teachers staff the Bay Team project and visit schools throughout Virginia demonstrating teaching strategies and disseminating new resources and information.  Associated activities include curriculum development and teacher-training workshops.  The Bay Team teaches in more than 700 classrooms each year and has provided instruction for some 140,000 students and their teachers since the program's inception.  The Bay Team is financially supported by the Commonwealth of Virginia.

**165.  Discovery Quest**
**Virginia Living Museum**
**Contact:  Peter Money, Newport News, (804) 595-1900, FAX:  (804) 595-4897, Internet:  n/a**

Based at the Virginia Living Museum, Discovery Quest involves K-12 science teachers in a summer program of hands-on science activities that emphasize the use of live animals, artifacts, and specimens.  The goals of the program are to encourage teachers to incorporate hands-on activities and field experiences into their science teaching, to increase their content knowledge, and to involve them in the development of curricular materials.  With funding from the National Science Foundation, Discovery Quest has provided teachers with lectures, demonstrations, workshops, discussion, and field work for 5 years.

**\*\*166.  Inservice programs**
**National Association of Biology Teachers**
**Contact:  Mary Louise Bellamy or Kathy Frame, Reston, (703) 471-1134 or (800) 406-0775, FAX:  (703) 435-5582, Internet:  n/a**

The National Association of Biology Teachers (NABT) offers inservice programs to hundreds of teachers each year.  The primary goal of these workshops is to bring biology teachers together to share classroom ideas and experiences, become familiar with new technology and diverse methods of teaching in the field, and improve student outcomes in their classrooms.  One such new program is the Shoestring Biotechnology Workshop, which requires each participant to establish a partnership with an industrial scientist and another educator to work together throughout a school year. A stipend, expenses, and continuing-education credit will be provided. NABT also publishes manuals to promote hands-on laboratory experiments, including "Biology on a Shoestring," "Neuroscience Classroom and Laboratory Activities," and "Working with DNA and Bacteria in Precollege Science Classrooms." NABT receives funding from various sources.

### 167. Teacher Intern Program
**Merck & Co.**
**Contact: Suzanne Auckerman, Elkton, (703) 298-4873, FAX: (703) 298-4194, Internet: auckerfp@merck.com**

Merck & Co. is a chemical and pharmaceutical manufacturing company with a wide range of operations. Among employees, scientific expertise is mainly in chemical engineering, chemistry, and microbiology. The company offers shadow programs, during which middle- and high-school students are matched with employees for a 1-day site visit at Merck. The Teacher Intern Program provides teachers with the opportunity to spend 2 weeks at Merck in activities that provide an overview of the facility. A second project develops business-education partnerships between K-12 education, higher education, adult education, and business and industry. Merck's goals are to improve educational quality, resource accessibility, educational access, and workforce preparation for persons in the greater Shenandoah Valley region. Additional outreach includes career fairs, equipment donations to schools, and classroom visits by Merck scientists.

### 168. Teacher Training Institutes
**National Association of Partners in Education, Inc.**
**Contact: Janet Cox, Alexandria, (703) 836-4880, FAX: (703) 836-6941, Internet: n/a**

The National Association of Partners in Education is a nonprofit membership organization that serves the schools, businesses, education, community groups, and individual volunteers that work together to help students achieve educational excellence. Specific projects include development of resource materials, a clearinghouse on partnerships, regional conferences, teacher-training institutes focused on the effective use of volunteers in the classroom, and other education-related initiatives. The training component often addresses how to develop partnership programs that target specific disciplines, such as science.

### 169. Fellowships in Biology and Chemistry
**Biology Department, College of William and Mary**
**Contact: Sharon Broadwater, Williamsburg, (804) 221-2216, FAX: (804) 221-6483, Internet: stbroa@facstaff.wm.edu**

With funding from the Howard Hughes Medical Institute, the Biology Department of the College of William and Mary offered a summer research program, Fellowships in Biology and Chemistry, to four junior- and senior-high-school teachers. The program engaged teachers in individual research projects with biology or chemistry faculty members for a 6-week period. Participating teachers were given a list of faculty members and research topics from which to choose. Although fellowship responsibilities focused on research, each participant was expected to complete a paper or offer a seminar on a project topic. In addition, the teachers spent 1-2 hours per day at the Governor's School on campus during 4 weeks of the fellowship. Stipends of $3,000 were provided. The project is looking for other sources of support to permit it to continue.

**170. Topics in Biology**
**Biology Department, College of William and Mary**
**Contact: Sharon Broadwater, Williamsburg, (804) 221-2216, FAX: (804) 221-6483, Internet: stbroa@facstaff.wm.edu**

Topics in Biology is a series of courses designed by faculty in the Biology Department of the College of William and Mary. The project objective was to update middle- and high-school teachers on trends and technologies in genetics and cell biology. Admitted on a first-come-first-served basis, 16-18 teachers attended the program each year. They received one graduate credit for each course. With funding from the Howard Hughes Medical Institute, the program provided lectures, seminars, demonstrations, workshops, and discussions. The project is looking for other funding sources.

**171. Introduction to Microscopy**
**Central Virginia Governor's School for Science and Technology**
**Contact: Cheryl Lindeman, Lynchburg, (804) 582-1104, FAX: (804) 239-4140, Internet: clindema@pen.k12.va.us**

The Central Virginia Governor's School for Science and Technology offers workshops for K-12 life-science teachers as needed in microscopy. Through hands-on laboratory activities, they explore the educational applications of microscopy using video microscopy equipment and a transmission electron microscope. Participants are given the opportunity to plan and record their own video tapes of living organisms and to make black-and-white prints of electron micrographs.

**\*\*172. Student-Centered Learning Using BIOQUEST Computer Simulations**
**Central Virginia Governor's School for Science and Technology**
**Contact: Cheryl Lindeman, Lynchburg, (804) 582-1104, FAX: (804) 239-4140, Internet: clindema@pen.k12.va.us**

High-School life-science teachers explore biological concepts, using computer simulations from the BIOQUEST library. The activities parallel classroom management for student-centered learning. Each group poses problems, solves problems, and persuades peers, using the computer as a tool. The simulations involve topics in genetics, physiology, and ecology.

**\*\*173. Utilizing Technology to Enhance Learning**
**Central Virginia Governor's School for Science and Technology**
**Contact: Tom Morgan, Lynchburg, (804) 582-1104, FAX: (804) 239-4140,**
**Internet: tmorgan@pen.k12.va.us**

As computer technologies become more prevalent in schools, it is essential that educators harness the capabilities of the technologies to enhance student learning. Participants in this hands-on seminar learn a simple strategy to use in planning and evaluating implementations of computer technologies to ensure that the technologies are being used to support student learning. The generic strategy derived from instructional design principles can be used for all grade levels and in all subjects.

**\*\*174. Using Computers in the Science Laboratory**
**Central Virginia Governor's School for Science and Technology**
**Contact: Bill Bishop, Lynchburg, (804) 582-1104, FAX: (804) 239-4140,**
**Internet: bbishop@cvgs.k12.va.us**

The Central Virginia Governor's School (CVGS) for Science and Technology offers this workshop to middle-school and high-school science teachers. Participants explore, through hands-on activities, how computers are used at CVGS to provide a variety of learning experiences. Emphasis is placed on using computers as tools for data collection, data analysis, accessing information on the Internet, and simulations of situations not suitable for actual experimentation in the high-school laboratory.

**\*\*175. Selecting and Using Data Collection and Analysis Technology for**
**Math and Science**
**Central Virginia Governor's School for Science and Technology**
**Contact: Bill Bishop or Jane Simms, Lynchburg, (804) 582-1104, FAX:**
**(804) 239-4140,**
**Internet: bbishop@cvgs.k12.va.us or jsimms@cvgs.k12.va.us**

This workshop is offered for teachers and administrators in mathematics and science for grades 9-12. It is an introduction to calculator- and computer-based data-collection sensors, TI-82 sensors, and data-analysis software. Guidelines for selecting and using computer-interfaced data-collection sensors, TI-82 CBl sensors, and data-analysis software in mathematics and science classes are presented through a variety of hands-on activities.

## WASHINGTON

### 176. "Science in a Box" Elementary Science Curriculum
### Olympic Educational Service District 114
### Contact: Brian Bennett, Bremerton, (360) 692-3239, FAX: same,
### Internet: bbennett@orca.esd114.wednet.edu

The Olympic Educational Service District 114 (ESD 114) "Science in a Box" supports the idea that an activity-based program should be the core of elementary-school science curricula. The program offers at least four subject kits at each grade level, K-6. The kit lessons teach students science-process skills through hands-on lessons covering the earth, life, and physical sciences. All kits include a teacher guide, student worksheets, and consumable and nonconsumable materials for presenting 8-10 lessons to classrooms of 32 students. The Olympic ESD 114 Science Kit Center provides the material-support system to restock and maintain the kits and provides training opportunities for the teachers who use the program. Through using and restocking each kit several times during the school year, the Science Kit Center is able to provide an efficient and cost-effective method of supporting elementary-school science education. In addition, the Science Kit Center staff provides resources, technical assistance, and in-class model lessons and demonstrations for region teachers and students.

### 177. Practical and Creative Ways to Strengthen Student Achievement in Science
### Puget Sound Educational Service District
### Contact: Ron Thompson, Mercer Island, (206) 232-8042, FAX: same,
### Internet n/a

This program will enable participants to modify their current science programs to meet the new national science recommendations. Emphasis is on adding award-winning problem-solving laboratory activities to existing courses. A hands-on workshop also provides a variety of laboratory-performance-based assessment tools for evaluating student progress. This offering is appropriate for science teachers of grades 3-12. Participants will receive student-ready activities specific for their grade levels. Some of the curriculum materials used are from a 1-year high-school biology curriculum titled "Biology: As Scientific Inquiry."

**178. Padilla Bay Teacher Workshops**
**Western Washington University**
**Contact: G. Alexander, Mount Vernon, (360) 428-1558, FAX: (360) 428-1491, Internet: alex@padillabay.gov**

Through a series of half-day workshops, K-12 teachers gain experience in estuarine ecology, discuss the importance of problem-solving in environmental education, and learn how to integrate topics into their classroom curriculum.

**179. Project WILD**
**Washington Department of Wildlife**
**Contact: Margaret Tudor, Olympia, (360) 902-2808, FAX: (360) 902-2157, Internet: tudormtt@dfw.wa.gov**

For 8 years, the state of Washington's Department of Wildlife has sponsored Project WILD, a course developed by and for K-12 teachers with input from biologists. Results of this grass-roots effort to improve teaching and student outcomes include district adoption of a curriculum for sixth-graders, the development of over 50 habitat projects, and widespread use of activities derived from the course. The program also produces a newsletter and issues grants to develop school habitat programs. There is also a nature mapping program in which data collected on fish, wildlife, and habitats can be contributed to the state biological database.

**180. Science-Education Partnership**
**Fred Hutchinson Cancer Research Center**
**Contact: Nancy Hutchison, Seattle, (206) 667-4486, FAX: (206) 667-6525, Internet: nhutchi@fred.fhcrc.org**

To help teachers introduce current biomedical research concepts into the classroom, the Fred Hutchinson Cancer Research Center developed a summer program in 1991 to pair middle- and high-school science teachers with scientists at the center, local biotechnology companies, and the University of Washington. The program immerses teachers in hands-on, current research techniques through laboratory experiments and aims to familiarize them with inquiry-based learning. Teachers participate in a spring workshop, a 2-week summer immersion experience, and followup days during the academic year. For their participation, teachers receive a $500 stipend, University of Washington credits, opportunities to borrow biotechnology-laboratory equipment kits, and classroom visits from the scientist-mentors. Initial funding for the program came from the center; current funding is from the Howard Hughes Medical Institute, the Discuren Charitable Foundation, and other local foundations. The McEachern Foundation, for example, helped to establish a teaching laboratory and equipment kits to loan to teachers.

### 181. The University of Washington Science/Mathematics Project
### College of Education, University of Washington
### Contact: Carole Kubota, Seattle, (206) 543-6636, FAX: (206) 543-8439, Internet: kubota@u.washington.edu

The University of Washington Science/Mathematics Project is a 2-year graduate program leading to a master of education degree in science or mathematics education. The project links people working in industry, public schools, and the university to integrate work experience in science and mathematics with academic study and leadership training. The project is supported by the local business community. The primary goal is to foster leadership skills among teachers of science and mathematics. Participants partake in leadership training institutes and seminars, a master of education program that includes advanced study in mathematics and science, a collegial team that includes an experienced science or mathematics teacher to answer questions and provide professional support, and a summer internship in a business or industry. Fellows are chosen on the basis of their leadership potential, teaching ability, and interpersonal skills.

## WEST VIRGINIA

### 182. Leadership Institute in Science-Technology-Society Education
### Pennsylvania State University; West Virginia University
### Contact: Peter Rubba, University Park, (814) 863-2937, FAX: (814) 863-7602, Internet: par4@psuvm.psu.edu

In August 1991, the National Science Foundation awarded a grant to Pennsylvania State University and West Virginia University to develop and support a cadre of science-technology-society (STS) teacher-leaders in rural central Pennsylvania and northern West Virginia middle and junior high schools. The two universities developed a 3-week Leadership Institute in Science-Technology-Society Education at the University Park Campus of Pennsylvania State University. Through a combination of lectures, discussions, demonstrations, and hands-on activities, 30 participants addressed the sources and effects of global warming and developed curriculum units for their classrooms. In addition, they tried to identify the components of STS instruction that led students to take action on STS issues (acid rain, global warming, waste management, and species extinction). The project ended in July 1995.

## WISCONSIN

**183. Biotechnology Inservice Program for Secondary Life Science Teachers and Agricultural-Education Teachers**
**University of Wisconsin-River Falls**
**Contact: Karen Klyczek, River Falls, (715) 425-3364, FAX: (715) 425-3785, Internet: karen.k.klyczek@uwrf.edu**

In response to a needs assessment of area high-school teachers, the University of Wisconsin-River Falls has been offering a 3-week workshop on life-science and agricultural education to increase biotechnology literacy and assist in the development of new classroom materials. Funded by money from the Eisenhower Mathematics and Science Education State Grant and the National Science Foundation, the program, now in its sixth year, encourages continuing activities among workshop participants during the school year.

**184. Teachers as Change Agents: An Integrated Curriculum**
**Cooperative Educational Service Agency 11**
**Contact: Juliette Vajgrt, Elmwood, (715) 986-2020, FAX: (715) 986-2040, Internet: n/a**

With funding from the Wisconsin Department of Public Instruction, this project helps school districts in rural northwestern Wisconsin to develop an issue-based, rather than textbook-driven, K-12 biotechnology curriculum. The objectives are to design and carry out environmentally oriented biotechnology school-community projects in the schools, to foster leadership among teachers, and to support the districts' teachers in implementing the new curriculum. In addition, the project facilitator helps teachers to develop effective procedures for evaluating pilot-teaching strategies and secure input from area universities and private industries.

**185. Institute for Multicultural Science Education/Teacher to Teacher Program**
**Center for Biology Education, University of Wisconsin-Madison**
**Contact: Lisa Wachtel, Madison, (608) 262-5266, FAX: (608) 262-6801, Internet: lwachtel@macc.wisc.edu**

With funding from the National Science Foundation and the University of Wisconsin-Madison (UWM), the UWM Center for Biology Education established the Institute for Multicultural Science Education in 1990. The institute's goals have been to provide K-12 teachers with opportunities to learn about the strengths and needs of minority-group students, to develop strategies for implementing a problem-solving approach to science teaching, to introduce and encourage cooperative-learning experiences among teachers and students, to recruit teams of teachers working at the same school (in addition to individuals) to the program, and to encourage the incorporation of new techniques into teachers' daily teaching strategies. To accomplish these goals, the institute offers a 5-year program made up of two 10-day summer sessions and numerous academic-year activities. Through curriculum-development activities, discussion, workshops, demonstrations, and lectures, the program emphasizes the importance of exploring issues of multicultural understanding and of teaching science as a process of investigation.

### 186. Science Workshops for Elementary and Middle School Teachers
**University of Wisconsin-Madison; Madison Education Extension Programs**
**Contact: Linda Shriberg, Madison, (608) 262-4477, FAX: (608) 265-5813, Internet: shriberg@mail.soemadison.wisc.edu**

The partnership of the University of Wisconsin-Madison School of Education and Madison Education Extension Programs offers a number of workshops in the biological sciences for classroom and science teachers of K-12 students. All workshops have a science focus but cover a variety of formats, such as infusing science concepts across the curriculum (how to learn about science in mathematics, language arts, social studies, and other subjects); meeting national and state guidelines in science education (e.g., becoming familiar with the Benchmarks for Science Literacy and Science for All Americans); exploring one science subject intensively (e.g., the rain forest, whales, the timber wolf, cranes, and other endangered species); tapping into science resources on the Internet (e.g., the Protein Databank, the National Library of Agriculture, and the Smithsonian Institution); learning about the research process in science (observation, hypotheses, investigation, and conclusions; how to write a science report; and tracking animals through radio telemetry); and general subjects in the biological sciences (e.g., environmental science, DNA and genetics, and biotechnology). The workshops also are offered to learning and curriculum coordinators, coordinators of programs for talented and gifted children, biology and life-sciences teachers, and librarians. Generally, attendees do not need to have a science background to participate in the programs.

### 187. Wisconsin Fast Plants
**Department of Plant Pathology, University of Wisconsin-Madison**
**Contact: Coe Williams, Madison, (608) 263-2634, FAX: (608) 263-2626, Internet: fastplants@calshp.cals.wisc.edu or http://fastplants/cals.wisc.edu**

Funded primarily by the National Science Foundation, the Wisconsin Fast Plants program offers a nationwide professional-development program. Based at the University of Wisconsin-Madison in the Department of Plant Pathology, the program disseminates instructional materials on rapid-cycling Fast Plants developed by a university research scientist for research purposes. The program sponsors regional teams of teachers and scientists to lead workshops on the use of these plants for investigative studies in plant growth, life spirals, inheritance, ecology, and plant technology. Workshop goals include encouraging teachers to learn science by doing it themselves, helping them to make their own experiments with the low-cost and recyclable materials, and helping to foster in them a sense of ownership about their classroom science projects. Additional services include the availability of instructional materials, a biannual newsletter, troubleshooting tips, slides and scripts, publications, and opportunities for networking among scientists and teachers at all levels.

**188. Wisconsin Teacher Enhancement Program in Biology**
**University of Wisconsin-Madison**
**Contact: Ruth Owens, Madison, (608) 262-1006, FAX: (608) 262-2976,**
**Internet: reowens@facstaff.wisc.edu**

Since 1985, the Wisconsin Teacher Enhancement Program in Biology, at the University of Wisconsin-Madison has provided a summer institute for teachers at the elementary-, middle-, and high-school levels. The Wisconsin Teacher Enhancement Program in Biology: Summer Institute offers quality education in the biological sciences. Teachers are provided an opportunity to review and update their science education through modules offered in a variety of subjects, including human genetics; molecular and cell biology; plant, animal, and environmental biology; and elementary science. Courses are offered in systemic-change issues, special education, and alcohol- and other drug-abuse issues. The summer institute offers a variety of 1- and 2-week modules during a 10-week period. All modules emphasize an inquiry-based, problem-solving approach to science. Activities developed by participants during each module reflect course content and can later be used in the teachers' classrooms to help to make biology exciting, relevant, and understandable for students. Teachers earn credits at the graduate level.

**\*\*189. BioNet**
**Waunakee High School**
**Contact: Lynn Gilchrist, Madison, (608) 265-3168, FAX: n/a, Internet:**
**lgilchrist@macc.wisc.edu**

Organized in 1991, BioNet aims to provide a forum for area biology teachers to meet statewide and share ideas and activities related to teaching biology and to establish communication and professional relationships with university biology teachers to see where other biology teachers work. BioNet, funded by a grant from the Center for Biology Education at the University of Wisconsin-Madison, meets four times per year at various high schools. Each of the 12 BioNet regions conduct two to four meetings per year.

**190. The Wisconsin Society of Science Teachers**
**Contact: Lynn Gilchrist, Madison, (608) 265-3168, FAX: n/a, Internet:**
**lgilchrist@macc.wisc.edu**

The Wisconsin Society of Science Teachers (WSST) is dedicated to the promotion and improvement of science education in Wisconsin. As the state science-teachers organization, it serves pre-K through grade 16 teachers. Membership numbers 2,000. This active organization provides teachers with the latest information in science education primarily through forums, newsletters, and an annual convention. It also has a foundation dedicated to the promotion of science education in Wisconsin.

# Professional-Development Programs, Organized by Grade

## K-6
3, 5, 41, 42, 44, 49, 67, 72, 83, 86, 92, 94, 106, 118, 120, 121, 124, 130, 139, 148, 157, 158, 176

## K-8
9, 23, 32, 35, 47, 52, 101, 111, 138, 159, 159, 186

## 6-8
26, 28, 33, 51, 53, 99, 113, 119, 123, 135, 140, 146, 156

## K-12
2, 10, 11, 13, 14, 17, 18, 19, 20, 24, 25, 27, 30, 31, 36, 38, 39, 40, 41, 42, 43, 45, 49, 54, 55, 60, 62, 63, 66, 72, 74, 76, 78, 79, 80, 81, 85, 88, 89, 91, 93, 97, 102, 107, 127, 133, 134, 136, 137, 140, 141, 142, 143, 147, 148, 149, 151, 152, 153, 154, 160, 161, 163, 164, 165, 166, 167, 168, 171, 173, 178, 179, 184, 185, 187, 188

## 9-12
12, 13, 15, 16, 46, 50, 52, 56, 57, 69, 70, 71, 82, 84, 87, 90, 93, 95, 96, 104, 105, 108, 109, 112, 122, 114, 115, 116, 117, 125, 128, 129, 132, 144, 145, 172, 175, 183, 189,

## 7-12
4, 6, 15, 24, 29, 34, 35, 59, 61, 65, 68, 77, 107, 112, 113, 126, 131, 138, 169, 170, 174, 177, 180

# Professional-Development Programs, Organized by Subject Matter

**All sciences K-12:**
2, 18, 19, 27, 30, 33, 75, 89, 91, 105, 130, 147

**Agriculture and soil ecology**:
3, 56, 99, 126, 183, 187

**Animal use in science education:**
85, 105, 140, 148, 174

**Atmospheric sciences:**
23, 42, 43

**Bioethics:**
6, 59

**Chemistry:**
31, 53, 136

**Computer use:**
24, 35, 51, 109, 172, 173, 174, 175, 177

**Cross-disciplinary interaction:**
38, 41, 88, 129

# Committee's Methods

The committee made extensive efforts to identify a broad range of professional-development activities in the sciences at the K-12 level. In the winter of 1992, the committee advertised requests for information in a variety of journals and newsletters of professional teacher and scientific organizations. It sent the same request directly to the members of some organizations and to principal investigators of programs sponsored by federal agencies and private foundations. It also posted the request electronically on electronic bulletin boards. Almost 200 programs responded to our requests for information. Those programs represented a wide range of activities—short, topical workshops, 1- to 3-week institutes during the summer, lecture series during the academic year, and programs designed to influence systemic reform. The activities were housed in numerous places—university science departments, schools or colleges of education, community colleges, museums and science and technology centers, nature preserves, professional societies, and industrial settings. A list of the programs is found in Appendix A.

An informal questionnaire was sent to all programs that responded to the committee's request for information. The questionnaire was designed to collect more specific information about each program but was not designed to be used to draw statistical inferences from the data. It was impossible to conduct a thorough review of all programs that responded to the questionnaire. Instead, committee members reviewed the questionnaires and selected a number of programs for followup telephone calls and a smaller number for site visits during the summer of 1992. Programs that were selected for further review had the following characteristics: each had been in existence for a number of years, each had some type of evaluation process, and each used the results of the evaluations to revise and improve itself. During the visits, committee members met with both program directors and teachers who had participated in the program. In several instances, committee members talked directly with teachers separately from the program directors.

The generalizations about professional-development programs found in this report are derived from both the committee members' professional experiences and the information gathered from programs around the country. The committee recognizes that many of its conclusions and recommendations are not based on empirical evidence, because such data do not exist. Instead, in the absence of empirical data, the committee drew useful conclusions and inferences from information learned from both program directors and teachers who participated in programs. The committee's intention is to draw attention to characteristics of programs that seem to be having an impact on the professional lives of teachers and therefore on the teaching and learning of the nation's students.

**NATIONAL RESEARCH COUNCIL**
**COMMISSION ON LIFE SCIENCES**
**BOARD ON BIOLOGY**
Committee on Biology Teacher Inservice Programs

**QUESTIONNAIRE FOR SCIENCE INSERVICE PROGRAMS**

**FEBRUARY 1992**

The goal of the National Research Council's Committee on Biology Teacher Inservice Programs is to identify successful biology inservice programs and assess the reasons for their success in order to make recommendations for improving opportunities for teachers' continuing education.

The purpose of this questionnaire is to determine some characteristics of science inservice programs at the K-12 level, not only biology inservice programs. Your responses will remain confidential.

Answer each question as completely as possible. If more space is needed, please attach additional pages. Skip any questions you feel are not relevant to your program.

PLEASE FILL OUT ONE QUESTIONNAIRE BOOKLET FOR EACH INSERVICE PROGRAM. YOU MAY MAKE A COPY OF THIS BOOKLET FOR EACH ADDITIONAL INSERVICE PROGRAM.

**Name of program:** _____

**Address:** _____

_____

**Name of respondent:** _____

**Telephone number:** _____

*Inservice Questionnaire, page 1*

**1.** **What are the distinctive features of your program?**

**2.** **What has been the most significant impact of this program?**

**3.** **Has your program been institutionalized within a local school system?**

**4.** **How does your program encourage participation by underrepresented populations or minority groups?**

**5.** **Is teacher inservice a component of a larger program?**

## PROGRAM DESCRIPTION

6. **Who initiated the teacher inservice program?** *(Circle the letter(s) of your answer)*
   - a. K-12 teachers
   - b. school or system administrator
   - c. college/university science faculty
   - d. college/university education faculty
   - e. college/university administrators
   - f. business or industry scientists
   - g. other (specify)_____

7. How long has the teacher inservice program been in operation? _____

8. How many teachers participate in the inservice program per year? _____

9. **How are participants in the inservice program selected?** *(Circle the letter(s) of your answer)*
   - a. mandatory...all teachers must participate
   - b. all science teachers
   - c. self-selected
   - d. recommended
   - e. other (specify) _____

10. How many hours of instruction does each teacher receive during the inservice program?

    _____

11. What is the average direct cost for each participant in the teacher inservice program?

    _____

12. What is the total direct cost of the teacher inservice program? _____

13. What percentage of funding for the teacher inservice program comes from each of the following sources?
    - ____ a. federal agencies (specify)_____
    - ____ b. state department of education
    - ____ c. state department of higher education
    - ____ d. private foundations and individuals
    - ____ e. corporations
    - ____ f. local education agencies
    - ____ g. colleges and universities
    - ____ h. other (specify)_____

14. **Does the local school system provide any of the following:** *(Circle the letter(s) of your answer)*
    - a. operating funds for the program
    - b. in-kind contributions
    - c. released time for participants
    - d. direct program support
    - e. pay for substitute teachers
    - f. none of the above

15. On a scale of 0 to 5, how important is each of the following goals to the teacher inservice program? For each item, enter a number (0 = least important; 5 = most important).
    - _____ a. improve content knowledge of the participants
    - _____ b. increase the range of teaching strategies for the participants
    - _____ c. improve student outcomes
    - _____ d. network teachers with scientists
    - _____ e. network teachers with each other
    - _____ f. develop curricular materials
    - _____ g. change teacher behavior
    - _____ h. other (specify)_____

16. What is the primary unit of participation in the teacher inservice program?
    *(Circle only one letter)*
    - a. individual teachers
    - b. teams of teachers
    - c. entire school or department
    - d. entire school system
    - e. other (specify) _____

17. Which of the following components are included in the teacher inservice program?
    *(Circle the letter(s) of your answer)*
    - a. demonstrations
    - b. pedagogy
    - c. scientific knowledge
    - d. designing and conducting investigations
    - e. field work
    - f. mentorship training
    - g. curriculum assessment
    - h. curriculum development
    - i. hands-on investigations
    - j. lectures
    - k. discussions
    - l. access to additional information

18. What percentage of time is spent on each of the following activities in the teacher inservice program?
    - _____ a. lecture/seminar
    - _____ b. demonstrations
    - _____ c. workshops (hands on)
    - _____ d. discussion
    - _____ e. computer instruction
    - _____ f. field work
    - _____ g. other (specify)_____

19. Does the teacher inservice program involve any of the following computer elements?
    *(Circle the letter(s) of your answer)*
    - a. software (existing)
    - b. software (developing)
    - c. interactive video
    - d. computer networking
    - e. telecommunications
    - f. CD-ROM
    - g. multimedia
    - h. other (specify)_____

20. **Which follow-up activities are part of the teacher inservice program?**
    *(Circle the letter(s) of your answer)*
    a. classroom visits by scientists
    b. networking with teachers
    c. networking with scientists
    d. return to institution where inservice activity occurred
    e. equipment loans
    f. additional experiments
    g. second/third year access to inservice activity
    h. compiling of materials developed by teachers
    i. mentoring
    j. ongoing materials support
    k. seminars, symposia, etc.
    l. funding for purchasing materials
    m. no follow-up activities

21. **Use the table below to indicate which of the following groups or agencies are involved or participate in the teacher inservice program and how each has participated.** *(Check all that apply)*

| | designing the program | developing lab materials | actual instruction during the program | providing equipment/materials | funding | providing space |
|---|---|---|---|---|---|---|
| parents | | | | | | |
| K-12 teachers | | | | | | |
| university scientists | | | | | | |
| industrial scientists | | | | | | |
| faculty in schools of education | | | | | | |
| school administrators | | | | | | |
| K-12 students | | | | | | |
| undergraduates | | | | | | |
| extension service agents | | | | | | |
| government agency personnel | | | | | | |
| educational societies/ organizations | | | | | | |
| community service agencies | | | | | | |
| scientific societies | | | | | | |
| foundations | | | | | | |
| private sector | | | | | | |

## PROGRAM EVALUATION

22. Use the table below to indicate what effects of the teacher inservice program you have measured and by what method(s). *(Check all that apply)*

| | questionnaire | observation | interview | test | other |
|---|---|---|---|---|---|
| changes in knowledge base of teachers | | | | | |
| changes in teacher behavior in the classroom | | | | | |
| changes in student learning | | | | | |
| changes in content of biology curriculum | | | | | |
| changes in colleagues of participants | | | | | |
| changes in administrators | | | | | |

If you have indicated that you use other methods to collect data, please summarize your methods here:

23. Estimate the level of awareness/knowledge about the teacher inservice program in the following individuals or groups in your local school district. For each item, enter a number (0 = no awareness; 5 = high level of awareness).

     ____ a. superintendent
     ____ b. district administrative staff
     ____ c. principals
     ____ d. teachers
     ____ e. parents
     ____ f. students
     ____ g. president of local teachers union
     ____ h. scientists

24. Have any elements of the teacher inservice program been adapted or used by others?

*Thank you for your time and effort. Please return the completed questionnaire to:*

*Board on Biology*
*NAS 356*
*National Research Council*
*2101 Constitution Avenue, NW*
*Washington, DC 20418*

# APPENDIX C

# Glossary

**Administrators**

Persons who provide academic or operational leadership beyond the classroom in any educational institution from kindergarten to grade 12 and at colleges and universities.

**Curriculum**

A set of experiences designed to help students to learn a body of concepts and supporting skills and knowledge; usually includes consideration of learners' experiences and understanding, current level of awareness, and factors likely to enhance their learning. Emphasis depends on context.

In the context of a school district or set of districts, such as a state, curriculum can be the body of learning that the schools provide for students. The conceptual framework and program themes are identified using suggestions for connecting the curriculum at various grade levels and in various subject contexts.

In the context of a teacher in an individual classroom, curriculum refers to specific concepts to be taught. In addition to concepts to be learned, the classroom curriculum will offer specific experiences to illustrate these concepts, opportunities for data collection to verify them, student-assessment materials and activities, and suggested experiences to augment conceptual understanding. A complete curriculum guide includes resource lists of laboratory and instructional technology, materials, and local field trips.

### Educator

A person involved in assisting others to learn at any level of the educational system. *Science educators* are persons whose educational endeavors are concentrated on the teaching of the natural sciences. *Teacher educators* are persons who assist college and university students in academic or pedagogic preparation for a career in teaching.

### Individual-Based Programs

Professional-development programs whose first goal is to enhance the abilities of individual teachers. In contrast, the goal of *systemic programs* (defined in Chapter 6) is to extend exemplary teaching and learning to larger groups, such as a department, a school, a school system, a district, a state, or an entire educational system.

### Pedagogy

Includes the complexities of educational theories and teaching strategies that facilitate the process of communicating subject matter, concepts, and skills from teacher to student through learning experiences.

### Professional Development

Term chosen by the committee to encompass the commonly used terms *inservice, staff development,* and *teacher enhancement.* Refers to the broad range of teacher involvement in out-of-school activities that are designed for professional growth. Includes the continuing process of professional development of teachers and long-term commitment on the part of scientists and teachers.

### Science Supervisor

An employee of a school district or regional or state education agency who coordinates professional development or curriculum development and implementation activities for science teachers.

### Scientist

A scientist is anyone whose higher education was concentrated in the natural sciences, usually including preparation and experience in research. A *research scientist* is one who is specifically actively engaged in research.

## Systemwide or Systemic Reform

Reform activities that involve all stakeholders in improving education systems (students, teachers, administrators, community members, and parent). The goal of systemwide reform is to target the entire system, rather than individual aspects of schooling. Issues can include teaching and learning; the culture of schools; professional development, curricular structure, assessments, and articulation between K-12 schools and universities; partnerships with other institutions; boards of education; and reward structures for faculty.

## Teacher-Education Professor (Science)

University faculty members whose graduate work focused on the study of teaching and learning to prepare upper-division undergraduates or graduate students for teaching positions. Courses on such topics as curriculum and instruction (also known as science methods) are usually taught by a professor who holds a baccalaureate or master's degree in science and has public-school science-teaching experience. A science-teacher educator might also supervise science student teachers.

## Teacher Preparation

Prospective teachers' formal course work and teaching practice before certification or employment in teaching at the undergraduate or graduate level. (Also called preservice.)

## Teachers

In this document, the term *teacher* refers specifically to persons who teach students in K-12.

**K-6 Teachers of Science** teach all subjects to about 20-40 students in a self-contained classroom.

**K-6 Science Specialists** are elementary teachers with extra background in science who teach science to elementary students. They might work in regular classrooms or have specially equipped laboratories.

**Middle- and Junior-High-School Science Teachers** usually teach science only to 12- to 14-year-olds in a departmentalized school setting.

**High-School Science Teachers** might teach classes in one or more of the sciences—such as biology, chemistry and physics—and possibly in general science.

### Two- to Four-Year College/University Science Instructors/Professors

Persons who teach science, usually in courses defined by a specialty, such as biology, botany, or zoology. Might also teach science to students in general education and nonscience majors, including prospective elementary teachers. Depending on the state and college/university systems, can work as professors at colleges or universities who teach science to prospective elementary and secondary teachers, as community-college instructors who teach science to nonscience majors and core courses for science majors, or as science professors at colleges or universities who teach graduate or upper-division undergraduate courses for science majors.

# Suggested Reading List

This reading list was developed to provide background material for scientists interested in participating in K-12 science education. Annotations provide thumbnail sketches of the contents of citations.

## THE TEACHING EXPERIENCE

The sources below address issues in the professional lives of K-12 public-school teachers—some of which can be generalized across academic disciplines. As with all professions, the experience of teaching varies with each individual, geographic area, and specific work environment. Often, individual experiences differ greatly within one school. The committee hopes that these materials provide insight into the teaching profession, but it believes, as stated in the report, that the best way to learn about the rewards and challenges of teaching is to develop continuing professional relationships with teachers. A good way to begin is to make arrangements with a teacher to visit a classroom for a day. And then perhaps another.

Freedman, S. G. 1990. Small Victories: The Real World of a Teacher, Her Students and Their High School. New York, NY: Harper & Row.
   Jessica Siegel teaches at a high school that ranks among the worst 10% in New York. Yet, she and her colleagues send 92% of their graduates to college. The author recounts what he has learned about Siegel's classroom

activities and her students' experiences by tracking her professional life throughout the 1987-1988 academic year.

Hendrix, J. R., and T. R. Mertens. 1986. Attracting and retaining qualified high school science teachers: views from those on the firing line. American Biology Teacher 48(1):32-36.

Presents findings from a 20-item questionnaire given to secondary-school life-science teachers selected for an NSF-funded honors workshop on human genetics. The questionnaire, submitted to two groups of teachers, aimed to identify what motivates teachers to maintain excellence in their teaching and ways to attract and retain quality science educators.

Herbert, C. 1974. I See a Child. Garden City, NY: Anchor Books.

Written by a teacher, this creative book captures the intricacies of student-teacher relationships. Includes photographs and written work by students to provide their perspectives on the issues addressed.

Kidder, T. 1989. Among School Children. New York, NY: Avon Books.

A poignant account of the author's 9-month experience with a schoolteacher and her students in Holyoke, Massachusetts.

Kohl, H. 1967. 36 Children. New York, NY: New American Library.

A teacher's narrative of his first year working in the New York City public schools in 1967. Illuminates issues still pertinent today.

National Research Council. 1990. Fulfilling the Promise: Biology Education in the Nation's Schools. Washington, DC: National Academy Press.

A report on high-school biology teaching today. Includes analysis of how the scientific community can help to improve the teaching of biology in the nation's schools.

Rosen, W. G., ed. 1989. High-School Biology Today and Tomorrow. Washington, DC: National Academy Press.

Papers developed from conference proceedings addressing issues in biology education. Includes current teacher perspectives.

## THE POLITICS AND SOCIOLOGY OF SCHOOLS

The following books describe some of the political and sociological forces influencing today's schools that have shaped many current school reform initiatives. In addition, these sources are intended to help readers understand the complex processes involved in changing schools or programs involved in large-scale, systemic reform efforts.

American Association for Higher Education. 1990 and 1991. Improving Student Achievement Through Partnerships: Three Presentations From AAHE's First and Second National Conference on School/College Collaboration. Washington, DC: American Association for Higher Education.

Contains presentations by Kati P. Haycock, Phyllis P. Hart, and Jacqueline J. Irvine on problems and strategies regarding achievement of underrepresented and minority-group students. Haycock asserts that the partnership movement needs to keep its focus primarily on student achievement, to look "beyond pet projects" and build a cohesive movement for reform, and to work toward establishing "a continuum for systematizing teaching and learning excellence in grades K-16." Hart, a teacher of 18 years, discusses "remarkable" academic improvement among minority-group students participating in a model partnership program. Irvine discusses how a "discontinuity" between an African American student's culture inside and outside school can limit achievement.

Atkin, J. M., and A. Atkin. 1989. Improving Science Education Through Local Alliances: A Report to Carnegie Corporation of New York. Santa Cruz, CA: Network Publications.

Describes examples of successful alliances between businesses, universities, and local school districts. Includes programs with interesting evaluation components.

Crawford, J. 1989. Bilingual Education: History, Politics, and Theory and Practice. Trenton, NJ: Crane Publishing Company.

A very readable analysis of bilingual education in the United States public schools. Contains useful glossary of related terms. Addresses past and current debates.

Gardner, H. 1991. The Unschooled Mind: How Children Think and How Schools Should Teach. New York, NY: Basic Books.

Basing his critique on his research in cognitive science, Gardner challenges current notions about what children should "know" and "understand" in school. He describes how children's minds work, the educational processes in schools, and how schools, owing mostly to low expectations of their students, tend to be unresponsive to students' abilities to gain in-depth understanding of classroom material. He sets forth a new framework for understanding how children learn and makes recommendations for applying these principles to the current school-reform agenda.

Gaudiani, C. L., and D. G. Burnett. 1986. Academic Alliances: A New Approach to School/College Collaboration. Washington, DC: American Association for Higher Education.

Provides a succinct history of the partnership movement between school and college educators. Introduces a partnership model known as the Academic Alliance and describes how discipline-based, voluntary partnerships build productive, collegial relationships among K-12 and post-secondary-school teachers.

Goodlad, J.A. 1984. A Place Called School: Prospects for the Future. New York, NY: McGraw Hill.

An in-depth, nationwide study of whole schools and classrooms. Contains data, descriptions, and analyses of specific schools and genres of schools and identifies issues deemed critical to educational change. Asserts that individual schools should be collecting education data that goes well beyond test scores. Offers other recommendations for school improvement but emphasizes that no single agenda can be created for all U.S. schools.

Hord, S. M., W. C. Rutherford, L. Huling-Austin, and G. E. Hall. 1987. Taking Charge of Change. Alexandria, VA: Association for Supervision and Curriculum Development.

Using the "concerns-based adoption model," this work describes how to implement effective strategies for change. Considers factors that traditionally have defeated many strategies. Required reading for anyone considering implementing systemwide, institutionalized innovations.

Joyce, B., H. Wolf, and E. Calhoun. The Self-Renewing School. Alexandria, VA: Association for Supervision and Curriculum Development.

An example of how one school "buys time" so that teachers can work together on school planning and reform. A good reminder to scientists who have not yet visited their area schools that many of their colleagues are already actively developing and participating in reforms.

Kozol, J. 1991. Savage Inequalities: Children in America's Schools. New York, NY: Crown Publishers.

Through research drawn from visits to schools in poor urban areas of several major cities and his earlier experience teaching in the Boston public schools, Kozol documents the racial and economic inequalities that have persisted over the last 25 years.

Oakes, J. 1985. Keeping Track: How Schools Structure Inequality. New Haven, CT: Yale University Press.

Describes how the traditional "tracking" systems in public schools hurt the less-advantaged students, yet do not help the more advantaged students. Explains the benefits of creating groups of students with mixed abilities (academic strengths and weaknesses).

Rigden, D. 1992. Businesses and the Schools: A Guide to Effective Programs. 2nd edition. New York, NY: Council for Aid to Education.

Describes industry's role in education today.

Sizer, T. R. 1992 (previously published in 1984 and 1985). Horace's Compromise: The Dilemma of the American High School. Boston, MA: Houghton Mifflin Company.

Chronicles the experiences of the fictional Horace, a reform-minded high school teacher, developed from the author's study of the American high school. Describes familiar, ineffective practices that take a heavy toll on all Horaces trying to improve their teaching. An afterword describes the principles of the secondary-school reform movement, the Coalition of Essential

Schools, which developed out of this study of high schools across the country.

Sizer, T. R. 1992. Horace's School: Redesigning the American High School. Boston, MA: Houghton Mifflin Company.

Serves as the first report of the Coalition of Essential Schools, a group of schools dedicated to reform. Summarizes what the author has learned since 1984, when he first published findings from a study of U.S. high schools, through the eyes of a fictionalized character, Horace. Conveys what he learned about processes of change within individual coalition schools through conversations with teachers, students, and others. The Coalition of Essential Schools is housed at Brown University, Providence, Rhode Island.

## SCHOOL REFORM

From Risk to Renewal: Charting a Course for Reform. By the Editors of Education Week newspaper. 1993. Washington, DC: Editorial Projects in Education.

Chronicles school reform efforts in the United States since 1981.

Hord, S. M., W. C. Rutherford, L. Huling-Austin, and G. E. Hall. 1987. Taking Charge of Change. Alexandria, VA: Association for Supervision and Curriculum Development.

See description under "The Politics and Sociology of Schools."

Joyce, B., H. Wolf, and E. Calhoun. The Self-Renewing School. Alexandria, VA: Association for Supervision and Curriculum Development.

See description under "The Politics and Sociology of Schools."

Leonard, G. 1987. Education and Ecstasy. Berkeley, CA: North Atlantic Books.

Leonard has reissued this popular book on education reform, which was first published in the 1960s. This version includes an essay, "The Great School Reform Hoax," which provides commentary and a general warning about current school-reform activities. Offers an exciting vision of what schools *could* become.

Little, J. W. 1993. Teachers' Professional Development in a Climate of Educational Reform. New York, NY: National Center for Restructuring Education, Schools and Teaching at Teachers College, Columbia University.

Describes a problem of "fit" between existing school reform activities and models of professional development. Points to some of the newer, alternative models of professional development as a remedy to this problem.

Toch, T. 1991. In the Name of Excellence: The Struggle to Reform the Nation's Schools, Why It's Failing and What Should Be Done. New York, NY: Oxford.

A review and analysis of school reform since 1983. Gives insight into a range of issues influencing the status of the nation's schools, including politics, unions, and the role of schools of education at the nation's colleges and universities.

## SCIENCE-EDUCATION JOURNALS FOR TEACHERS

American Biology Teacher. Reston,VA: The National Association of Biology Teachers.
> Articles cover a wide range of biological topics targeted for middle- and high-school teachers.

Journal of College Science Teaching. Arlington, VA: National Science Teachers Association, Society for College Science Teaching.
> Focuses on lower-division science courses for general education and science majors taken primarily by prospective elementary- and secondary-school teachers.

Journal of Research in Science Teaching. Manhattan, KS: National Association for Research in Science Teaching, Kansas State University's Center for Science Education.
> Keeps readers up to date monthly (except June and July) on research related to the teaching of science. For subscription information, contact John Wiley and Sons, Inc., (212) 850-6645.

The Kappan. A journal of Phi Delta Kappa.
> A scholarly publication, well read by K-12 practitioners, filled with articles addressing pedagogy.

Science and Children. Arlington, VA: The National Science Teachers Association.
> Focuses on hands-on science activities for elementary- and middle-school teachers.

Science Scope. Arlington, VA: The National Science Teachers Association.
> Provides activities, strategies, and reviews for middle-school teachers.

The Science Teacher. Arlington, VA: The National Science Teachers Association.
> Includes articles on topics in the sciences and related current research. Targeted for high-school teachers but recommended for elementary-school teachers as well.

Today's Education. Washington, DC: National Education Association.
> Contains articles on both the difficulties and successes in American schools.

## RESEARCH IN SCIENCE EDUCATION

Blank, R. K., and D. Schilder. 1990. State policies and state role in curriculum. In Politics of Education Association Yearbook: 37-62. Taylor and Francis Ltd.

In the 1980s, mathematics and science policy reform at the state level was aimed largely at raising standards in elementary and secondary education. This chapter delivers findings from a 50-state comparative analysis of those policy reforms; mathematics and science curriculum reforms receive particular focus.

Mechling, K. R., and D. L. Oliver. 1983. Activities, not textbooks: what research says about science programs. Principal 62(4):41-43.

A two-page article addressing the need for greater interface between good science-education research and classroom practice. Asserts that hands-on, activity-oriented curricula and inquiry-oriented instruction should replace textbooks as tools for improving science education.

Office of Educational Research and Improvement, U.S. Department of Education. 1992. Helping Your Child Learn Science. Washington, DC: U.S. Department of Education.

A part of a series of publications intended to help parents extend their children's learning experiences beyond the classroom. This publication provides science information and activities to help parents engage their children in science learning at home and foster their natural curiosity about their environment.

National Center for Improving Science Education, a Partnership of the NETWORK and the Biological Sciences Curriculum Study (BSCS). Summaries of Reports. Andover, MA: The NETWORK.

The National Center for Improving Science Education "synthesizes and translates the findings, recommendations and perspectives embodied in recent and forthcoming studies and reports" by top researchers in science education. Readers can learn about the range of topics and titles included in the center's resources through this document (e.g., *Getting Started in Science: A Blueprint for Elementary School Science, An Integrative Report* and *Developing and Supporting Teachers for Secondary School Science Education*), but they will benefit most by reading the reports on their own interests. To order a list of titles, call 1-800-877-5400.

Shymansky, J. A. 1989. What research says . . . about ESS, SCIS, and SAPA. Science and Children (April):33-35.

The author reviews and synthesizes research on the effectiveness of three science programs, the Elementary Science Study (ESS) Science Curriculum Study (SCIS), and Science—A Process Approach (SAPA). He provides recommendations for future programs.

## DIVERSITY AND EQUITY IN SCIENCE EDUCATION

As stated previously in the report, the committee encourages scientists to participate in professional-development activities that help teachers maintain high expectations of all students while considering the diversity among them. The following sources address some of the complex issues related to diversity in teaching and learning. The term *diversity* refers to gender, language, ethnic, racial, cultural, and economic differences.

Beane, D. B. 1988. Mathematics and Science: Critical Filters for the Future of Minority Students. Washington, DC: The Mid-Atlantic Center for Race Equity, The American University.

A collection of resources intended to help define and evaluate the principal's role in improving mathematics and science education for minority-group students. Offers data related to the underrepresentation of African-Americans, Hispanics, and American Indians in advanced classes, components of programs that have been successful in improving minority-group student achievement, and tools for assessing this progress. Its purpose is to help implement successful prevention and intervention initiatives at the local level.

Butler, W. T., et al. 1991. Baylor's program to attract minority students and others to science and medicine. Academic Medicine 66:305-311.

Describes Baylor College of Medicine's summer enrichment program designed to recruit and support students from underrepresented minority groups. Highlights the element of collaboration between faculty from Baylor and surrounding public schools as a reason for its success and states the need for assessment, participation, and financial support.

Cole, M., and P. Griffin, eds. 1987. Improving Science and Mathematics Education for Minorities and Women: Contextual Factors in Education. Prepared for the Committee on Research in Mathematics, Science, and Technology Education, Commission on Behavioral and Social Sciences and Education, National Research Council. Madison, WI: Wisconsin Center for Education Research, School of Education, University of Wisconsin-Madison.

A committee representing multiple disciplines, developed by the National Research Council, explores how contexts (e.g., the school, the classroom, and the home) affect the learning process of underrepresented students in the sciences and mathematics. Reviews existing research and identifies areas of research, institutional policies, and current programs that need further study.

Dilworth, M. E., ed. 1993. Diversity in Teacher Education: New Expectations. San Francisco, CA: Jossey-Bass Publishers.

See description under "Teacher Professional Development."

Goodlad, J. I., and P. Keating, eds. 1990. Access to Knowledge: An Agenda for Our Nation's Schools. New York, NY: The College Board.

A collection of articles by leaders in school reform concerned with educational equity for students. Includes works by James Comer, John Goodlad, Jeannie Oakes, and Linda Darling-Hammond.

Kahle, J. B., and M. K. Lakes. 1983. The myth of equality in science classrooms. Journal of Research in Science Teaching 20(10):1-10.

Analyzes a 1976-1977 survey concerning male and female attitudes toward science. Concludes that by age 9 female students have less contact with classroom-related and extracurricular science activities and acquire negative attitudes toward the discipline. This widely cited paper describes issues pertinent to elementary- and middle-school classrooms today. Offers suggestions to combat the problem.

Kahle, J. B., and J. Meece. Research on girls in science lessons and applications. In Handbook of Research in Science Teaching & Learning, D. Gabel, ed. Washington, DC: National Science Teachers Association.

An extensive review of literature on the performance and retention of girls in mathematics and science education. The authors criticize existing research models for focusing on "what's missing" in girls' skills or upbringing. Rather, they suggest considering cognitive, psychological and sociocultural variables, with race and class, in studies of school and career achievement among females in mathematics and science. Has a thorough bibliography.

Kahle, J. B., L. H. Parker, L. J. Rennie, and D. Riley. 1993. Gender differences in science education: building a model. Educational Psychologist 28(4):379-404. (Requests should be sent to Jane Butler Kahle, Miami University, School of Education and Allied Professions, Oxford, Ohio.)

The authors propose a model for studying gender and science in the schools intended for researchers, as well as practitioners. Based on a review of international research, the model is informed by existing models used to study gender in mathematics and a series of Australian and American studies exploring how teachers' perceptions of gender and science affect student achievement. The authors' model is proposed as a means of studying existing and new factors influencing girls' interest, confidence, achievement, aspiration, and retention in science.

Linn, M. C., and J. S. Hyde. 1989. Gender, mathematics, and science. Educational Researcher 18(8):17-27.

The authors summarize trends in cognitive, psychosocial, and physical gender differences in mathematics and science education. Using meta-analysis, a means of synthesizing results from several studies, and process analysis, a technique for characterizing cognitive skills used in complex tasks, they argue that gender differences in "earning power" and "career access" can best be explained by cultural and situational contexts, rather than cognitive and psychosocial differences. They assert that these differences can be lessened through the design of learning and earning environments that promote gender equity.

Making Schools Work for Children in Poverty: A New Framework Prepared by the Commission on Chapter One. Summary. December, 10, 1992, Washington, DC.

In December 1990, a committee of diverse professionals formed the Independent Commission on Chapter One to examine the status of economically disadvantaged children in American public schools, to evaluate how Chapter 1 of the Elementary and Secondary Education Act of 1965 has influenced the achievement of these children in school, and to write a new Chapter 1 statute based on their conclusions. This paper describes the commission's process and rationale for arriving at its recommendations and summarizes its proposed Chapter 1 framework.

Nelson-Barber, S., and T. Meier. 1990. Multicultural context a key factor in teaching. Academic Connections (A newsletter of the College Board) (Spring):1-11.

This paper addresses factors involved in teaching increasingly culturally pluralistic classrooms. Authors look at nonverbal cues, methods of questioning, and other subtleties as factors contributing to both student achievement and cultural misunderstandings.

Rosenberry, A. S., et al. 1992. Cheche konnen: scientific sense-making in bilingual education. HANDS ON! (a Newsletter of TERC) 15(1):1, 16-19.

Authors discuss how to teach science to limited-English-speaking children as a way not only to improve their skills in English, but to "attain scientific ways of knowing and thinking."

Tierney, D. 1988. Teaching content through a multicultural lens: a social studies case study. Journal of Educational Issues of Language Minority Students (a journal of a teacher-preparation program at Boise State University) (Summer):15-21.

An article based on a study looking closely at strategies used by teachers to explain information to their students. Explores how issues of diversity might affect teaching strategies, particularly when metaphors are used, and therefore affect student understanding. Results of the study led the author to conclude that greater attention to ethnic and cultural diversity can enhance teaching and learning.

## TEACHER PROFESSIONAL DEVELOPMENT

Arons, A. B. 1983. Achieving Wider Scientific Literacy. Daedalus 112(2):91-122.

Arons attributes the current state of scientific literacy among students to poorly designed preservice and inservice training programs. He relates the problem directly to the kinds of science courses taught at college and universities attended by potential teachers. He asserts that teachers are educating their students in the same ineffective manner in which they are taught in these preparation courses and concludes that no short-term inservice program, curricula, or set of materials can correct this problem.

Dilworth, M. E., ed. 1993. Diversity in Teacher Education: New Expectations. Developed for the American Association of Colleges for Teacher Education. San Francisco, CA: Jossey-Bass Publishers.

Addresses some of the major problems and challenges in teacher education related to issues of ethnic and cultural diversity. Provides tangible suggestions for improving teacher programs so that they can successfully address diversity as related to curricula, the teacher work force, and student learning. Contains articles by seasoned practitioners who call for the "development of better programs, better teachers, and. . . better education for all children."

Little, J. W. 1993. Teachers' Professional Development in a Climate of Educational Reform. New York, NY: National Center for Restructuring Education, Schools and Teaching at Teachers College, Columbia University.

See description under "School Reform."

Shulman, L. S. Those who understand: knowledge growth in teaching. Educational Researcher (February):4-15.

Traces the history of the dichotomy between content knowledge and methodology in procedures for evaluating teachers. Criticizes current teacher certification, research, and evaluation practices for focusing too heavily on teacher methodology and for overlooking the importance of teachers' content knowledge, their organization of subject matter, and other aspects of classroom teaching. Proposes the use of discipline-based case studies in the classroom as a means of effectively integrating content and process among all aspects of the teaching profession.

## SCIENCE-TEACHING STRATEGIES

Biological Sciences Curriculum Study (BSCS). 1993. Developing Biological Literacy: A Guide to Developing Secondary and Post-Secondary Biology Curricula. Colorado Springs, CO: BSCS.

Provides resources and suggestions for developing secondary and postsecondary science curricula and considers how to teach science as a "process and a way of knowing." Recommends science teaching that encourages students to explore and understand the natural world through inquiry, interest, and technology. Suggests an approach to science teaching that integrates biological concepts and themes that are contemporary and personal, and spark students' interest.

Elstgeest, J. 1970. Teaching Science by Posing Problems. Prospects: UNESCO 8(1):66-72.

The author describes why helping children approach and solve problems logically and thoroughly is crucial for life-long learning and asserts that the acquisition of problem-solving skills should be the objective of science education.

Gurley-Dilger, L. 1992. Gowin's Vee, linking the lecture and the laboratory. Science Teacher 59(3):50-57.
This article demonstrates how to use the pedagogical tool "Vee Heuristicis" to support a conceptual approach to science.

Hunter, M. 1984. Knowing, teaching, and supervising. In P. Hosford, ed. Using What We Know About Teaching. Alexandria, VA: Association for Supervision and Curriculum Development.
A good introduction to one expert's teaching method. Hunter is a veteran and a leader in the field.

Leonard, W. H., C. Fowler, C. Mason, N. Ridenour, and C. Stone. 1991. A minimum core curriculum for introductory high school biology. American Biology Teacher 53(October):219-222.
Based on a national inquiry, this article reflects the members of the National Association of Biology Teachers opinions on what topics, at a minimum, should be addressed in a high-school biology course.

Mechling, K. R., C. H. Stedman, and K. M. Donnellan. 1982. Preparing and Certifying Science Teachers. An NSTA Report.
The report cites the lack of attention given to K-12 teacher certification standards across the country as a major problem in science education. Provides recommendations for focusing on elementary-teacher preservice programs.

Mestre, J. P. 1991. Learning and instruction in pre-college physical science. Physics Today (September):56-62.
Refutes the notion that teachers can best "transmit" knowledge to students through lectures and other forms of traditional classroom communication. Advocates the constructivist approach to teaching and learning, which aims to engage students in activities that illuminate scientific concepts through the process of doing as well as listening. The author also states the need to strengthen students' problem-solving skills through science activities. To improve science education, he states that preservice and inservice programs should better inform teachers about scientific content knowledge, how students think and learn, and instructional strategies. He also asserts that the reform movement in science should include the participation of teachers, cognitive scientists, and textbook publishers.

National Science Resources Center. 1988. Science for Children: Resources for Teachers. Washington, DC: National Academy Press.

A comprehensive resource guide to encourage the use of hands-on science activities in school systems. Contains a wealth of information on programs, curriculum materials, books and magazines, professional associations and organizations, and other sources related to science education currently available for elementary-school science.

Novak, J. D. 1991. Clarify with concept maps, a tool for students and teachers alike. Science Teacher 58(7):45-49.

A short presentation about how to use concept maps as a pedagogical tool for the purpose of enhancing student learning of concepts rather than knowledge bits.

Novak, J. D., and D. B. Gowin. 1984. Learning How to Learn. New York, NY: Cambridge University Press.

The book covers the rationale for meaningful learning. Advocates teaching students through the development of a conceptual framework rather than a sequence of memorized bits. Illustrates how to use concept mapping in the classroom. Addresses the kind of learning that empowers students to develop their own knowledge—knowledge that is conceptual and connected to what they already know.

Raghubir, K. P. 1979. The laboratory-investigative approach to science instruction. Journal of Research in Science Teaching 16(1):13-17.

Outlines an approach to teaching laboratory activities that allows for student-initiated and student-directed projects. Describes how this approach fosters scientific thinking, a deep understanding of science, important cognitive processes, and positive attitudes toward laboratory activities—such as curiosity and responsibility—that are needed for students to become successful laboratory scientists.

Watson, B., and R. Konicek. 1990. Teaching for conceptual change: confronting children's experience. Phi Delta Kappan (May):680-685.

The article describes how teachers who track children's assumptions and misconceptions about science through journals and other methods can help each of their students gain a clearer and deeper understanding of scientific concepts.

## SCIENCE-CURRICULUM DESIGN AND REFORM

Several national and regional science-education reform efforts in science curriculum are under way. Below are some brief descriptions.

Alridge, B. 1988. Essential Changes in Secondary School Science: Scope, Sequence & Coordination. Arlington, VA: National Science Teachers Association.

This article launched the national Scope, Sequence, and Coordination Project that is helping secondary schools to rework their traditional course offerings.

American Association for the Advancement of Science. 1989. Project 2061: Science for All Americans (Overview Report). Washington, DC: American Association for the Advancement of Science.

A report on Project 2061's first phase, which outlines a vision of what scientific information all high-school graduates should know in the year 2061. Other documents from the Project describe the types of curricula, programs, courses, and teaching strategies that will be needed to implement that vision.

National Research Council. 1996. National Science Education Standards. Washington, DC: National Academy Press.

The "Science Standards" report is described and cited in several chapters of the present report.

National Science Teachers Association. 1993. The Content Core: Scope, Sequence, and Coordination of Secondary School Science: Volume I. A Guide for Curriculum Designers. Revised edition. Arlington, VA: National Science Teachers Association.

Provides a framework for designing or restructuring secondary-school science courses. Emphasizes coordinating or integrating separate high-school courses in scientific subdisciplines. Includes an Apple IIe computer diskette.

National Science Teachers Association. 1992. Scope, Sequence, and Coordination of Secondary School Science: Volume II. Relevant Research. Arlington, VA: National Science Teachers Association.

A sampling of research articles that support the Scope, Sequence, and Coordination arrangement of science content.

## BUILDING COMMUNITY SUPPORT FOR
## SCIENTIST-TEACHER PARTNERSHIPS

Alberts, B. M. 1991. Elementary science education in the United States: how scientists can help. Current Biology 1:339-341.

A scientist describes his experience learning about elementary science education. Discusses how and why scientists should participate in science-education reform.

Atkin, J. M., and A. Atkin. 1989. Improving Science Education Through Local Alliances: A Report to Carnegie Corporation of New York. Santa Cruz, CA: Network Publications.

See description under "The Politics and the Sociology of Schools."

Gaudiani, C. L., and D. G. Burnett. 1986. Academic Alliances: A New Approach to School/College Collaboration. Washington, DC: American Association for Higher Education.

See description under "The Politics and Sociology of Schools."

Moore, P., and E. Richards. 1992. Science for Science Teachers ($S_4ST$). Berkeley, CA: Regents of the University of California.

A guide to designing and implementing an institute for junior-high-school science teachers aimed at enhancing and updating both scientific knowledge and laboratory teaching skills. For science teachers working to improve science education through efforts that bring together junior-high-school and college and university science teachers.

Rowe, M. B. Science education—a framework for decision-makers. Daedalus 112(2):123-142.

Rowe offers a new framework for evaluating recommendations, plans, and policies regarding science education that are often voiced by a variety of professional communities. Provides recommendations for improving science instruction.

Schwartz, B. B., and J. J. Wynne. 1991. Pre-college physics education programs from the research community. Physics Today (September):48-54.

This article describes a sampling of programs intended to improve K-12 science education that were developed by physicists in response to the 1989 education summit. The article examines programs run by physicists from all sectors of the physics community—the professional societies, the national laboratories, and industry.

Sussman, A., ed. 1993. Science Education Partnerships: Manual for Scientists and K-12 Teachers. San Francisco, CA: University of California, San Francisco.

Thirty-four articles by experienced practitioners (scientists, teachers, funders, curriculum developers, education administrators, and museum staff) working on partnerships between scientists and teachers. Authors address how to design, fund, implement, and evaluate programs, drawing from their own experiences with specific programs. A preface by Bruce M. Alberts and several articles come together to describe a national picture of science-education reform and how partnerships can interact with systemic reform efforts.

# University Statements of Policy Regarding Recognition of Faculty Contributions to Professional-Development Programs

## UNIVERSITY OF CALIFORNIA, IRVINE
## COMMITTEE ON PRECOLLEGE EDUCATION

To ensure that precollege education could become recognized as part of a faculty member's ongoing teaching responsibility, the Academic Senate at the University of California, Irvine, established a Committee on Community Education in 1985, which has the following charge:

### Committee for Community Education

(A) Membership

(1) The Committee for Community Education shall consist of ten division members, appointed by the Committee on committees for three-year terms, and ex-officio, the Chair of the Department of Teacher Education, the Director of the Office of Relations with Schools, and the Dean University Extension.

(2) There shall be one member from each department and program offering instruction in subject matter taught in the public schools, i.e., biology, chemistry, computer science, English, fine arts, foreign languages, history, mathematics, physics, and social sciences.

(B) Duties

(1) To recommend to the Academic Senate and to the university administration proposals to assure faculty awareness of the university's current and potential relations and involvement with K-14 education.

(2) To examine the possibility of the re-institution of Master of Arts in Teaching programs supervised by the university faculty and to develop other programs to assure effective continuing education of school personnel and to promote curriculum and instructional research and development.

(3) To explore the possibility of the university administration's creating an office for community education to implement the above.

(4) To review reports and recommendations intended to improve the quality of education at all levels; and to recommend appropriate actions that would involve the university faculty and administration.

## UNIVERSITY OF ARIZONA PROCEDURES FOR EVALUATION OF FACULTY MEMBERS WHO PLAY A SUBSTANTIAL ROLE IN PRE-COLLEGE MATHEMATICS AND SCIENCE EDUCATION

(Adopted by the Faculty of Science 7/23/92)

Although there has been substantial support within several Faculty of Science departments for involving competent mathematicians and scientists in pre-college education, the promotion and tenure committees and peer review committees of some of those departments have expressed frustration when trying to evaluate faculty who have been significantly involved with pre-college education activities. The following procedures and the accompanying criteria are meant both to assure high quality scholarship and to assure faculty who choose to participate in such activities that they will be evaluated in an appropriate manner. No faculty member will be evaluated using these procedures without a written agreement between the faculty member and the department head. We urge department heads to consult with their entire faculty before reaching such agreements.

The procedures and criteria are written broadly enough so that some faculty whose primary appointment is in the College of Education may appropriately be evaluated by them.

• A written agreement should be reached between each individual faculty member and his or her department head as to what percent of the faculty member's time is to be spent on pre-college mathematics or science education.

• When the percent agreed to in item 1 is greater than 0, and the faculty member wishes to be evaluated by the Science Education Promotion and Tenure Committee (SEPTC), appropriate papers should be submitted to SEPTC concurrently with or previous to submission of such papers to the Departmental evaluation committee. The percent agreed to in item 1 should also be communicated to SEPTC.

• SEPTC will solicit evaluations from appropriate outside and inside referees. These must include scholars in the appropriate content who have an interest in education, and distinguished educators who have an interest in the appropriate content.

• Before making a formal report, SEPTC will meet with the faculty member to advise him or her about SEPTC's preliminary evaluation and to consult with the faculty member about possible further information and alternative actions.

• SEPTC will evaluate all materials and send them, with SEPTC's recommendation, to the appropriate department head and evaluation committee. SEPTC's report will become part of the permanent record.

## UNIVERSITY OF ARIZONA CRITERIA FOR EVALUATION OF FACULTY MEMBERS WHO PLAY A SUBSTANTIAL ROLE IN PRE-COLLEGE MATHEMATICS AND SCIENCE EDUCATION

### Introduction

The purpose of mathematics and science education is to improve the teaching and learning of mathematics and science. Evaluation of faculty members who play a substantial role in mathematics and science education should take into account the impact they have, and are having, and are likely to have, on the teaching and learning of mathematics and science. Both the magnitude of the impact and its direction should be considered.

Written evaluations by distinguished colleagues and others, both within and without the University, will necessarily play an important role in determining the magnitude and the quality of a professor's impact. Efforts that will be evaluated for science and mathematics education should be directed towards the systematic improvement of science and mathematics education beyond the faculty member's own classroom and advising activities. Examples of such efforts might include: scholarly works that made a contribution to teaching and learning, innovative textbooks that substantially impact on teaching and learning, leadership in service activities, etc., but in all cases, the magnitude and quality of the impact is the essential issue.

Further evidence of achievement may come from initiation and development of education programs, from obtaining and managing grant support, from service on advisory and policy boards that have substantial influence, and other similar activities.

Traditional categories (research, teaching, service) may be inappropriate for evaluating science and mathematics educators because the lines between the categories are often blurred. If these categories are to be used, however, caution must be exercised to avoid assigning creative scholarly work to the service or teaching category (where it ordinarily receives less weight in the overall process) simply because it is different from traditional research.

*Research or Its Creative Equivalent*

The *University of Arizona Faculty of Science Guidelines for Judging Stature and Excellence in Research* includes the following statements:

> "Excellence in research means, among other things, performance that earns international stature."
>
> "In evaluating research, Standing Committees should look especially for publications and other efforts that reflect existing or developing international stature, e.g., refereed publications, invitations to substantial conferences, grants and awards."

The criteria are appropriate for mathematics and science education, but some of the specifics may differ from more conventional evaluations within the Faculty of Science.

Worthy contributions could include scholarly books that make a significant contribution, textbooks that are substantially different from, and better than, previous textbooks (if any) on a worthy subject, articles in refereed respected journals that describe and advocate better practice or that present research results relating to learning science or mathematics, improved methods and instruments for evaluation, computer software, movie or television productions that enhance education, and so on.

No one person, of course, will make contributions in all of these ways, but any of these activities, and many similar ones, should be thought of as legitimate research or creative activities. The quality and impact of the work must be seen as the important issues.

Evaluation committees must, of necessity, consider with some care the actual origin of materials. If a textbook, for example, was designed and largely developed by employees of the publishing company, the "author" should receive little credit for it. If co-authored articles or books were written largely by the other authors, that fact should be considered. In situations where possibilities of this sort exist, the evaluation committee has an obligation to establish the nature and magnitude of the faculty member's contribution.

*Service*

The *University of Arizona Faculty of Science Guidelines for Judging Stature and Excellence* say that: "Service . . . must be of such a character as to add to the professional reputation of the faculty member and of the University at the local, national, and international level." Because a major goal of university mathematics and science education is to improve teaching and learning in the schools, service is of greater importance than for most members of the Faculty of Science. It may include service to professional organizations, to government and other agencies, to the University, to the College, to the Department, to local schools, etc. It may also include speeches and workshops at professional meetings, and similar activities.

There may appear to be some overlap between "research or its creative equivalent" and "service" as used here. Many of the opportunities to provide service on a national or international level may be indicators of a distinguished reputation, and therefore of high quality research and creativity. However, speaking, service, etc., should not be taken as *ipso facto* evidence of research and creativity. The research and other contributions must be considered directly, and the opportunities for service taken as only one indicator of the quality of that research and creative contribution.

### Teaching

The *University of Arizona Faculty of Science Guidelines for Judging Stature and Excellence in Teaching* say that: "In order for the University's commitment to quality teaching to be a practical reality, it is essential that teaching quality be evaluated, recognized and rewarded. . . . It is the responsibility of departments to devise evaluation procedures and to collect systematic information on teaching performance. As a minimum, student evaluations, peer evaluations, measures of student learning, and evaluations by department heads are required."

In addition to the normal faculty teaching responsibilities, special consideration will be given to the development of new and innovative courses, and to the creation of new courseware or laboratory activities that substantially enhance existing teaching practice. Unusually strong commitment to student advising (such as being Faculty Fellow) should be taken into account. It is appropriate to consider the career outcomes of former students, and to solicit their evaluations of the faculty member.

It is also important to recognize and evaluate activities that impact the quality of science and mathematics teaching in the schools. This includes inservice training of teachers, and the development of courses or materials that substantially benefit instruction in the schools.

# Organizations That Support Activities in Science and Mathematics Education

Many organizations support science- and mathematics-education activities and partnerships throughout the country. Some activities are organized through scientific professional societies, others through professional science-teaching associations, and still others through state academies of sciences and departments of education. The following list provides a starting point for scientists interested in becoming involved in K-12 science education and professional development.[1]

## GENERAL INFORMATION REGARDING SCIENCE EDUCATION

American Association for Higher Education
One Dupont Circle, NW
Washington, DC  20036
(202) 293-6440

American Association for the Advancement of Science
James Rutherford, Chief Education Officer and Director of Project 2061
Shirley Malcom, Head, Directorate for Education and Human Resources
Programs
1333 H Street, NW
Washington, DC  20005
(202) 326-6670

---

[1]Two valuable sources of information are the American Association for the Advancement of Science *Sourcebook for Science, Mathematics, & Technology Education,* from which some of the following information was obtained, and the Department of Education *Guidebook to Excellence, 1994, A Directory of Federal Resources for Mathematics and Science Education Improvement.*

American Federation of Teachers
Albert Shanker, President
555 New Jersey Avenue, NW
Washington, DC  20001
(202) 879-4440

Association for the Education of Teachers in Science
Paul Kuerbis
Colorado College
Education Department
Colorado Springs, CO  80903
(719) 389-6726

Association of Science-Technology Centers
Contact: Andrea Anderson
1025 Vermont Avenue, NW, Suite 500
Washington, DC  20005-3516
(202) 783-7200

Biological Sciences Curriculum Study
Contact: Joseph McInerney
Pikes Peak Research Park
5415 Mark Dabling Blvd.
Colorado Spring, CO  80918-3842
(719) 531-5550

Department of Education's Dwight D. Eisenhower Mathematics and
Science Education Program
State Programs Contact: Doris Crudup
(202) 401-0841
National Programs Contact: Eve Bither
(202) 219-2164

Education Development Center, Inc.
Millie LeBlanc
EDC Publishing Center
55 Chapel Street
Newton, MA  02160
(800) 225-4276

Lawrence Hall of Science
University of California, Berkeley
Berkeley, CA  94720
(510) 642-5132

Margaret Cozzens, Division Director
Elementary, Secondary and Informal Education
4201 Wilson Boulvard
Arlington, VA 22201
(703) 306-1620

National Association for Research in Science Teaching
Barry Frasier, President
Contact: John Staver, Executive Secretary
College of Education
Kansas State University
219 Bluemont Hall
Manhattan, KS 66506-5301
(913) 532-6294

National Education Association
Keith Geiger, President
1201 Sixteenth Street, NW
Washington, DC 20036
(202) 833-4000

National Research Council
2101 Constitution Avenue, NW
Washington, DC 20418
(202) 334-3628 (Science Standards)
(202) 334-2500 (Life Sciences)
(202) 334-3061 (Physical Sciences)
(202) 334-3294 (Mathematics)

National Science Foundation
Janice Eale, Office Director
Office of Systemic Reform
(703) 306-1682

National Science Resources Center
Douglas M. Lapp, Executive Director
900 Jefferson Drive, SW, Room 1201
Arts and Industry Building
Smithsonian Institution
Washington, DC 20560
(202) 357-2555

National Science Teachers Association
Jerry Wheeler, Executive Director
1840 Wilson Boulevard
Arlington, VA  22201
(703) 243-7100
*Activities: Professional publications, newsletters, activities for teachers
and students, curriculum development*

Society for College Science Teaching
Eleanor D. Siebert, President
Physical Science and Mathematics
Mount St. Mary's College
12001 Chalon Road
Los Angeles, CA  90049
(310) 476-2237

State Academies of Sciences
*Activities: Professional publications, activities for students and teachers,
newsletters, speakers' bureau, symposia for students and general public*

State Departments of Education
*Activities: Responsibility for elementary and secondary science- and
mathematics-education programs*

State Science-Teacher Associations

Technical Education Research Centers
Robert Tinker, Chief Scientist
2067 Massachusetts Avenue
Cambridge, MA  02140
(617) 547-0430


**LIFE SCIENCES**

American Association of Immunologists
9650 Rockville Pike
Bethesda, MD  20814-3994
(301) 530-7178

American Institute of Biological Sciences
Roy H. Saigo, Chair, Education Committee
President for Academic Affairs
Southeastern Louisiana University
Hammond, LA 70402
(504) 549-2316
*Activities: Professional publications, newsletters, activities for students and teachers, career information*

American Physiological Society
Marsha Matyas, Education Officer
9650 Rockville Pike
Bethesda, MD 20814
(301) 530-7164
*Activities: Professional publications, newsletters, activities for students, career information*

American Society for Biochemistry and Molecular Biology
Peter Farnham, Public Affairs
9650 Rockville Pike
Bethesda, MD 20814
(301) 530-7147
*Activities: Professional publications, activities for teachers, career information*

American Society for Cell Biology
9650 Rockville Pike
Bethesda, MD 20814-3992
(301) 530-7153
*Activities: Publish "Resources for Scientists Involved in Pre-College Science Education"; education workshops for scientists at annual meetings; research experiences for teachers*

American Society for Microbiology
Amy L. Chang, Assistant Director, Office of Education and Training
1325 Massachusetts Avenue, NW
Washington DC 20005
(202) 737-3600
*Activities: Professional publications, newsletters, curriculum development, career information, activities for scientists, teachers, and students*

American Society of Human Genetics
9650 Rockville Pike
Bethesda, MD  20814
(301) 571-1825
*Activities: Program at annual meeting for teachers and students*

American Society of Plant Physiologists
Melvin Josephs, Executive Director
15501 Monona Drive
Rockville, MD 20855
(301) 251-0560
*Activities: Professional publications, newsletters, curriculum development, activities for teachers and students, career information*

Biophysical Society
Norma M. Allewell, Chair, Education
Committee
Department of Biochemistry
University of Minnesota
St. Paul, MN
(612) 624-7755
*Activities: Professional publications, newsletter, career information, activities for students*

Coalition for Education in the Life Sciences
Dr. Sharon Zablotney, Executive Committee
c/o Board of Education & Training
American Society for Microbiology
1325 Massachusetts Avenue, NW
Washington, DC  20005
*Activities: Meetings to convene scientists and educators interested in improving undergraduate life-science education*

Ecological Society of America
Marjorie Holland, Director, Public Affairs Office
2010 Massachusetts Avenue, NW, Suite 420
Washington, DC  20036
(202) 833-8773
*Activities: Professional publications, newsletters, curriculum development, career information*

National Association of Biology Teachers
Mary Louise Bellamy, Education Director
11250 Roger Bacon Drive, #19
Reston, VA 22090
(703) 471-1134
*Activities: Professional publications, newsletters, activities for teachers and students, curriculum development, career information, award programs*

Society for Developmental Biology
Dr. David G. Capco, Chair, Education Committee
Department of Zoology
Arizona State University
(602) 965-3571

Society for Neuroscience
Mary Beth Altenberg
11 Dupont Circle, NW, Suite 500
Washington, DC 20036
(202) 462-6688

## CHEMISTRY

American Chemical Society
Sylvia A. Ware, Division Director, Education
1155 16th Street, NW
Washington, DC 20036
(202) 872-4388
*Activities: Professional publications, publications for high-school students, newsletter for teachers and students, activities for teachers and students, curriculum development, career information*

## PHYSICS

American Association of Physics Teachers
Jay Zimmerman, Chair, Physics in High School
2530 Anita Drive
Brookfield, WI 53005
(414) 785-3910
*Activities: Professional publications, newsletters, activities for teachers and students, curriculum development, career information*

American Institute of Physics
Donald F. Kirwan, Manager, Education Division
One Physics Ellipse
College Park, MD 20740-3843
(301) 209-3000
*Activities: Professional publications, newsletters and activities for teachers and students, curriculum development, career information*

American Physical Society
Brian B. Schwartz, Associate Executive Secretary
335 East 45th Street
New York, NY 10017-3483
(212) 682-7341
*Activities: Professional publications, newsletters, activities for teachers and students, career information*

## EARTH SCIENCES

American Geological Institute
Marilyn Suiter, Director of Education and Human Resources
703-379-2480

American Meteorological Society
David Houghton, Chair, Education and Human Resources Commission
Department of Meteorology
University of Wisconsin
Madison, WI 53706
(608) 262-0776
*Activities: Professional publications, newsletters, career information*

National Association of Geology Teachers
Robert A. Christman, Executive Director
(206) 650-3582

National Earth Science Teachers Association
Frank Ireton, Manager, Pre-College Education Programs
2000 Florida Avenue, NW
Washington, DC 20009-1277
(202) 462-6910

# APPENDIX G

# An NSTA Position Statement on Science Teacher Professionalism

## PREAMBLE

The teacher is the key to making science teaching a profession and to providing quality science education. For American society to accept science teachers as professionals, science teaching needs to conform to society's *professional practice model.*

*Society's professional practice model* is knowledge based and content oriented. It is a pact between society and members of an occupation whose work "requires discretion and judgment in meeting the unique needs of clients . . . (A profession organizes itself) to guarantee the competence of its members in exchange for the privilege of controlling its own work structure and standards of practice. "The profession assumes collective responsibility for defining, communicating, and enforcing professional standards of practice and ethics. It develops and maintains a process which ensures both the research and craft knowledge accumulated in the field are communicated and used effectively by all its members. That knowledge is also used to prepare, induct, certify, select, and evaluate new members. Further, the profession ensures continuous generation of new knowledge. Differences in knowledge levels, expertise, responsibility, and productivity result in differentiated roles, status, and compensation.

Science teaching requires an individual to exercise discretion and judgment in meeting the needs of students. Thus it is fitting for science teachers[1] to assume the rights and responsibilities of professionals in our society. To do so, the

---

[1]Science teachers herein are defined as in the NSTA Visions paper which includes underrepresented groups: African Americans, Hispanic Americans, Native Americans, Asian Americans, the disabled, and women.

educational enterprise in the United States must eliminate the existing hierarchy. The roles of all participants in the enterprise must change. Such initiatives are emerging throughout the country and are supported by research publications and position papers from professional societies. This position statement *describes changes in structure and expectations which must occur* to enable a science teacher to assume the role of a professional within society's *professional practice model.*

## POSITION STATEMENT

*NSTA supports the restructuring of schooling in the United States so that science teaching can become consistent with the professional practice model.*

Teachers must collectively (1) establish and continually revise standards for the profession and (2) enable individuals to make choices exercising their own discretion and judgment in their professional work within the parameters of the collective standards.

## DECISIONS

Since making decisions collectively is critical to establishing science teaching as a profession, interaction among teachers and the time to interact are essential. Sharing, mutual commitment, and caring about community must be facilitated. This means establishing new priorities for how teachers allocate their work time so they can collaborate with each other and other stakeholders to make policies and regulations relating to science teaching. Teachers' success is evaluated in terms of these new priorities.

Decisions cover the entire range of school activities that impinge on science teaching. Some examples are monitoring science education programs and practice; identifying changes needed in schools so the needs of the local school population and the specific community in which students live are met; relating disciplines, selecting curricula, materials, instructional approaches, and assessment procedures; allocating resources; hiring new teachers and influencing their preparation, induction, certification, selection and evaluation; and more.

## TIME

The multifaceted nature of professional science teachers' responsibilities requires their work time be divided between interaction with students and interaction with parents, peers, administrators, scientists and other professionals, and other community members including people from business and industry. Community expectations and school structures (e.g., schedules, assignments) must be flexible enough to allow teachers to exercise discretion and judgment in meeting their obligations to the students and the adults with whom they interact.

## SUPPORT

Teachers must have both technical and human support in order to make time available for the necessary interactions and to facilitate communication. Technical support includes ready access to a telephone, computer, modem, fax, photo copy machines, expertise to make maximum use of current hardware and software, and personal work space outside the classroom. Human support includes people such as a laboratory assistant, teacher assistant, and secretary to do tasks that do not require the unique expertise of the science teacher.[2]

## PROFESSIONAL GROWTH

Exercising discretion and judgment to make effective decisions requires information from many diverse sources about the specifics of each situation and current scientific technology, and pedagogic knowledge, information and skills. Therefore, teachers must continue to grow professionally, and life-long-learning must be supported. Teachers should determine what they need to learn and when they need to learn it. Learning opportunities tailored to the point of need should be available to enhance teachers' decision making and activities. Any behaviors which contribute to professional growth should be supported and rewarded (e.g., being active in professional associations, organizing and attending conferences, participating in bulletin board conferences and networks, taking courses and seminars, reading publications, visiting other classrooms, and informal interactions with other professionals). Learning opportunities should also include teachers as reflective practitioners who do research on their own experiences and their students' experiences, thus continuing to increase the knowledge base of the profession.

## SYMBOLS OF PROFESSIONALS

Symbols are used in our society to nurture and build professional images. They identify a person's professional status to others and aid in interaction and communication. For example, students and adults with whom one interacts can recognize the accomplishments and subsequent status of a teacher when teachers frame and display diplomas and certificates of licensing, of participation in study seminars, of appreciation, and awards. The code of ethics displayed on a wall announces the existence of professional standards. Business cards facilitate net-

---

[2]Laboratory assistants collect, set up, and break down laboratory equipment, run inventories and order materials and equipment, and conduct safety inspections. Teacher assistants perform classroom clerical tasks, acquire teacher selected materials, and follow up on contacts within the community to set up field trips, guest speakers, funding, etc. Secretaries do paperwork that includes attendance reports, book inventories, copying, running computer searches, and making transparencies. Functions such as monitoring a hall, bus, or cafeterias are also assumed by others.

working. The profession and individual teachers should develop deliberate public relations initiatives to build a public image supporting science teacher professionalism.

## RESPONSIBILITY

In order to effectively meet the needs of students, science teachers assume responsibility for enabling each learner to reach his/her own potential. This means cultivating the varied capacities of students by empowering them to think with all their senses: responding to their ethnic, cultural, and linguistic differences; focusing on learning in contrast to focusing on the content of the discipline and "covering the material"; and relating science to the whole of what students learn in schools.

Professional science teachers facilitate the construction of science concepts for learners. They are decision makers who employ knowledge of science, pedagogy, and change to fulfill their individual responsibilities. They are continuous learners who stay current in scientific, pedagogic and change literature and are reflective practitioners who generate new knowledge and share knowledge. They assume collective responsibility for the profession, model ethical behavior in keeping with the profession's standards of practice, and are accountable for their actions.

## SCIENCE TEACHER PROFESSIONALISM

NSTA supports the restructuring of schooling necessary to enhance science teacher professionalism so that:

- Science teachers collaborate with each other and with stakeholders to make decisions about policies and regulations for science teaching
- Science teachers allocate their time among students, parents, peers, administrators, scientists, and other community members.
- Science teachers have both technical and staff support in order to be available for interaction with students and other stakeholders.
- Science teachers' professional growth continues throughout their careers. They select learning opportunities that meet their needs. They are reflective and share research findings from both their own and their students' experiences.
- Science teachers use society's symbols such as business cards, displaying diplomas, certificates, and awards to reflect professional images.
- Science teachers assume responsibility for enabling learners to reach their potential. Science teachers collectively establish and continually revise standards of practice, model ethical behavior, and account for their actions.

—Adopted by the NSTA Board of Directors in January 1992.

# Example of an Inquiry-Based Laboratory Exercise

## LAB 1: ECOLOGY OF DUCKWEED

NAME _____ PER _____ DATE DUE _____

GRADED _____ FIX/FINISH/RETURN _____

### INTRODUCTION

Have you spent any time collecting samples of plants in ponds and streams? Ponds are an interesting aquatic ecosystem with numerous forms of life to study. One of the plants common to this ecosystem is a plant called duckweed.

If you have a pond or stream near your home or school, collect some of these plants for the class experiment. You could also compare the plant structure of duckweed to that of the pond or stream algae. Think about the function of the various plants in the freshwater ecosystem.

Many aquatic ecosystems have become endangered by human interference. When the pond or marsh is filled in or polluted, there is no longer a balance within that habitat and many organisms are endangered or killed.

You will be using duckweed in the lab. In the first demonstration lab, you will set up a growth culture and graph the growth of the duckweed under normal conditions.In the second part of the lab, you will design an approach that will test some variables that affect the growth of duckweed.

Which of the following growth curves do you think will illustrate the growth pattern of a small population of duckweed introduced into a container and left to grow for two weeks?  Discuss this with your team.

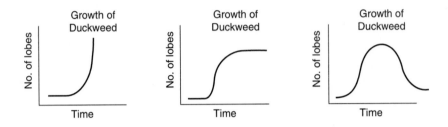

The following are some questions that you can discuss in you group before your start the lab:

- Can you name some biotic and abiotic factor that would influence the rate of growth of the duckweed in a pond or in the classroom?
- Can you think of some natural or human induced factors in the environment that could alter the rate of growth of the duckweed population?
- What economic factors relate to environmental pollution such as acid rain?
- What political factors are involved in preventing or cleaning up environmental pollution?

## SAFETY NOTES

- Use care when working with glassware.
- Wash your hands before and after the lab.
- Use care when working around electrical sources.
- Use care when using any chemicals in the lab.

## PART A:

### Materials:

### Each team should have/obtain:

- 400-ml beaker or similar container to hold the initial culture of duckweed.
- Light source.

- 10 duckweed structures. Each unit includes several lobes attached and roots growing beneath. Try to have structures with 3 lobes/structure or a total of 30 lobes per container.
- Pond water.
- Inoculating loop or similar device to pick up and transfer duckweed from source to team vessel.
- Graph paper.

**Procedure for Part A of the Investigation:**

1. Microscopic examination under stereo microscope or hand lens.

- Take a "plant" from the pond water provided or that you collected yourself.
- The duckweed floats on the surface of the water and is made of 1-4 lobes. It usually occurs as a three-lobed structure. Each lobe is considered a separate plant.
- Note the arrangement and structure of the lobes.
- Note the roots that extend into the water.
- Can you find any invertebrates living on the duckweed?
- Sketch the arrangement of the lobes on the duckweed.

2. Set up a culture of duckweed to observe over 1-2 weeks, depending upon the instructions of your teacher.

- Obtain a 400-ml beaker or similar container.
- Add 300-ml of pond water to the beaker/container.
- With the inoculating loop or similar device, select 10 "plants" from the stock of duckweed. Remember that each "plant" is made of several real plants that look like lobes.
- Set up a chart to record your observations of the population of lobes of duckweed over the period of the lab. The chart should include the total number of lobes from all "plants" added together.
- Record the number of lobes in your original sample of duckweed.
- Label your beaker/container with your team members.
- Place the container in the light source provided by the teacher.

**DATA ANALYSIS AND INTERPRETATION**

- Make daily observations and count the lobes. Record these data.
- At the end of the 1-2 weeks, make a final count of the lobes and record on your chart.

- Graph your results with the independent variable on the $x$ axis (days) and the dependent variable on the $y$ axis (number of lobes).
- Explain your results.

## PART B

## HYPOTHESIS OR PREDICTION

Now that you have completed the preliminary part of this lab and have recorded the growth patterns of duckweed, design a procedure for testing one factor that would influence the growth of the duckweed.

From the information that you have about this topic, develop a hypothesis that could be tested in a controlled experiment that will gather quantitative data. Explain the reasoning behind your hypothesis.

Answer the following questions to develop your hypothesis:

1. What is the question you are investigating?
2. What variables are you testing?
3. What are the controls for the experiment?
4. What hypotheses could you propose?

## PLAN OF INVESTIGATION

Design a controlled experiment based on your hypothesis. Make a number list of steps, similar to a recipe, that anyone could follow. Design a table that will be convenient for recording your data. Answer the following list of questions as you design your experiment:

1. What procedures would you use to test your hypothesis?
2. What will you measure?
3. How will you show your results in graphs?

## QUESTIONS/ANALYSIS

1. How do your data relate to your hypothesis?
2. What caused any errors in your experiment?
3. What other questions came from your results?
4. To what other biology topics is this lab related? Explain.
5. What did you learn from this activity?
6. How does this lab relate to topics studied in the classroom?

# APPENDIX H-2

# Example of A Traditional Laboratory Exercise

**LAB #2: THE EFFECT OF pH ON THE GROWTH OF DUCKWEED**

NAME _____ PER _____

## INTRODUCTION

Duckweed is a common aquatic plant that can be grown in the lab in a simple nutrient culture medium. The growth of these plants occurs by mitosis and can be quantified by counting the number of new buds found on the plant after a period of time. The growth of a population of plants establishing itself in a new area typically follows an S-shaped curve. This curve consists of three phases:

1. A period of slow growth, the lag phase, followed by;
2. Exponential growth and finally;
3. An equilibrium phase where the population levels off.

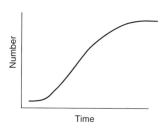

Biotic and abiotic factors influence the growth of individuals and populations. The pH of an aquatic environment is an abiotic factor which dramatically influences its inhabitants and their growth. In this experiment, you will determine the optimal pH for the growth of duckweed, along with the effects of sub-optimal pH values on the growth of duckweed.

## MATERIALS

50 ml graduated cylinder
6 containers of culture media each with a specific pH (4, 5, 6, 7, 8, 9)
6 petri dishes
duckweed
marking pens
inoculation loops

## PROCEDURE

1. Take 6 sterile petri dishes and label each with your initials and one pH value starting with 4 for the first dish, continuing until the last dish is labeled 9. Label on the bottom or side of the dish.

2. To the petri dishes add 25 ml of the culture media (decholorinated tap water plus liquid fertilizer) at the given pH.

3. With an inoculating loop transfer 15 duckweed plant lobes to each of the petri dishes. Record the total number of lobes per petri dish. Each lobe is actually a plant, although you often consider a three-lobed structure a plant. For statistical tests, it is IMPERATIVE that each group start with as close to 15 lobes as possible.

4. Place your 6 labeled petri dishes on the counter under the lights and allow them to remain undisturbed for one week or more, depending upon the success of the experiment.

5. Observe the plants in the petri dishes each day and record the number of

| pH | 4 | 5 | 6 | 7 | 8 | 9 |
|---|---|---|---|---|---|---|
| DAY 1 | | | | | | |
| DAY 2 | | | | | | |
| DAY 3 | | | | | | |
| DAY 4 | | | | | | |
| DAY 5 | | | | | | |
| DAT 6 | | | | | | |
| DAY 7 | | | | | | |
| DAY 8 | | | | | | |
| DAY 9 | | | | | | |

| DAY 10 | |
|---|---|
| DAY 11 | |
| DAY 12 | |
| DAY 13 | |
| DAY 14 | |

lobes in each dish. Count weekends as one day. Do this up until 14 class days and record data below:

6. With all the growth data for each pH as one population, do an ANOVA F test on your data to see if each group is similar. Your Null Hypothesis here would be that all the populations of duckweed grew at the same rate despite the pH.

F test value = _____
Degrees of freedom for numerator = _____
Degrees of freedom for denominator = _____
Critical F value on the ANOVA chart = _____

Do you reject of fail to reject your Null Hypothesis? _____
Explain in complete sentences:

7. Collect class data on the following charts so you can compare growth per pH for all of the 8 groups, using the statistical ANOVA F test.

# APPENDIX I

# Funding of Professional Development

This appendix presents information on the funding of professional-development programs. Programs cannot be successful unless they are adequately funded. The federal government is redefining how it categorizes the education programs that it supports, and recent data were not available. However, the issue of funding is too important to neglect so the committee has included the information available to it at the time of publication in this appendix rather than as part of the main report. The recommendations at the end of the appendix are important for the advancement of professional-development programs.

Science-based professional-development activities are funded by a variety of federal, state, local, and private sources. The increase in the number of programs over the last decade suggests a response to a perceived need for professional-development activities. The primary sources of funds are federal agencies, state departments of education (including flowthrough funds from national programs), national and local private foundations, industry, and professional organizations. Because programs and funding sources change constantly, we describe here only major sources of funding, and the descriptions might not be current.

## FEDERAL SOURCES

The primary sources of federal funding for professional-development activities are the National Science Foundation (NSF) and the Department of Education, but a few other federal agencies have some education activities at the K-12 level.

The FY 1993 appropriation for professional development (called teacher enhancement) was about $93 million through NSF's Directorate for Education and Human Resources, Division of Elementary, Secondary, and Informal Education. The FY 1994 request for teacher enhancement was $106.5 million (CRS, 1993). NSF awards most of its teacher-enhancement grants to principal investigators in colleges and universities through a competitive, peer-reviewed process. Some funds are also granted to private organizations and professional societies for programs that directly benefit teachers.

The Department of Education, through the Dwight D. Eisenhower Professional Development Program (formerly the Mathematics and Science Education Program), supports professional development of teachers. The Eisenhower program has two components. The state component awards funds to state education agencies, which then apportion funds to local education agencies through a formula-grants program that considers both overall school-age population and state shares of Chapter 1 basic grants. (The Chapter 1 program provides aid to local education agencies for the education of disadvantaged children). The state component is designed to provide support of elementary- and secondary-school teachers for training and retraining only in the sciences and mathematics. Funds are to be used primarily for teachers' professional-development activities. Some Eisenhower funds are also used to enable teachers to attend national or regional meetings of professional teachers organizations (NSTA Reports, 1993; SRI, 1990). Some state organizations use Eisenhower funds to provide opportunities for staff-development presentations by teachers. The national component supports such national- or regional-level projects as the National Clearinghouse for Science, Mathematics, and Technology Education Materials and regional mathematics and science education consortia. The FY 1993 appropriation for the whole Eisenhower program was $275 million; the appropriation for the state component was $246 million.

The Eisenhower program was reauthorized in October 1994 as part of the General Education Provisions Act and its Title II, Improving Teaching and Learning. A new Part A of Title II authorizes the Dwight D. Eisenhower Professional Development Program to support professional development of elementary- and secondary-school teachers in core academic subjects. It replaces the Dwight D. Eisenhower Mathematics and Science Education Act programs. Despite the change in name and the inclusion of other fields, the new program is designed to place emphasis on professional-development programs at the state level in science and mathematics; 94% of the funds are directed toward science and mathematics. Most other provisions of the previous Eisenhower program appear to remain in force, including support of the clearinghouse.

Several agencies have designed programs that correspond to their own scientific missions. The Department of Energy has a program that pays a stipend to selected teachers to work in national laboratories during the summer. The National Institutes of Health (NIH) awarded nearly $6 million in grants in FY 1991 in its Science Education Partnership Award (SEPA) program, whose goal was "to link scientists with creative educators to produce projects that foster excitement about the health sciences in young people and the public." For example, in Seattle, a SEPA grant has linked Group Health Hospital, the University of Washington Nursing School, and the Pacific Science Center to create a multi-faceted professional-development program. For middle-school teachers and students, the Brain Power van has hands-on activities that accompany a student-centered school-assembly program.

## STATE AND LOCAL SOURCES

Most funds for science and mathematics education at the state and local levels consist of flowthrough funds from federal agencies. Most of the flow-through funding used for professional-development activities comes from the Department of Education's Eisenhower funds. Those funds flow through state education agencies for elementary and secondary education and are distributed to local education agencies, to state demonstration and exemplary projects, or to state agencies for higher education for cooperative projects or competitive grants to institutions of higher education.

Most local funds for science and mathematics education also come from federal formula-grant programs, primarily the Department of Education's Eisenhower state funds. In the midst of severe budgetary constraints in most local economies, science often has a low priority, as do professional-development activities for science teachers. In some areas, utility companies and some community organizations and special-interest groups offer small grants for teacher-initiated special projects.

## PRIVATE FOUNDATIONS AND INSTITUTIONS

Private foundations are an important source of funds for professional-development activities. In the life sciences, a major contributor in the last few years has been the Howard Hughes Medical Institute (HHMI). Its Undergraduate Biological Science Education Program focuses on improving undergraduate life-science education through institutional grants, many of which provide an opportunity for biology and other science teachers to enhance their skills. Through the outreach mechanism of the grants, several institutions have summer institutes specifically for teachers. About $65.5 million (23%) of the $290 million spent on the program in 1987-1994 was awarded to expand relationships between higher education and precollege institutions with an emphasis on professional development of teachers. HHMI estimates that in 1988-1994, about 11,500 elementary- and secondary-school teachers participated in outreach activities sponsored by the 213 institutions that received Undergraduate Biological Science Education Program awards.

Another HHMI initiative, the Precollege and Public Science Education Program, focuses more on elementary-school children and has awarded $20.8 million beginning in 1992, when $6.4 million was awarded to 29 science and children's museums for programs targeted primarily at K-8 children and their teachers and parents. The initiative encourages cooperation and collaboration between science-resource centers and elementary schools. In 1993, HHMI awarded $4.2 million for similar initiatives at 22 institutions, this time including aquariums, botanic gardens, and zoos. For 1994, the program provided $10.3 million to 42 biomedical research institutions for outreach programs with students and teachers in their areas. HHMI reports that in 1992-1993, as a result of the above efforts, nearly 79,000 students (65% from underrepresented minorities and 55% female), 3,500 teachers, and 31,000 family members visited museums, attended summer science camps, participated in mentor programs, or helped to conduct research.

Local and regional philanthropic organizations are another potential source of funds. *The Foundation Directory* (Foundation Center, 1992*)*, *Sourcebook Profiles*, and *Taft Foundation Reporter* are good places to start searching for information about local giving priorities. Those references are available in many university development offices and in libraries.

## INDUSTRY

Industry has become more involved in professional-development activities for science teachers. Its involvement reflects a variety of motivations, including public service to the local community, concern about entry-level workforce needs, and concern about the science pipeline. Several notable examples are Pfizer (Connecticut), Hoffmann-La Roche (New Jersey), Immunex (Seattle), and Industry Initiatives in Science and Mathematics Education, a consortium of companies in the San Francisco Bay area. In general, their programs are designed primarily for highly selected teachers, who are given the opportunity to work in research laboratories over the summer with a competitive salary. At a small expense to the companies, teachers are offered a unique opportunity not only to conduct research, but also to see what types of career opportunities are available to their students. In 1992, the Council for Aid to Education published a comprehensive document that lists the range of educational activities that industry is involved in supporting.

Industry has also established a number of partnerships. The Science Education Advisory Board of the University of California, Irvine, for example, comprises representatives of 16 corporations, 16 faculty members, and six community members. The adjunct honorary board comprises 13 members of the National Academy of Sciences, the National Academy of Engineering, and the Institute of Medicine. The Advisory Board has overseen the development of science-education programs and has contributed $100,000 per year to support those programs over the last 10 years. Another major partnership in the Los Angeles area is Project LEARN, which has formed a partnership among corporations, district administrators, educators, parents, and community agencies to revitalize science and mathematics teaching in the Los Angeles School District. The partnership is funded at $10 million per year.

## PROFESSIONAL ORGANIZATIONS

During the last few years, scientific professional societies have developed activities to engage teachers in their own communities. Most events are in the form of special sessions at annual meetings. Opportunities for teachers to work in research laboratories on university campuses during the summer, however, are growing in popularity. Teachers participate in research projects, develop supplementary classroom activities, and foster teacher-scientist collaborations. Some of the most active life-science societies in this regard are the American Physiological Society, the American Association of Immunologists, the American Society for Cell Biology, the Society for Neuroscience, and the American Society for Biochemistry and Molecular Biology. In some cases, funding comes directly from the professional organization; in others, the organization receives a grant from a federal agency, such as NSF or NIH.

## RECOMMENDATIONS

Federal agencies and private organizations directly and indirectly provide a large proportion of funds that are used for the professional development of science teachers. Because teachers' continuing education relies so heavily on the availability of those funds, it is important that the organizations provide continuing support for programs that have been shown to be working. As noted in Chapter 5, lasting change must be supported in a variety of ways.

The recommendations offered here are directed primarily to federal agencies, although many also apply to private organizations.

• Increase the duration of education grants. Improving science education takes time, but the short duration of most federal and private grants, usually 3 years, inhibits institutionalization of change. Unlike conventional research grants, education grants require collaboration between people with different backgrounds, goals, and interests. In addition, the chief goal of an effective education program—better learning for students—is a long-term goal and cannot be effectively measured by testing students' knowledge immediately after the intervention. An average duration of 5-10 years would be more conducive to promoting effective education partnerships. This extended duration requires a well-developed, rigorous plan for continuing and overall program evaluation.

• Provide long-term funding for effective professional-development programs. Many effective programs disappear because they fail to receive funding renewals. Programs that have shown evidence of success should receive long-term funding.

• Create more education "add-ons" to research grants. An efficient and cost-effective way to have an immediate impact on science education would be for granting agencies to allow an education components as parts of research grants. Add-ons to grants would create opportunities for undergraduates, teachers, and even some high-school students to participate in laboratory or field research. They would also lead university scientists to become involved in education endeavors. An effective research laboratory where students, faculty, technicians, postdoctoral fellows, and others participate in a common scientific research effort is a model of an ideal intellectual community of learners—a community suggested in much of the education-reform literature. Such research-laboratory communities can be particularly supportive of  members of under-represented minorities and women.

• Fund professional, third-party evaluation to determine the effectiveness of major programs. As noted in Chapter 6, principal investigators often are responsible for evaluating their own programs. We recommend that a separate funding pool be created to support the evaluation of clusters of similar programs. In particular, funding should be made available to look for clear evidence that evaluate how well programs have succeeded in being used in classrooms in penetrated into the schools and school districts.

• Encourage programs that focus on systemic change. When designing future program announcements, funding agencies should require program planners to identify how specific projects will support, supplement, or initiate systemic-reform efforts at the local level. This will require that proposals will include clear evidence that program planners have researched existing science-education programs. Systemic efforts can build on the efforts of creative and innovative people who have established an atmosphere within a school or school district where change can occur.

• Fund programs that eliminate barriers and stimulate cooperation between science and teacher-education departments in colleges and universities. Science and education departments at colleges and universities collaborate, or even cooperate little, but we believe that each community can benefit from collaboration. We encourage funding agencies to develop requests for proposals that will foster closer linkages between education research and educational practice.

• Provide substantial grant funds for supplies and equipment to support implementation of programs by teachers in their classrooms. Most federal education grants do not allow grantees to buy supplies and equipment. For science programs, this is particularly troublesome, in that all effective programs require some kind of hands-on activities and supplies. We recommend a change in the rules so that teachers will be able to purchase the supplies they need to conduct inquiry-based activities in their classrooms.

• Link funding of curriculum development with professional development.

Many good science curricula already exist, especially at the elementary-school level. If curriculum development is proposed, grantors should require that those programs include a strategy for linking curriculum development with professional development and demonstrate that new curricular initiatives do not duplicate ones that already exist.

• Involve both scientists and educators in the peer-review process. Peer-review panels should include scientists who are well informed about science-education reform efforts, education researchers, and outstanding teachers.

• Fund activities to improve that are aimed at determining methods of evaluating how professional-development programs affect students' learning of science. As noted in Chapter 6, there is a paucity of evaluative methods to determine the impact of programs for teachers on student achievement. More research must be conducted, and grants should be given to encourage research in this field. A granting mechanism should also be set up to direct research into evaluation of the relative effectiveness of different kinds of programs in terms of both costs and impacts on students.

• Fund the establishment of an information and dissemination center for professional-development programs. NSF has funded hundreds of science-education programs over the years, but there is no central repository of programs. Descriptions of programs and their successes would be particularly useful for scientists who want to become involved in professional development of teachers and for others who want to become involved in science education.

## REFERENCES

(CRS) Congressional Research Service, U.S. Library of Congress. 1992. Eisenhower Mathematics and Science Education Act: Overview and Issues for Reauthorization. CRS Report for Congress 93-5 EPW, by J. B. Stedman. Washington, DC.

Foundation Center. 1992. The Foundation Directory. New York, NY: Foundation Center.

National Science Teachers Association. 1992-93. Standards for the preparation & certification of teachers of science, K-12. In NSTA Handbook. Arlington, VA: National Science Teachers Association.

SRI International, Policy Studies Associates, and Inverness Research Associates. 1991. The Eisenhower Mathematics and Science Education Program: An Enabling Resource for Reform. Technical Report. A National Study of the Education for Economic Security Act (EESA) Title II Program. Prepared by M. S. Knapp, A. A. Zucker, N. E. Adelman, and M. St. John for the Office of Planning, Budget and Evaluation of the U.S. Department of Education. Washington, DC: U.S. Government Printing Office.

# Index\*

Add-on grants, 8, 51
Administrators, 4, 56, 59-60
    enlisting support of, 2, 6-7, 26, 28-29, 46, 58-59
    university, 5, 51
Advertisements, 55-56
Alliances, *see* Partnerships and alliances
American Association for the Advancement of Science (AAAS), 24, 52, 65, 72
American Association of Physics Teachers, 52
American Chemical Society (ACS), 51-52
American Physical Society, 51-52
American Physiological Society, 44
American Society for Biochemistry and Molecular Biology (ASBMB), 44
American Society for Cell Biology (ASCB), 44, 52
American Society for Microbiology, 52
American Society of Human Genetics (ASHG), 52, 53
Association of Science-Technology Centers (ASTC), 44

Beginning teachers, 22-23
*Benchmarks*, 65
Business and industry, 8, 31

City Science Project, 56, 66
Class presentations, 3, 32
Classroom supplies and equipment, 60, 64, 78
    funding for, 5, 8, 28-29, 42, 58, 60
    laboratory kits, 38-39, 44
    sharing of, 38, 58
Collaboration and cooperation, 2, 26, 27, 32, 33, 42-43
    among university departments, 8, 54
    in reform efforts, 62, 63, 65, 67-68, 72
Colleges, *see* Universities and colleges
Collegial relationships, 2, 4, 17, 26, 27, 57
Computers and computer networks, 28, 41-42
Conceptual-change perspective, 20
Consortia, 58, 229
Content learning, 16, 17, 19-20, 37, 63, 68
Continuing-education credits, 4, 5, 6, 40, 57
Conventions, *see* Meetings and conventions

---

\*Because of the structure and content of the appendixes to this volume, they do not lend themselves to regular indexing; therefore, they are not represented here.

LIBRARY
copy #1

EDUCATION
Acc # 8561

# DISCARDED
Exploratorium
Learning Studio

## For Reference

**Not to be taken from this room**

**Exploratorium Library**
**3601 Lyon Street**
**San Francisco, CA  94123**

GAYLORD